3

PORTRAIT OF SHEFFIELD

Portrait of
SHEFFIELD

B. BUNKER

ROBERT HALE · LONDON

© B. Bunker 1972
First published in Great Britain 1972

ISBN 0 7091 3245 X

Robert Hale & Company
63 Old Brompton Road
London, S.W.7

PRINTED IN GREAT BRITAIN
BY EBENEZER BAYLIS AND SON LTD.
THE TRINITY PRESS, WORCESTER, AND LONDON

CONTENTS

		page
	Foreword	9
I	The Canvas is Prepared	11
II	Invaders	25
III	Church and Manor	39
IV	Hard Times	51
V	The Beginning of Sheffield Cutlery	66
VI	The Town at War	77
VII	Religion and Education	86
VIII	Scientific Solutions	95
IX	The Importance of Trade	115
X	Reforms	125
XI	A Growing Population	134
XII	Festival Days	150
XIII	The Queen Comes	162
XIV	The School Board	175
XV	Murders at the Theatre	187
XVI	The Threatened Canal	197
XVII	All Kinds of Houses	206
XVIII	Church into Cathedral	219
XIX	The Portrait is Framed	227
	Bibliography	230
	Index	233

ILLUSTRATIONS

facing page

1 High Neb, Sheffield's highest point   32
2 Sheffield Town Hall   33
3 Sheffield University: one of the oldest parts   48
4 The City Hall   48
5 The Cutlers' Hall, Church Street   49
6 Sheffield Cathedral: the new extension at the west end   64
7 Sheffield from Wincobank   65
8 Long Causeway, the Roman road   80
9 The Anglian cruck timbers in Stumperlowe cottage   81
10 The shaft of the Sheffield Cross   81
11 Castle Market, on the site of the Norman castle   96
12 View down the Don Valley to the east   97
13 The two 'hulls' of Shepherd Wheel in Whiteley Woods   112
14 The Abbeydale Industrial Hamlet   113
15 The Tilt Hammer 'Shop' at the Abbeydale Industrial Hamlet   128
16 An example of Old Sheffield Plate   128
17 Grindstones lying unused below Burbage Edge   129
18 The Iron Wharf on the Sheffield and South Yorkshire Navigation in about 1880   144
19 Part of the Sheffield Basin in 1961   144
20 Sheffield Central Library   145
21 Paradise Square   160
22 The City Museum and Mappin Art Gallery in Weston Park   160

23 The Cholera Monument in Clay Wood   161

24 The War Memorial in Barker's Pool   176

25 The Castle Square pedestrian underpass or 'the hole in
       the road'   177

26 A carved post in 'The Old Queen's Head', Pond Hill 192

27 Bishops House, Meersbrook   193

28 Detail of the plaster-work over a chimney breast in
       Bishops House   193

29 Another view of Sheffield from Wincobank Hill Fort 208

30 Looking down the Haymarket to Waingate   209

PICTURE CREDITS

N. V. Bell: 1; R. H. Bird: 2, 3, 4, 5, 6, 7, 8, 11, 12, 13,
14, 15, 17, 20, 21, 22, 23, 24, 25, 29, 30; Sheffield City
Museum: 10, 16; Firth Brown Ltd: 18; R. Frost: 19;
The City Engineer and Surveyor's Office: 9, 26, 27,
28.

MAPS

Sheffield: the City in its Setting   12–13

Sheffield: the City Centre   207

FOREWORD

THE Portrait of Sheffield is not a 'history' in the generally accepted sense; it is an attempt to portray—briefly—the main factors which have, from prehistoric times, helped to shape the large, interesting city we know today. An attempt has been made to delineate our city's *character*—a character which spells Sheffield. From the first beginnings of Escafeld, through periods of sadness and tragedy, of progress and happiness, our Portrait inevitably shows the unchanging hues of integrity, of good humour, of friendliness, of skilled craftsmanship—and love of the hills which so beautifully cradle our city.

Grateful use has been made of the writings of both early and contemporary authors, and also of invaluable sets of notes made available. Assistance of many kinds has generously been proffered from a variety of sources for all of which the author is sincerely appreciative.

Many of the pictures were specially taken by Mr. R. H. Bird; others were kindly provided by Sheffield Corporation (City Engineer and Surveyor's Office), Messrs. Firth Brown Ltd., and Mr. N. V. Bell. For this valuable help and for the maps drawn by Mr. D. Cathels the author is most grateful. To my husband, whose encouragement and advice gave much practical help, thanks are expressed. And to Sheffield people throughout the centuries whose courage and skill have helped to fashion today's fine city, grateful recognition is recorded.

Holmesfield   B. Bunker
Sheffield

I

THE CANVAS IS PREPARED

THE canvas on which Sheffield's Portrait is painted is large, and of interesting texture. Its extent must of necessity be considerable, for how else could the portrait of our country's fifth largest city be adequately limned? When we view the size and complexity of our Portrait today, depicting a city which, in area, is the second largest in the country, covering some 18,202 hectares (45,000 acres), being about 24 kilometres (15 miles) across, and with levels ranging from 27 to 458 metres (89 to 1,502 feet) above sea level (High Neb, the highest point in the City is 1,502 feet in height and 8 miles from the city centre), we shall be impressed by the diversity of contours and the fascination of the hills. This is a 'border' area, dropping steeply from the Pennines to the valley of the River Don, and lying across the dividing line between north Derbyshire and south Yorkshire.

Today, Sheffield's citizens need no reminding of the wonderful heritage they enjoy; that their city, long regarded as 'isolated' by hills on three sides and marshland on the east, has combined the undoubted skills and traditions of past centuries with today's dramatic architecture and modern techniques. This fine city, with its sad history of periods of depression and industrial disease, has today a proud tradition of excellent medical service and fine hospitals; of notable educational facilities, ranging from efficient primary schools through secondary and comprehensive schools to colleges and a fine university—a university famed for its Metallurgy Department (frequently described as the best in the country), having the world's first Chair of Glass Technology and also of Landscape Architecture, and where modern research is carried out in spina bifida, in computer use, in the behavioural sciences and in the documentation of scientific information.

For many years in the world of sport both men and women

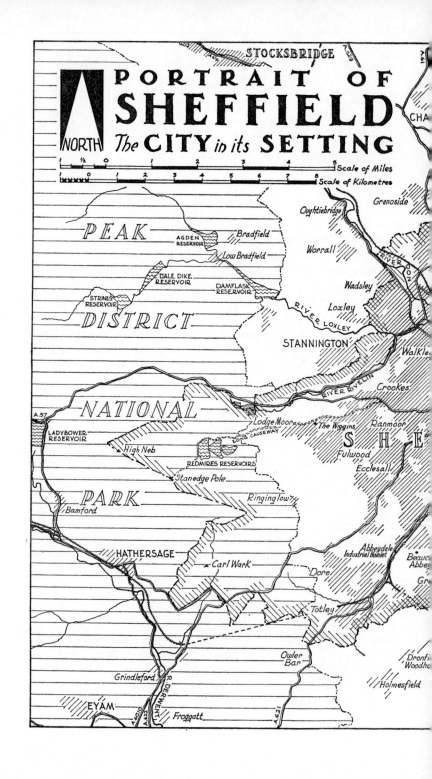

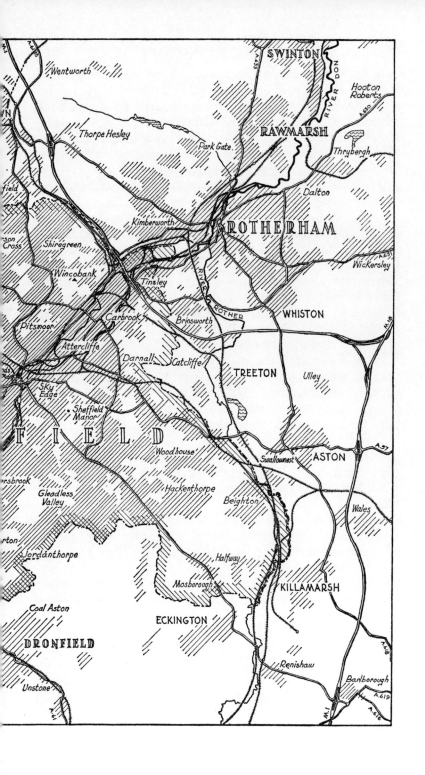

have made their mark at international level; cricket, football, bowling, tennis, golf, hockey, rugby, climbing, skiing, swimming, rowing, sailing, archery, boxing, cycling, fishing, yachting, athletics, wrestling, dancing, ice skating, speedway, pony trekking are all remarkably well provided for. It has been truly stated that Sheffield is a city of sportsmen, where leisure time is employed healthily and actively, where people live, work and play with enthusiasm. Sheffield has a greater area of public parks and open spaces than any other city in the country.

Sheffield's libraries, museums and art galleries house well-known, important collections, and all have modern buildings.

On her doorstep, but a few miles from the city centre, Sheffield has a wealth of stately homes and castles of historic interest—Chatsworth House (the home of the Duke of Devonshire), Haddon Hall (the home of the Duke of Rutland), Hardwick Hall, Bolsover Castle, Peveril Castle, Conisbrough Castle, Wentworth Castle, Wingfield Manor, Barlborough Hall and Manor—to name several of the better known.

In the city centre is the fine town hall, with a striking statue of the god Vulcan high on the tall tower; there is the magnificent City Hall and the Cutlers' Hall. And at the city's heart stands the historic parish church cathedral on its age-old site. There are good theatres, to which the modern, thrust-stage Crucible Theatre is about to be added.

The M1 passes through the city's boundaries, with modern road connections. There is an efficient railway system, and a fine water-highway to the sea which secures for Sheffield the enviable facilities of an inland port.

And Sheffield's long connection with the metal industries—notably iron, silver, and steel—and with engineering, and the reliability and skill of the Sheffield craftsmen, is known throughout the world. Modern techniques might be expected to have affected the traditional skill of the Sheffield craftsman, who a generation ago worked in an area often darkened by smoke from hundreds of chimneys, and who dourly stated "where there's muck there's money" (though whose house-proud women even in the tiniest, most inconvenient and insanitary 'back-to-backs' kept spotless homes); but the skill inherited from generations of craftsmen, remains. And although today's smoke-control methods happily have removed much of the 'muck', the age-old uprightness and integrity and addiction to quiet, plain-spokenness is still evident. Only recently a not-so-young 'little mester' was heard to pass quiet judgement on an 'up-and-comer' who was somewhat over emphasizing his idea of his own importance, with: " 'Im? E's only penny-'ead and fardin-tail."

It is known that Sheffield's attitude to research has lead to its development as an international leader in many fields of activity; as many as sixteen major research industries are based in Sheffield.

In the modern Sheffield new hotels have been built, and the city is now recognized as a convenient and attractive conference centre. It has even been claimed that there are more departmental stores here than in any city north of London, that Sheffield has the largest toy-shop in England, and the biggest night club in Europe!

In her *Sheffield. Its Story and its Achievements* Miss M. Walton— who, like the present author, is a child of Sheffield—states: "The natural riches which her rocks, streams and trees provided were only made fruitful by constant unremitting toil, and during long periods of poverty and loneliness. That is why, great as is the achievement which crowns her homely face, she wears it rather like a bonnet than a crown. . . . With characteristic simplicity these people have always taken more pride in the splendid sur- roundings of their city than in their own achievements."

The true Sheffielder has an inborn love of music and of the open country, is friendly and practical; and looks askance at anyone exhibiting 'side'.

As we glance back through the hundreds of centuries of prehistory when our canvas was slowly—and sometimes violently—being prepared, we shall realize why the outline of our Portrait began to appear at a comparatively late date; and why today it shows areas of significant contrast and undoubted interest.

Indeed it could well be claimed that this is a *unique* portrait.

The geology of Sheffield and its surrounding area is complex, and noteworthy; this is the very stuff of which our canvas is woven. It would be impossible to estimate how many centuries slipped by as the canvas was being prepared. Although several Ice Ages played an important part in shaping the landscape it is unlikely that the outlines we know today appeared until after the ice cover

of the last Ice Age had slowly receded northward to the Arctic
Regions. But the departing ice cover left an amazing, complex
'canvas' open to the skies, and the wind and rain; amazing because
of its great diversity of texture, and complex by reason of its many
sudden changes in elevation.

Geologists remind us of ranges of Mesozoic and Palaeozoic
rocks climbing more or less steadily from the low elevations in
the east of our area to the Pennine uplands of the west; from the
Keuper Marls, through the Bunter sandstone, through the ridge
of Permian limestone, westward across the ups and downs of the
sandstones and shales of the coal measures; westward, still climbing, to the striking millstone grit moorlands with their 'edges',
and then to the smoother heights of the carboniferous limestone.
This is not the place to attempt any detailed description of our
area's complex geological formation; but brief mention is
essential.

A significant component is provided by the rivers and streams.
Most of them have undergone considerable direction changes
through the centuries, as well as showing a gradual decrease in
volume of water carried; but the importance of the five conver-
gent valleys whose streams, as we shall see, have played such an
important role in the siting and development of Sheffield on the
abrupt, right-angled turn of the River Don, cannot be overlooked.

The River Don has its headstreams at elevations of some 1,500
feet on the gritstone moorlands to the north, in the cloughs of
Grain Moss and Harden, west of Thurlstone Moors; and it flows
in a generally easterly direction through Penistone, to the east of
which high land compels a curve to the south-east. This direction
is continued through some dozen miles or so of gorges and twist-
ing narrow valleys, many streams from the Pennine moorlands
rushing to join it, until a spectacular approach to high land block-
ing the way to the south-west and south necessitates a dramatic
swing from a south-east to a north-east direction. And here is
Sheffield's beginning.

The turbulent River Don flows more calmly once it has made
its sudden right-angled turn to lower land and wider valleys. But
we must take a closer look at the course of the Don after it leaves
the high moors of its birth.

We note how the young river, having swung to the south-east
below Penistone continues swiftly around many bends and hill-

gaps until it is met at Stocksbridge by the equally swift-flowing Little Don from the high Langsett Moors to the west. About 2 miles farther south the Ewden Beck comes in from Margery Hill and the Broomhead Moors of the high western area. The growing river swirls determinedly round the confining rocky outcrops until at a point some 5 miles or so farther along its course, at the place we know as Owlerton, the River Loxley approaches, again from the western hills where its headstreams rise on the Bradfield Moors; and about 1 mile before joining the Don the Loxley has received a tributary from the south-west, the River Rivelin, which has approached swiftly from the Hallam Moors. At the point where the River Don is compelled to make its dramatic sweep to the north-east, from the high moors of its birth to the low-lying plains and 'wastes' beyond, it is joined by the River Sheaf from the south-west, which has itself been joined by the little Porter Brook a short distance before the junction with the Don. Both these short tributaries have come from the high lands of the south and west, the River Sheaf from the heights of Totley Moor and the Porter Brook from Brown Edge.

The important contribution of these rivers cannot be over-estimated; we shall see that without them there would have been no Sheffield. Having been compelled to swing to the north-east the River Don flows more gently through a wider valley past Grimesthorpe, past historic Wincobank, past Attercliffe and Brightside, through Tinsley and Templeborough to Rotherham, where it is joined by the River Rother from the south.

Another essential constituent of the landscape was provided by the slow development of the varied vegetation we know, which spread over the area many centuries ago. As the last ice-cap moved slowly northward, probably some 10,000 or more years ago, the sparse vegetation was mainly of the moss and lichen tundra type, and many centuries would pass before the slowly rising temperature encouraged the growth of forests, and the diverse geology and land-heights provided conditions for a wide variety of plant and tree growth. The area's vegetation owes much to the various types of good soil, to the elevations of the hills and the slopes of the valleys and to the plentiful supply of water, as well as to the climate—which our school books described as 'equable', inferring that neither prolonged droughts nor intense frosts occurred to hinder plant growth. By the time man had penetrated to the regions round the Don's great curve and decided to settle—although his 'settlements' may well have been of the nomadic type—forests abounded, giant oaks being particularly evident in the Rivelin Valley region. The coal measures area must have been particularly beautiful; here dozens of tiny streams babbled through flower-decked valleys and wider grassy nooks, with trees boldly climbing the hill sides. It was here that the more acid soils of the moorlands had yielded to the fertile stretches of the coal measures. And here Sheffield grew.

The earliest outlines of our Portrait, faint and indistinct, began to appear perhaps more than 40,000 years ago. With modern intensive techniques of agriculture and industrial development many signs of those early dwellers in our area have been eradicated, but at Cresswell in Derbyshire, some 15 miles south-east of Sheffield, there have been found in caves in that magnesian limestone region relics of Old Stone Age man of the Palaeolithic period.

Of the Sheffield region A. Leslie Armstrong has written:

Archaeologically, the north Midland region is unrivalled in Britain for its complete record of prehistoric occupation from the dawn of the Palaeolithic to the end of the Bronze Age and beyond; also, for the significant evidence which it has provided indicative of the continuity of culture and its gradual development and adaptation to changing conditions. It extends from the Pennine watershed eastward to the Trent valley and beyond it to Scunthorpe and Lincoln Cliff, but all the most important prehistoric sites with the exception of the Hilton gravel pits, are situated within easy access of Sheffield.*

Beginning in 1875 Sir William Boyd Dawkins and the Reverend Magins Mello investigated the caves of Creswell Crags, and their discoveries proved that early man was in existence during the same period as the mammoth. Thousands of flint and quartzite tools were unearthed in the various caves—the Pin Hole Cave, Robin Hood's Cave, Mother Grundy's Parlour and the Church Hole—and numbers of bone and ivory tools, and quantities of bones and teeth of musk ox, glutton, hippopotamus, woolly rhinoceros etc. were discovered at various levels.

* David L. Linton (ed.) *Sheffield and its Region*, a scientific and historical survey compiled for the Sheffield Meeting in 1956 of the British Association for the Advancement of Science.

In 1955, when walking on an old trackway near Town End Farm Lieutenant-Colonel Gell of Hopton Hall found a prehistoric flint hand-axe, some 150,000 years old, of the Lower Palaeolithic Age. This site is some 22 miles south-west of Sheffield.

How cleverly those Palaeolithic people adapted themselves to their surroundings. The conditions then existing in our immediate area around the Don and its hills must have been quite unappealing to those early folk, but the caves and conditions in the Creswell area satisfied their needs. Only on the extreme south-east and south-west of the area therefore, do we find signs of the early Stone Age folk.

The centuries passed, and the next lines drawn on our Portrait are attributable to the Neolithic, or New Stone Age folk. Climate and vegetation had become much more favourable than when the Old Stone Age people managed to exist in the Creswell area.

It has been claimed that the Neolithic people of our area were typical of the Highland Zone, and despite the long centuries which had passed, there is evidence of direct descent from the Old Stone Age folk as well as admixture with incoming immigrants. It seems likely that by about the period 2500 B.C. the Neolithic folk, who introduced a pastoral pattern as a definite advance on the earlier entirely hunting economy, had clearly penetrated the outer edges of our environment. The hills in the Sheffield area had the good pasturage they sought, and more and more of their living sites as well as their burial places of important folk are being discovered. They made pottery and used stone axes and leaf-shaped arrow-heads.

Towards the end of the Neolithic period, in addition to their known chamber-tombs burials on the heights near Sheffield, such as Minning Low, Harborough Rocks, Green Low, Five Wells, Long Low, there is on the carboniferous limestone at a spot some 19 miles south-west of Sheffield the striking Arbor Low, which has been called the 'Avebury of the North'. This impressive 'henge' type construction, with all its great limestone blocks lying flat, is quite near the course of the much later Roman road running south-east from Buxton. At the Bee Low cairn, near Arbor Low both Neolithic and 'Beaker culture' burials have been found.

Signs of the occupation sites of these Neolithic people have quite recently been found within 8 miles of the centre of Sheffield.

The Beaker people (who earned their name because of the distinctive shape of some of their pottery) arrived at the end of the Neolithic period. It was around 1600 B.C. that these round-headed folk were arriving on the hills which dominate Sheffield. The artifacts found near Sheffield, at Dronfield Woodhouse, Wharncliffe Edge, near Birley Spa and above Bradfield, at Moscar and near Baslow, and which are still being discovered, show that it is likely that the various cultures and economies in many places had gradually merged over the centuries.

The Bronze Age, which followed the Beaker Period, produced men similar in type to the Beaker folk, and indeed some bronze implements appear to have been used before the Bronze Age people arrived to settle. And all the time the area—except the steep, marshy and heavily wooded river valleys—was attracting more and more tribal peoples. In about 1500 B.C. the Middle Bronze Age folk reached the area. These people were armed and led by warrior chiefs, who subdued the earlier pastoral dwellers. These newcomers are sometimes called the Urn people; their whole economy was distinct from that of the earlier people. They constructed many stone circles, both large and small, examples of which exist at Moscar Moor, Froggat Edge, Ewden Moor, Barbrook, Ramsley Moor and Redmires, to name a few. Bronze tools and weapons were widely used, but they seem to have been brought to the area by traders over well-established trade routes. Cremation was widely practised, the ashes, in a cinerary urn, being buried with, or without the building of a cairn. Two such urns were found at Crookes. As these lines are written it has been proved that these are Early Bronze Age urns. Three Middle Bronze Age barrows were found at Lodge Moor.

After the coming of the Beaker people the pattern spread inwards from the edges of the region. The Millstone Grit uplands, the source of the River Don tributaries in the area, were being settled, albeit somewhat sparsely, and so was the coal measures area. The arrival of more and more Urn people expedited this settlement, and the forest-clearing activities which had been started several centuries earlier to provide more pasture-land, continued. A Bronze Age hoard of six implements was found at Kilnhurst, a village some 8 miles north-east of Sheffield. It has been attributed to the Late Bronze Age, c. 800–400 B.C.

Throughout history and prehistory our area has, because of its position far from the coasts, been slow to receive new bands of immigrants. But they came nevertheless, and because of the apparent safety of this 'border' area they remained to mingle eventually with the next newcomers. Due to the comparative isolation of the region the Iron Age people, who were the next new arrivals, seem to have reached this area late in the fifth century B.C., and their rather slow penetration permitted them to mingle with the native population.

Perhaps the most outstanding feature added to our Portrait by the Iron Age people was their hill-fort construction. Each hill-fort had its own characteristics, but each construction usually required a rampart and ditch together with a counterscarp bank. Always the contours were cleverly used for the maximum defensive plan. At least sixteen hill-forts have now been identified, of which one of the most important is the fort on Wincobank Hill, almost central in our Portrait, overlooking the Don's sharp bend in Sheffield. Still nearer to the river bend is a hill-slope fort in Roe Wood, and there is the Canklow hill-fort some 6 miles downstream overlooking the junction of the Don with its tributary the Rother coming from the south. A hill-fort at Langsett overlooks the course of the infant Don in the north-west; at Scholes Coppice, a few miles north of Wincobank is a hill-slope fort, and beyond Castleton, west of the River Derwent is the well-known Mam Tor hill-fort. All these hill-forts are remarkable features of our landscape, and those which lie within the confines of our area add to the increasing clarity of our Portrait. It is worthy of note that at both the Wincobank and Canklow hill-forts Mesolithic (pre-Neolithic) flint tools have been found.

As the cultivation of grain increased, methods of grinding the grain to make flour were needed, and it is of considerable interest to learn that stone rotary querns were fashioned in our locality. Mr. L. H. Butcher has investigated a large quern-factory at Wharncliff, near the River Don just north of Sheffield. The stone at this site evidently was utilized over a long period, as querns of Roman as well as Iron Age types have been found there.

It has been stated that the hill-forts were probably the work of the Brigantes, who by the time of the Roman invasion were in control of most of Yorkshire north of our area, so that the hill-forts may have been constructed along the southern borders of their territory. Another view is that certain of the peoples who were included in the Brigantian tribe-federation used the hill-forts as headquarters for cattle-raiding activities. Recent investigation supports the suggestion that some hill-forts were being built as early as 250 B.C. Whatever causes were responsible for their construction, it is impossible not to admire the choice of site, the labour needed to build them and the superb views they command over the surrounding terrain, particularly over strategic routes. Excavation in several hill-forts has produced a little hand-made Iron Age pottery, and at Wincobank there was found some Roman pottery in the filling of one of the ditches. Much work remains to be done on hill-fort excavations.

From Sheffield, in an east-north-east direction there runs for some ten miles the interesting 'Roman Ridge', or 'Roman Rig'. This is a man-made trackway, apparently beginning in the area we know as Grimesthorpe, on Wood Hill about a mile north of the Don; and it could well have climbed from a river crossing by the Don's spectacular bend, although today there is no sign of it in that section. From Grimesthorpe the 'Ridge' continues past the lower slopes of Wincobank on the south-east, running parallel to the Don, and it is seen again to the north-east of Scholes Coppice, and yet again as it swings more to the east towards the junction of the Don with its tributary the River Dearne just beyond Mexborough. Despite its name, it has been established that 'Roman Ridge' is not Roman; it could well be an Iron Age trackway established by the Brigantes.

The Romans seem to have been concerned in our area for two reasons, the first being their interest in the lead mines of the carboniferous limestone region between Wirksworth and Castleton, the other being that they must get control of the warlike, troublesome Brigantes, on whose southern border the future Sheffield would grow. Cartimandua, the Queen of the Brigantes, was pro-Roman—perhaps because she was astute enough to realize that the Romans were powerful, and if she could be established in their favour they would support her against possible enemies. Her surmise proved to be correct, for many of her own people were opposed to her pro-Roman activities and would gladly have deposed her.

As they pushed northwards the Romans had a good deal of trouble with the Iron Age Brigantes, and in A.D. 48 a rising of the tribes caused the Romans to forsake their planned expedition into North Wales, so that they could suppress the rebellion. In A.D. 51 the Queen's surrender to the Romans of Caractacus, who had sought shelter at her Court, angered her people and caused further Brigantian risings. Cartimandua was kept on her throne only by Roman help.

That the folk in the Wincobank hill-fort played a determined role against the Romans would seem to have been partly the reason for the building of the Roman fort at Templeborough near the far bank of the Don some 3 miles east of Wincobank and about 2 miles north-west of the Canklow hill-fort. It was not until A.D. 71–72 that the Romans crushed the Brigantes for the time being, and it is thought that after his arrival in Britain as governor in A.D. 77–78, Agricola, in his plans to secure the North, caused a road to be made (or improved) from Ermine Street just north of Lincoln, to ford the River Trent at Littleborough and continuing westwards to pass over the magnesian limestone ridge and down to the coal measures area, passing south of the Templeborough Fort and through the Sheffield we know to start the long climb up through Sandygate, up over the high gritstone moors via the Long Causeway, and steeply down the 'edge' to cross the River Derwent to their Fort Anavio, by the River Noe at Brough on the carboniferous limestone. At Brough they were near the valuable lead mines at Castleton, they could keep an eye on the hill-fort on Mam Tor above Castleton; and at Brough their road divided, the north-westerly branch climbing over the moorlands to their Fort Melandra Castle near Glossop, and the other branch, Batham Gate, running south-west to Buxton.

Despite today's tendency to minimize or even ignore the contribution made by the Romans to the area's development, the author recognizes certain 'site evidence' of their work, particularly of the lines of their roads. Indeed, how could they utilize the lead they valued so much from our Peak District lead rakes unless they had adequate, logical routes over which this heavy, valuable commodity could be carried to suitable collecting points for despatch to Rome or where needed? Such a collecting point was Chesterfield, just 12 miles south of Sheffield, on the ancient Ryknild Street, and believed to be Lutudarum.

To Chesterfield run several direct roads from various lead-mine areas: one runs down to Chesterfield through the significantly named village of Walton; another is Rumbling Street, which borders the southern boundary of the village of Holmesfield, 8 miles from Sheffield, to continue down through Barlow to Chesterfield. There are several other significant roads leading direct to Chesterfield from the Peak District's lead mines, though north of Chesterfield the actual line of Ryknild Street is difficult to trace in places.

To date, no signs of villas or farms have been noted, and this may have minimized an appreciation of the importance of our area in Roman times. One detail of interest is the discovery, in 1761 on the Stannington side of the Rivelin Valley, of a broken bronze diploma, conferring Roman citizenship on a discharged soldier (whose name is missing) and on his family. This diploma seems to have been issued around A.D. 124, and when found in 1761 was hailed as the first discovery of its kind in Britain.

The 360 years of Roman control of Britain, which ended in A.D. 410 added little to the lines of our Portrait except in their long-forgotten road improvements. This area had little appeal to the Romans, at any rate as a settlement region. The Romans were in Britain to control it as a useful part of their empire, particularly because of the lead obtainable in Derbyshire and the Mendips, the tin obtainable in Cornwall and its wheat obtainable especially in the southern parts of the country. The immediate area around the Don's great bend offered none of these things. And so the Romans came—and went. But their more than 300 years of control had established a sort of peace and had left the dwellers to pursue their own way of life without fear of attack from invading tribes. They had also left several good roads. Their more or less sudden departure must have caused a somewhat bewildered reaction in the scattered settlements of the Britons.

II

INVADERS

IN THE year A.D. 410 the Romans departed. There was still no Sheffield. Except that the natives were existing, more or less at peace, and that their livelihood depended on the conditions of their environment, we know little of their lives. We know that few of them would be affluent enough to afford 'luxuries' occasionally brought through the area by traders, and it seems unlikely that the Roman way of life made any impact. After all, the only Romans they saw were marching between Brough and Templeborough, or were having occasional skirmishes with troublesome tribes.

Our area has always been 'border' country—the borderland between the Pennine uplands in the west and the plains and marshes in the east. Unknown to those early dwellers, and indeed to the inhabitants for several centuries to come, it was an area of hidden wealth. Its borderland status was responsible for both advantages and disadvantages.

Today, our area still is borderland, with the special conditions of such an area.

And then, in the fifth century came the people who gave Sheffield—and indeed England—its name; practical, resourceful people who knew what they sought. The 'civilized' Roman way of life meant nothing to them. Perhaps one of the attractions offered by our remote border area was its un-Romanized state. The new-comers were Angles, people to whom 'kin' was of great importance; they came seeking land—the right kind of land on which to settle.

It was after the Romans had gone that the three Teutonic peoples from across the North Sea came to this country, seeking homes. They were the Jutes, the Saxons and the Angles. The Jutes advanced into the southern areas of Britain; the Saxons gradually occupied all the rest of the southern half of the country; and the Angles eventually after many years spread over the northern half. Even during the Roman occupation there had been 'hit and run' raids on Britain's east and south coasts by these peoples, and the Romans had found it necessary to appoint a Count of the Saxon Shore to repel them. But desirable land had been noted, and after it was realized that the Romans had left these shores plans were made to leave their old homes and to seek new settlement sites in this country. Their sea-going boats were loaded with their 'kin' and all their possessions, and their journey to a new life began.

The early comers would have first choice of sites and they settled near the coast, possibly driving away or enslaving the native Britons of that area. Later comers would need to continue up the rivers in their boats until they found a desirable site, and the Humber, the Trent and the Don would be anxiously navigated, the higher, well-forested land to which they gave access being particularly desirable. It would take time for these later new-comers to reach our area, especially as the Don above Doncaster would be difficult for the passage of sea-going boats except in times of flood. Eventually their boats would be abandoned and the 'kin' with their trusted leader would continue slowly on foot, leading their valuable team of plough oxen, dragging their great wooden plough, carrying their looms and cooking pots and their treasured wood-working tools. And at last—we do not know exactly when—the first Anglian family reached our area, probably during the last quarter of the fifth century.

Since the 'invaders' almost certainly approached via the Don Valley, one of the first sites to attract attention would be Winco-bank Hill. Oak trees flourished there, the land sloped south to the Don; it was an easily defensible site, and the new-comers doubtless decided that this should be *home*. Their first task after carefully surveying the site would be to choose the right spot to erect their great cruck-constructed aula, for which all the materials were to hand. Their skill with wood-working tools, axe, adze, auger and wedge resulted in the great timber building being 'raised' on massive 'arches' fashioned from great riven oak trees, and thatched as soon as was consistent with thoroughness, and with all the 'kin' helping. The massive arches which supported and secured the whole building have been known throughout the ages as crucks, and today we know the whole structures as cruck buildings. The sturdy building raised on Wincobank would be at least 60 feet long and 16 feet wide; it was the main building of the new settlement, and would withstand the vicissitudes of the centuries.

Today, a building is still on the same site—long, low, unmistakeable. Centuries later, after a hamlet had grown and extended around it, the site with its acres of agricultural land became known as Grange Farm. Much later a well-built stone house was erected nearby for the farmer's family and the centuries-old cruck building adapted for farming use. The timber walls already had been replaced by stone, the thatched roof had been given a stone-slate roof, and the valuable crucks with their main timbers eventually were removed for use in the roof construction of new buildings. But today several sections of the cruck timbers can be seen, re-used, in the long barn which occupies the original site. Until some twenty or so years ago, when modern housing schemes claimed much of Wincobank, Grange Farm had at least several hundred acres of excellent land, and the pattern of the wide ridge-and-furrow ploughing first marked out by the great wooden, oxen-drawn Anglian plough, could still be seen.

The views from the Anglian homestead on Wincobank were superb to the east, south and west. The rise to the summit of Wincobank Hill from the Grange Farm site blocked much of the view to the north; but from the ramparts of the Iron Age hill-fort on the hilltop fine views extended in every direction—tree-clad hills climbing to the western moorlands with here and there a small patch of cultivated land worked by the remaining British people. Unattractive marshland bordered the lower reaches of the Don.

We can never know definitely which was the first site in our area chosen by a newly arrived Anglian family, but we know what they sought, and that they came up the Don Valley, perhaps traversing the Roman Rig trackway. The slopes of Wincobank would be an obvious choice.

From the Grange Farm site a view due south across the Don Valley to the top of the hill beyond would seem to suggest another desirable settlement site, with land sloping away on every side and with a particularly steep ravine on the south. A visit to the site reveals that this is Sheffield Manor. On a piece of neglected land—obviously once good agricultural land—is a ruined, long, low, roofless building almost hidden by shrub growth both inside and outside the thick walls; and pointing to the sky is one cruck of what must have been a remarkably sturdy set. In 1913 there were still two complete sets of crucks remaining in this building, which was known as The Laithes, and was not then in ruins. These details were stated in a lecture by Mr. Thomas Winder.

About a thousand years later, some 20 yards or so beyond the ancient, cruck-built, Anglian Laithes the large Manor Lodge was built. In Mr. Winder's opinion the Lodge was started in about 1516. Tragically associated with Cardinal Wolsey and with Mary Queen of Scots, it was built on much of the land which showed significant signs of 'the old ploughing' (as it is still spoken of by the area's long-established farming families), the early ridge-and-furrow ploughing which can be identified near many of our still existing early Anglian cruck buildings, indicating the use of their great wooden plough and team of plough oxen.

Following the arrival of the first Anglian families others came very soon, some being members of the same 'kindred', but always a separate site would be chosen.

About a mile north-north-east from the Wincobank site at Grange Farm is the fine cruck barn at Concord Park, on a hill-site near Shiregreen; half a mile west of this building is the long-neglected cruck barn at the interesting Hatfield House, at Sheffield Lane Top; nearly 2 miles north-west from here is a fine cruck barn at Hill Top Farm near Grenoside; $2\frac{1}{2}$ miles west of this site, on a hill across the Don is Low Hall at Onesacre, with two cruck buildings; $2\frac{1}{4}$ miles to the south-west brings us to a large cruck barn (sadly neglected) at Briers House Farm, on the hill-slope above the River Loxley. From this site it is a quarter mile south to Tom Hill at Dungworth, a farm with two cruck buildings. Three-quarters of a mile to the south-west brings us to Hall Broom with two cruck buildings, and half a mile from there is Sykehouse Farm, with massive crucks in a barn. From this site an old trackway leads to Stannington on a hill between the rivers Loxley and Rivelin, and here is Well House Farm with a cruck barn, and half a mile to the south-east is Park Side Farm on a hill-slope overlooking the River Rivelin, with three fine sets of crucks remaining. About $1\frac{1}{4}$ miles to the south-west on a remarkable hill-site on the far side of the River Rivelin is The Wiggins, a place of great historic significance where two fine cruck buildings were demolished a few years ago.

At The Wiggins beyond Hallam Head, just off the Roman road known as Long Causeway we are just over 5 miles south-west of our starting point on Wincobank Hill, and it is obvious that we are circling the hilltops of modern Sheffield. But we will continue. A distance of almost 1 mile south-east of The Wiggins brings us to the hamlet of Stumperlowe, in Fulwood, where there are three cruck buildings—one at Stumperlowe (Hall) Cottage, and two others some 300 yards beyond at Stumperlowe Grange Farm. Just over 1 mile to the west stands Bennett Grange with a cruck building on a fine site overlooking the valley of the Porter Brook; $1\frac{1}{4}$ miles to the south-east brings us to a cruck building at White House Farm at Whiteley Wood Green, high on a hill on the opposite side of the valley overlooking the Porter Brook; and $1\frac{1}{4}$ miles east of this site, again on a hilltop overlooking the Porter, stood High Storrs Farm with a remarkably fine cruck barn. Regrettably, this was demolished a few years ago although it was a 'listed' building. Just about $1\frac{1}{4}$ miles to the south-west stands Whirlow Hall, with two cruck buildings, high above the Limb Brook tributary of the River Sheaf. On the far side of the Limb Brook, on a hill just 1 mile to the south stands the village of Dore, well known to history, and here is a cruck building near the church. Dropping steeply from here to cross the Old Hay Brook, on a striking hill at the village of Totley, less than 1 mile from Dore is a cruck building at Cannon Hall. On a hilltop beyond the Abbey Brook tributary of the River Sheaf, some $2\frac{1}{2}$ miles north-east of Cannon Hall was a cruck building (recently demolished) at the Manor House in the village of Greenhill.

One mile to the east from Greenhill is Jordanthorpe Hall on land sloping to the headstreams of the Moss Brook, with a cruck building. Less than half a mile north from here, in the interesting village of Norton stood a fine cruck building (now demolished) at Norton House, near the church. Just over half a mile to the east on a fine slope overlooking the Moss Brook tributary of the River Rother stands Grange Farm at Mawfa (derived through several variations from the Anglian 'maegth', a group of kindred) with a cruck building, and three-quarters of a mile to the north-east on a striking hill-site between the Moss Brook and the Meers Brook tributary of the River Sheaf stood two fine cruck buildings (one now demolished) at The Herdings. Two and a quarter miles due north takes us to The Laithes, the now almost completely

destroyed cruck building at Sheffield Manor on its hilltop overlooking the Don, and across the Don Valley; on its hill slope
2¾ miles due north stands Grange Farm on Wincobank Hill with
re-used cruck timbers, from where we started.

Each of these fine sites had what the searching Anglian families
needed—a fairly high, defensible site with good water available,
slightly heavy land (after the forest growth was cleared) for their
great plough with its hard oaken ploughshare, and well above the
river marshes. Each site was an appreciable distance from the
next group of settlers, for each needed to be surrounded by acres
of fertile land as well as meadow and 'waste' (scrub land), for as
Tacitus wrote of these people, they "dwell apart".

All these sites encircling our modern Sheffield are significant
hill sites. In this area the only places where we find a cruck building in a valley is where it overlooks a river crossing, in fact the
trackway running down to the river crossing actually passes alongside the cruck building. A river crossing was of great importance,
and one would expect to find that there is, or has been, a cruck
building on the slope down to the early river crossing of the Don,
in Sheffield. There was such a building, on higher land command-
ing the Sheaf–Don junction and the Don crossing. Evidently
during the Norman period the cruck building was burnt and the
Norman castle built over the site. This fact was not known until
the site of the castle was being excavated in 1927–9 for the erection
of new shops; below the castle's foundations traces were found of
a long timber building, obviously of cruck construction, which
had suffered the effects of fire.

It is impossible to be certain how many years elapsed before the
sites surrounding the cruck buildings mentioned above were
cleared and worked to the standards the Angles required. Locally,
these settled areas can be found extending to the north, the south
and for a certain distance to the west, and their contribution to
our Portrait is considerable. Because it was border country between high moorland regions and the lower swampy valleys, few
main routes came this way, so the inhabitants were less involved
in the quarrels, raids and fighting that went on in many other
places. Historians have suggested that the Anglian settlers drove
out or enslaved the Britons living hereabouts, but it may well be
that after a number of years of fear and suspicion they gradually
adapted themselves and lived in peace together.

The name of the River Sheaf reminds us again that this was border country between highland and lowland, for it derived from the Old English word meaning a frontier or divide. It came to be recognized, with its tributary the Meers Brook, as part of the boundary between the Anglian kingdoms of Mercia and Northumbria. It would appear that the Anglian settlers lived here in a more or less quiet, industrious way; but we do not know exactly when the growing village or 'township' of Escafeld (the feld or open space by the Sheaf) was so named.

An important happening in 641 had tremendous, lasting effect on the area; this was the conversion of the heathen Angles to Christianity. The Christian teaching which converted much of Mercia and Northumbria came from the saintly Aidan's monastery at Lindisfarne and it was his monks, many of whom like Chad, Cedd and their brethren were themselves Angles, who made long missionary journeys throughout the two kingdoms, with surprising results. There may have been early heathen temples in some villages, but these were adapted for Christian worship; probably also, since the settlements were increasing in size new small timber churches were erected in important villages.

It is noteworthy that today a number of seventh- and eighth-century stone preaching crosses still exist in the area, their timber predecessors having yielded pride of place. Some of the still existing crosses are beautifully carved with Anglian motifs, and some are almost plain. They seem to have been erected on the south side of the church (which may have been of timber), in the churchyard. Later, in some cases before the end of the Anglian period in 1066, a stone church replaced the early timber building. Many of these crosses were broken or removed during the Reformation period, but many were hidden, and saved to be re-erected later. A beautifully carved stone Anglian cross stood in the 'yard' of the first small church in Sheffield, on the typical hill site overlooking the Don crossing, on the site of the present cathedral. This cross was removed in 1570.

The Anglo-Saxon Chronicle gives little information about this region, but an entry for the year A.D. 829 names an event which shows that in the 350 or so years since Anglian settlers first arrived here the land had been well cleared and cultivated and a number of small, well-managed townships had grown up around the original settlements. In the year 829 Ecgbert, King of Wessex, marched at the head of an army (a levy) to the village of Dore, just on the Northumbrian side of the Sheaf–Meersbrook border between that kingdom and Mercia. After years of struggles, most of which had left our area unscathed, Ecgbert had become master of six of England's seven kingdoms; and it was in 829 that he marched to Dore to meet King Eanred of Northumbria, who came and offered obedience and allegiance, "and with that they separated".

We can be quite certain that a meeting between two kings and their hundreds of followers would have been arranged only in an area where it was known there would be adequate supplies of food.

By this date an important change in the method of government was taking place. The descendants of the original settlers, in their thriving townships, found that gradually the war-chiefs assumed control, and then the most successful claimed control of the land they had acquired and proceeded to give land-grants on special terms to chosen followers known as thanes. Gradually the area's freemen, for defence purposes, acknowledged the supremacy and accepted the overlordship of this new aristocracy.

One facet of the region's successful—and on the whole peaceful —growth could well be followed up, and that is the development of water-powered wheels for grinding corn, and probably to work bellows for metal smelting. The streams rapidly falling from the high land to the River Don provided power which may well have been first utilized in the Anglian period. So important are the dozens of wheels in and around Sheffield that they will be discussed in a later chapter.

It was in A.D. 789 that the first Danish raids occurred on our coasts. They were 'hit and run' raids, similar to those of the Angles, Saxons and Jutes during the Roman period. Our isolated area seems to have escaped these attacks, perhaps because the Danes sailed their boats only a certain distance up the rivers, then landed to plunder, burn and slay, retreating quickly with their booty to their boats, getting away to sea and to their north European homes. Throughout the ninth and into the tenth centuries the raids continued, and like the Teutonic settlers in the fifth century the Norsemen eventually came seeking places to settle. Our area's comparative isolation from a fully navigable river stood it in good stead, for it would seem that not until much later in those troubled

High Neb, Sheffield's highest point

times, after the great King Alfred had forced their leader Guthrum to make peace at Chippenham in 878, allowing them to occupy the country east of the Roman Watling Street, did our area become part of Danelaw.

One of Alfred's conditions was that the Danes should accept Christianity, the result of this being that gradually they became less warlike. It may have been towards the end of this disturbed period, when the Danes seemed to be settling to live in peace with their English neighbours that a few families arrived as far west as our area, and settled here. Today there are very few signs of the Danish settlers, but several hamlets to the north-east of the early Escafeld—Grimesthorpe, Osgathorpe, Skinnerthorpe—have names of Danish origin. They may actually have come to settle here much later in the Danish period.

The Anglo-Saxon Chronicle, initiated by that fine scholar, King Alfred, mentions our area a second time; the chronicle was continued after Alfred's death in the year 901. Although Alfred had established a treaty with Guthrum the Dane in 878, it was an uneasy peace. Alfred's son Edward the Elder and grandson Edmund continued the struggle to subdue the Danes of the Danelaw, and it was in 942, the chronicle tells us, that Edmund recaptured Mercia "as where Dore divides" the kingdoms of Mercia and Northumbria. It therefore appears that the area was disturbed seriously and that the English King Edmund had his army here; but no major battle is mentioned, and this district seems to have escaped the devastation which overtook many other parts of the country. And the forest-clearance, the ploughing, sowing and reaping, milling, stock-rearing, spinning and weaving, extending of settlements, holding of moots, with all the essential activity of a growing community, continued.

It is not until after the Norman Conquest of 1066 that a document gives us important information about the period which had lasted from the last quarter of the fifth century and was now closing. The document is Domesday Book, compiled in 1086, twenty years after William of Normandy conquered England, and in it we are given scanty but valuable information about happenings in the reign of Edward the Confessor, the last of the pre-Norman kings except for the short reign of Harold. We learn that Earl Waltheof was lord of the manor of Hallam, and we gather that this was a manor of considerable extent, although from

3

Sheffield Town Hall

the information given it would be almost impossible to name its boundaries with conviction. We quote the Domesday Book entry:

> Manor. In Hallam with 16 berewicks there are 29 carucates of land for geld. Earl Waltheof had a hall there. There there can be 20 ploughs. Roger has this land of Countess Judith. [He] himself [has] there 2 ploughs and 33 villeins having 12½ ploughs. 8 acres of meadow there. Pasturable wood 4 leagues in length and 4 in breadth. The whole manor 10 leagues in length and 8 in breadth. In the time of King Edward it was worth 8 marks of silver. Now 40 shillings.
>
> II manors. In Attercliffe and Sheffield [Escafeld] Suuen had 5 carucates of land for geld where 3 ploughs can be. This land is said to have been inland in Hallam.
>
> In Hallam, Countess Judith 29 carucates. In Attercliffe, the same countess 3 carucates. In Sheffield, the same countess 3 carucates.

Before examining the Domesday Book information it is essential to try to assess the factors important in the growth of the region during the 150 years before the Norman Conquest. We have seen that the Anglo-Saxon Chronicle gives the information that by 942 King Edmund, Alfred's grandson, had recaptured the Danelaw area from the Danes as far as the northern boundary of Mercia. There is evidence that the Danes were becoming more friendly, for King Edgar (Edmund's son) actually appointed certain Danes aldermen, others bishops, and added several to his Witan. Local government was strengthened, and each hundred was compelled to answer for the misdeeds of any of its members.

England was at peace, and the inhabitants of the area prospered.

King Edgar died in 975, and then England's troubles increased. In 979 Danish attacks from overseas began again; Sweyn King of Denmark led a determined attack on the north of England. Even our usually isolated border area experienced very disturbed times. At last in 1016 Canute the Dane was appointed king by the Witan. He promised to give England the good government it had lost since the death of King Edgar and he succeeded remarkably well. Trade increased, and it could well be that the settlements north of Sheffield with Danish names were established at this time.

The Danish line of kings ended in 1042 and the Witan chose the English Edward (the Confessor) as king. He had dwelt for many years in Normandy and it was during his reign (1042–1066) that

Norman influence is first noted, although there is no indication
that this influence was felt in the Sheffield area.

Undoubtedly the great manor of Hallam already existed, and
may well have been known for several centuries. Its boundaries
are not known with any certainty, but in this area it extended as
a rapidly widening region from the River Don crossing at Escafeld, climbing up to the Hallam Moors in the west, occupying the
stretch between the Rivelin and the Porter Brook. The Roman
road, Long Causeway, runs east–west through the manor and
would be used by traders and travellers.

We do not know exactly when Waltheof inherited the manor.
Where exactly the 'Hall of Waltheof' was sited has led to much
speculation. One view is that it stood overlooking the River Don
crossing in Sheffield where the later Norman castle was built; but
in view of the fact that a small manor, Escafeld, not owned by
Waltheof existed here, it seems unlikely that Waltheof's great hall
would stand in another lord's manor. Another view is that it
stood on the east side of the hamlet of Hallam on a site later
occupied by Broomhouse Farm (now demolished). An inspection
of the whole length of the manor reveals a specially striking hill-
site, The Wiggins, on the west side of the hamlet of Hallam,
several hundred yards south of the Long Causeway. There was an
ancient trackway running north–south alongside the site connecting a crossing over the Porter Brook with one over the River
Rivelin, beyond which, on a hill, a cruck building, Park Side Farm
is reached, the track continuing uphill to pass Well House Farm.
Another trackway which has climbed from a lower crossing over
the Porter Brook near one of the ancient water-wheels, and up the
hill to pass alongside the cruck building Stumperlowe (Hall)
Cottage, continues up to The Wiggins, which until a few years
ago was a large farm with two very notable cruck 'barns'. The late
Mr. Colin Cooper knew the site and its buildings well, and gave
detailed descriptions of their massive construction.

The Hall of Waltheof!

The site is now covered with modern houses, but there is no
mistaking its former significance—and one of the old trackways
has now become Barncliffe Lane. Waltheof doubtless had many
manors, but none could have been more desirable than the manor
of Hallam, which with its sixteen berewicks (not named, unfortunately) had 29 carucates of land for taxation—a carucate was

the area of land which could be ploughed by a team of oxen in a year. There was adequate meadowland and a considerable acreage of pasturable woodland. Before the Norman Conquest it was worth 8 marks of silver.

It would be well at this point to consider the social conditions existing in the area at that period, almost 600 years after the first Anglian settlers had arrived. A land-loving rural community had spread over the district, grouped into hamlets or villages surrounded by the necessary land. They were entirely self-supporting, except for unusual luxuries. By Waltheof's time much of the land, as we have seen, had been acquired by powerful war-leaders, and many former freemen had lost that status.

The earls were the most powerful people and under them came the thanes, themselves large landholders; the yeomen came next, either as freeholders or as working, rent-paying tenants. There were smiths and metal-workers, wrights, tradesmen and secular clergy. There was no monastery in our Sheffield area at that time. Then came the unfree class, consisting of peasants who had a smallholding but had to work several days a week for their lord without pay, and there were the serfs who had no land and were engaged in menial tasks.

The country was divided into shires and it is interesting to learn that some years hence the manor of Hallam became known as Hallamshire, although its status seems never to have been on quite the same lines as that of the other shires. As elsewhere there would be the hundred court (governing a district containing originally 100 warriors) and of course the village moots, the laws (dooms) in the early days being handed on by word of mouth. Justice was strict and harsh, including the paying of blood-money (wer-gild), trial by the moots and punishment by death or scourging. If twelve men could be produced to testify to the accused's innocence, he could be acquitted; or he could elect to undergo trial by ordeal, the trial being carried out in the nave of the church.

How hard those people must have worked; and although their lack of 'education' is decried (few could read or write) their thoroughness, stability and courage must be admired. Even at the turn of the present century the old families of Hallam had a quiet integrity, a great pride in their work, were decidedly musical and had a very real love of that beautiful area. The spirit of those early settlers survived.

Such was the situation when the coming of the eleventh century heralded the approach of troublous times.

Waltheof's is the only name associated with the district at that period with which we are familiar today. History tells us that when King Harold, the last of the English kings of that period, had beaten the Norwegians under Harald Hardrada and his half-brother Tostig at Stamford Bridge on 25th September, 1066 and then began his epic march to oppose the invading Duke William of Normandy, he was only half-heartedly supported by the Northumbrian nobles Edwin and Morcar, and there is no mention at all of Waltheof. It was perhaps because Harold needed to leave a reliable man to watch the situation in the north that Waltheof lord of Hallam was not with Harold on his march south.

It was on 14th October, 1066 that the tragic battle of Hastings was fought, ending in defeat for the English when Harold was killed.

Another dynasty would now control the country. William of Normandy was elected king by the Witan.

The new king evidently pardoned Waltheof, and made him Earl of Huntingdon, giving also his niece Judith in marriage. Edwin and Morcar also were pardoned when they made their submission to William, and were allowed to keep their manors, although over most of the country the estates of those who opposed William at Hastings had been forfeited. An interesting point is that Edwin was lord of the manor of Laughton-en-le-Morthen where there is a striking hill-fort, some 14 miles east of The Wiggins.

William's heavy-handed government of England caused great unrest, and when he was in Normandy in 1067 several rebellions broke out, one of the most serious being in the north, in which Waltheof and Edwin were implicated. There is no doubt that the Sheffield area was considerably involved, and eventually the rising was put down. To punish the northern folk William 'harried the north', particularly the Vale of York and the area for miles around; everything that would burn was burned, for almost all the buildings were of timber construction. The inhabitants were slain, or driven away to die of starvation—for their crops and farms were ruined. The effect of this savage devastation was manifest twenty years hence, when the Domesday Book entries of 1086 mention manor after manor as "waste".

For his part in the northern rising William again pardoned Waltheof. But the period following the rebellions was very troubled indeed; William's Norman supporters had been given vast estates, and they made no secret of their opinion of the English, calling them 'Saxon dogs' and treating them with the utmost contempt.

When King William was again in Normandy in 1074 Earl Waltheof again was persuaded to take part in a rebellion. Again the rebellion was unsuccessful, and Waltheof was captured and beheaded, though his wife the Countess Judith was permitted to retain the manor of Hallam. Suuen's two manors, Attercliffe and Sheffield, were given to the powerful Norman Roger de Busli after the Conquest in 1066, and now de Busli became the tenant of Judith's manor of Hallam.

Domesday Book tells us that by 1086 the value of Hallam had fallen to just over one-third of its pre-Conquest value; and the manors of Attercliffe and Sheffield had deteriorated ominously. Domesday Book's brief information actually tells us much about the 'harrying' and wasting following Waltheof's rebellions.

We have noted above that Countess Judith was allowed to retain the manor of Hallam, to which she accepted de Busli as tenant. But shortly after 1086 Judith herself incurred the King's displeasure and her estates were declared forfeit. They passed to the King of Scots, who was her daughter's husband, and it seems that de Busli continued as the tenant.

Evidently the whole of our area was settled, and still wholly rural in character.

III

CHURCH AND MANOR

FOR many years following the accession of William the Norman
the Sheffield area suffered exceedingly. There was little or no
admixture of Norman peoples with the English they so openly
despised; the area was simply useful to a Norman lord as part of
the vast estates given to him, and neither he nor his people understood the English or their language. The feudal system imposed a
very heavy burden, and the fact that the Manor of Hallam came
into the hands of the King of Scots did not ease the situation.
Roger de Busli the Norman, who owned over sixty estates in
Yorkshire, to say nothing of his properties elsewhere, probably
had little interest in his small manors of Attercliffe and Sheffield
and his tenancy of Hallam.

However, at some date early in the twelfth century conditions
took a turn for the better, for William de Lovetot became tenant
lord of Hallam, and lord of Sheffield and Attercliffe. It is not
known with certainty how he acquired these manors but it has
been suggested that he may have married one of the de Busli
daughters. William de Lovetot decided to live in the area, and
built what came to be known as Sheffield Castle. This was probably
mainly of timber of the Norman motte and bailey type, and it
may have been erected in the reign of King Henry I (1100–1113) at
the period when the king issued a 'Charter of Liberties' promising
that 'aids' exacted from his feudal tenants should be fair and
correct, and that he would keep all the laws in force during the
reign of Edward the Confessor before the Norman Conquest.
The old shire courts and hundred courts were revived. All this
promised better days for our area.

De Lovetot erected his castle on the high ground near to and
overlooking the Don's great curve, where the Rivers Sheaf and
Don on two sides of the site and the digging of a substantial moat

between the rivers on the other two sides of the high ground completed his defences, for despite the promise of happier times there was the constant threat of trouble from the powerful barons. It was an attractive site surrounded by fertile, well-cultivated land, and of course overlooking an important Don crossing.

Fortunately de Lovetot was interested in this lovely if somewhat remote area, and he was of a type very different from the general run of domineering, land-grabbing Norman barons of the period. He has been claimed to be the founder of Sheffield and it was indeed propitious that during the turbulent days of the struggle between Stephen and Matilda for the throne, when more than ever before the arrogant barons were striving solely for their own ends, the de Lovetots were lords of Sheffield, Attercliffe and Hallam.

The population of the area slowly but steadily increased as its hidden wealth became manifest. It was probably the increased revenue from these new sources which permitted the de Lovetots to provide new services. A corn mill was established on the Don a short distance upstream of the castle, and the old trackway which led to this has long been known as Millsands. The mill became known as the Town Mill, and functioned right on into the nine-teenth century. From the early days when manors were established it was usual for the lord to have a corn mill known as the lord's mill, and his tenants were compelled to bring their corn to be ground there, the requisite dues being part of the lord's revenue. In fact it was a punishable offence to have corn ground elsewhere. It seems unlikely therefore that de Lovetot's mill was an innova-tion, although since this seems to be the first time a Norman lord actually resided in the manor, this could have led to the rebuilding of an older mill. The Town Mill of later days was built on the site of de Lovetot's twelfth-century corn mill.* It is known that early in the thirteenth century Lady Maud de Lovetot, who married Gerard de Furnival, gave to the Canons of Beauchief Abbey one mark of yearly rent . . . from her mill at Sheffield.

De Lovetot founded a hospital at a suitable distance from his castle and its precincts (there is still Spital Hill on the far side of The Wicker) and built a bridge over the Don, which may have been a replacement of a much earlier timber structure. And it was William de Lovetot who founded the *parish* of Sheffield and built

* According to Dr. A. Gatty, *Sheffield Past and Present*.

a parish church. It would be wrong, however, to assume that he built the *first* church on the site (on which stands today's cathedral).

In the year 667 a famous Greek scholar, Theodore, was appointed Archbishop of Canterbury, and he undertook the difficult task of uniting the Christian Church in the North of England with the Christian Church of the rest of the country which followed the Roman rites introduced by St. Augustine in 597. It was a task made more difficult because three years before Theodore became archbishop there had been a dreadful epidemic particularly in the northern part of the country, which greatly reduced the population, and many priests and Christian teachers had perished. In many areas in the north the small timber churches were left with no one to serve them. During his period as archbishop Theodore tried to introduce a system whereby the country was divided into *parishes* which could be served by a priest, but being such an innovation it was many years before this became effective.

One of the remarkable happenings following the conversion to Christianity of the Anglian kingdoms—particularly Northumbria and Mercia—in the eighth century was the erection of beautifully carved stone crosses which obviously replaced the timber crosses erected immediately upon conversion, the symbol of the new faith to each converted hamlet. Some of the stone replacements actually suggest the timber form which they followed; others, perhaps in the larger, wealthier hamlets, were given the elaborate crosses which are such a wonderful heritage today from the ignorantly styled 'Dark Ages'.

We have seen that during the years 1927–9 excavation on the site of the castle foundations indicated the earlier existence of a long cruck building. This would be the aula or hall of the first Anglian settler on that fine site, and the hamlet would be important, surrounding the great cruck building which controlled the tremendously important crossing of the Don. This hamlet was Escafeld, and without doubt when the area accepted Christianity in the mid-seventh century a timber church would stand on the ideal spot, the hill rising a few hundred yards west of the cruck building, at the crossing of two important ancient trackways, one running east–west to cross the Don near the Sheaf junction, and the other running north–south. And in the churchyard in the early eighth century was erected a beautifully carved Anglian stone cross.

As we have seen, the Domesday survey compiled in the eleventh century reveals that Escafeld is still only a small manor, and no mention is made of a church there, but that is no proof that a church did not exist. It is known that much of interest which existed in the North in 1086 was not recorded in the survey. Perhaps the surveyors were then working against time; travelling conditions could have been extremely difficult, and the English in the area, of sturdy Anglian descent, would give the minimum of information to the already weary investigators. We can be sure that the scant information in the Domesday survey concerning our area is correct, but it would be very unwise to assume that because certain items are not recorded they did not in fact exist. The typical church site existed, and on it stood the Anglian cross which continued to stand there for many more centuries. We may well conclude therefore that de Lovetot *rebuilt* the church in the twelfth century, and a definite *parish* was outlined which would be served by the parish church. After centuries of difficult times the township of Escafeld was entering a happier period, and the Parish of Sheffield was created.

The boundaries then established for the Parish of Sheffield seem to have continued for hundreds of years—until 1900, in fact—to mark the area covered by the City of Sheffield. Our Portrait from the twelfth century shows the extent of the parish area, which was rather large for that time, and stretched from Blackburn Brook in the east to Stanage Pole on the western hills and from the ancient boundary the Meers Brook in the south to the River Rivelin and the north of Wincobank Wood on the north.

From this area the de Lovetots would receive a considerable income, and enough was available to found the Priory of Worksop, towards the upkeep of which a third of the tithes of Sheffield was allocated. In return the priory provided a priest to serve the parish church.

The parish was still an agricultural district, and it continued thus for many centuries; but it was during the lordship of the de Lovetots that the first emphasis on the area's mineral wealth is noted, a development of the utmost importance. The attention of those who rely on 'documentary evidence' is attracted to this development by a charter of May 1161, in which Richard de Busli made a grant to the monks of Kirkstead Abbey.

We have seen that the Romans were interested in the limestone hills to the west of Sheffield because of their valuable veins of lead ores, but the iron-ore deposits in the coal measures of our area seem not to have interested them, although it would be rash to say that these deposits were not known. Over the centuries the lead industry gradually declined in importance although it continued to exist, with fluctuations. The iron industry increased but for some time to come was worked in conjunction with the area's agricultural pattern. The lack of good roads made the transport of heavy commodities almost impossible, so the long-known, slowly growing iron industry would be strictly localized. It was, however, of sufficient potential value to interest local Norman barons.

Richard de Busli was lord of Kimberworth, near Rotherham, and a neighbour of the de Lovetots who were lords of Ecclesfield as well as of Sheffield and Attercliffe. De Busli's charter concerned an area in Kimberworth through which ran an outcrop of the so-called Tankersley ironstone. The early method of mining this was to sink bell-bottom pits to a depth of about 20 feet and then to extract the iron from the ore and forge it by repeated heating and hammering.

The late H. G. Baker* investigated the antiquity of our area's iron-working and established the early period of a number of old furnaces and forges. Two of the recorded sites, at Clifton and Wincobank, possibly belong to prehistoric times; one at Templeborough to Roman times, and two, at Kimberworth and Morlay were medieval. It is pointed out that the comparatively recent removal of many long-existing slag heaps has removed much possible evidence of early workings.

De Busli's charter to Kirkstead Abbey cannot be regarded as a chance venture, or an experiment; clearly it was granted with the long-established knowledge that iron-ore was readily available with the necessary materials to hand for smelting and forging. The abbey was granted: "A site within the territory of Kimberworth for their houses and an orchard and four forges, to wit, two for smelting iron and two for forging it, whensoever they wished, and leave to dig for ore throughout the territory of that township, so much as would be sufficient for two furnaces."

The de Lovetots granted to the abbey some 200 acres of their neighbouring manor of Ecclesfield.

* Quoted in G. P. Jones, *Sheffield and its Region.*

Today, to climb the hill from the Blackburn Brook valley to the ridge of the hill at Thorpe Common gives an interesting insight into our area's story. By this swift-flowing tributary of the River Don is Grange Mill, the site of a very ancient corn mill; to quote the Reverend J. Eastwood, "Grange Mill is doubtless situated on the very spot where the monks of Kirkstead placed their mill nearly 700 years ago"; and as the hill is climbed dozens of uneven hummocks on the rising hillside tell of the mining and iron-working carried on by the monks. On the top of the hill to the east, standing back from the road is the lovely old Kirkstead Abbey Grange on Thorpe Common, a most interesting building. Here the monks lived and cultivated the land immediately surrounding it for their food. And less than a mile to the east along the ridge is Scholes Coppice, where there is an Iron Age hill-slope fort.

When Henry II ascended the throne in 1154 he set about curbing the excessive power of the Norman barons. He was a statesman. He imposed a tax known as 'scutage' (i.e. shield tax) on each 'knight's fee', so that the holding of land involved a payment to the king to provide a knight and his attendants in case of war. This payment to the king so that he could *hire* troops helped to weaken feudalism and permitted peaceful development in the manors and townships. The murder of Becket, Archbishop of Canterbury, in 1170, lost Henry the support of the Church, for he was held to be mainly responsible, because of his ill-guarded remarks, for the murder. Our own 'isolated' region felt repercussions of this unhappy affair, for in 1183 Robert Fitzranulph, lord of Norton, a valuable manor to the south of Sheffield, founded an abbey for Premonstratensian Canons at Beauchief, on a lovely site above the valley of the River Sheaf. Fitzranulph is supposed to have shared some of the guilt for Becket's murder, though this has never been definitely established. He founded the abbey in honour of St. Thomas the Martyr, became a brother himself, and is buried there. Although Beauchief was a comparatively small foundation, it was the first monastic house to be established near to Sheffield and stands some 4 miles from the early centre of Sheffield; it possessed a number of Granges where sheep-farming and coal- and iron-mining were carried on. It was only a few years after the abbey's establishment that the canons were given permission to mine coal in Fitzranulph's former manors of Norton and Alfreton.

Documentary evidence concerning our area's slow industrial development prior to the early thirteenth century is sparse but undoubtedly suggests that the working of iron and the digging of coal had existed over a very long period.

By the end of the twelfth century the de Lovetot estates passed by marriage to the de Furnivals, a family as adventurous in war and peace as the de Lovetots had been quietly unobtrusive. The de Furnivals were great supporters of the Crusades to the Holy Land which had started almost a century earlier, in 1099, and this caused changes in the region's story. Naturally, great sums of money and many men were needed to support the enthusiastic Crusaders, and this imposed a certain amount of hardship, intensified no doubt by the long absences of the lord, and by the various types of epidemics, including leprosy, brought back by the returning Crusaders. Substantial help was obtained by creating sub-manors in Hallam, the holders having to pay feudal dues and provide services to the de Furnivals. The manors of Owlerton, Shirecliffe, Darnall, Wadsley and Ecclesall were created, but only the latter manor actually continued, being held in turn by a succession of well-known families until manors were officially discontinued in the twentieth century.

It was in 1266, in the reign of Henry III, that Sheffield and Hallamshire were again involved in fighting. The de Furnivals were staunch supporters of the King against the rebellious barons under Simon de Montfort, and John de Eyvill, one of the rebel barons, attacked Sheffield, burning the castle, destroying many of the small town's buildings and slaying a number of townspeople. The name of the ancient Burnt Tree Lane in the early part of the town bears witness to this devastation.

Slowly, helped by the income from the iron and coal workings in the manor the town recovered. An award made at York in 1268 to Berta, widow of Gerard de Furnival, referred to 'a third part of all the moneys from all the smithies which shall have been farmed out in the park of Shefaud or in any woods of Thomas in Halumpshire . . . and from all smithies hereafter in the said woods and land to be farmed out . . . .'. This document refers also to "Riveling quarries".

The de Furnival whose castle of Sheffield had been burnt

petitioned the King for permission to rebuild it, and the charter permitting this is dated 1270. The charter gives permission to make strong a castle "at his manor of Sheffield". This is believed to be the first written reference to the Manor of Sheffield and is an indication of its growing importance.

Despite the devastation of 1266, succeeding de Furnivals seem to have taken increased interest in the manor's welfare.

What a compact little township it must have been, overlooking its main feature, the River Don. Narrow unpaved lanes traversed the township, deeply rutted in winter and deep in dust in summer, the drainage running down the middle of the alleyways. Only the homes of the more successful citizens would have dignity; but even the tiniest dwellings would have a small croft. The castle itself stood proudly on its raised site, its nursery gardens, orchards and greens nearby, with the majestic river curving alongside. The township's dominant building would now be the new castle of stone. The significance of today's Nursery Street, Orchard Street, Meadow Street, Castle Green, West Bar Green, High Street, Townhead Street, cannot be overlooked. There were Waingate and Fargate ('gate' meaning 'way'), and the pasturable 'wastes' of the Moor, and Shalesmoor. The Wicker, running through the lowest part of the township, also had significance, as we shall see later. There was still the common land, common to all the townsfolk, a heritage from Escafeld's Anglian settlers of some seven centuries earlier.

By the end of the thirteenth century it was evident throughout the country that the old feudal control was becoming outdated, and many lords already had granted greater freedom to their tenants. It was not until the year 1297 that Sheffield's lord, Thomas de Furnival, granted to his tenants a charter which may be regarded as the first real step in this direction.

The charter, which was signed on 10th August, 1297 contained some clauses that were re-affirmations of earlier privileges, but the new clauses established a class of free tenants, who were the forerunners of a corporation. In the charter the lord undertook to:

> demise, grant and deliver in fee farm to all my free tenants of the town of Schefeld and their heirs all the tofts, lands and holdings which they hold of me in the foresaid town of Schefeld to hold and to have of me and my heirs to the aforesaid tenants and their heirs with all their appurtenances belonging to the said tofts, lands and

holdings, within the town of Schefeld and outside, in fee and heredity, freely, quietly, well and in peace, for ever (provided that my free warren be not hindered by the said tenants or in any wise disturbed), the said tenants and their heirs paying yearly therefor to me and my heirs £3. 8s. 9¼d. of silver, in discharge of all services and demands, reserving nevertheless to me and my heirs fealty, escheats, and suit of court of the said tenants.

Further, I will and grant that the court of the said town of Shefeld of my aforesaid Tenants shall be held within the aforesaid town every three weeks by my bailiffs, as has hitherto been accustomed in the time of my ancestors.

And if it should happen that my said tenants, or any of them, are to be fined for any trespass in my said court, I will and grant for myself and my heirs that they be fined by their peers, and that according to the measure of the offence.

Furthermore, I will and grant for myself and my heirs, as well buyers as sellers, shall everywhere throughout all Hallamshire be quit from all exaction and demand of toll, as they were wont to be in the time of my ancestors, for ever.

And I, the aforesaid Thomas, and my heirs will warrant all these matters aforesaid, with their aforesaid appurtenances, as is aforesaid, to my aforesaid tenants and their heirs, against all people, for ever.

His witnesses were the lords of his submanors, which we have seen were established to ease the financial situation—namely Robert de Ecclissale, Robert de Waddisley, William de Darnale, Thomas de Schefeld (Owlerton) and Thomas de Mountney (Shirecliffe), as well as his steward Robert le Breton, and Sir Edmund Foliot and Thomas de Furneys.

There is no doubt that de Furnival was very short of money; he saw it would be an advantage to be able to collect dues in place of feudal service. The lord was still the master of his manor, but there was now a class of Free Tenants with definite rights.

After the Norman Conquest, and the death of Waltheof of Hallam in 1074 no Englishman seems to have his name recorded in official 'history' in our area. The Conqueror's 'harrying of the north' following the northern rebellions had served the purpose of making it clear to the English of the region that they had lost all pretence to freedom. Vast areas were seized by the King himself for his royal hunting forests—the Royal Forest of the Peak being one, and Sherwood Forest another; and in the Royal Forests the laws were very severe indeed. The creation of these forests had caused many people to lose their homes and means of livelihood. Not surprisingly, bands of homeless 'outlaws' frequented the forests, poaching the king's deer and subsisting as well as they could, doing the best possible in many cases to help other unfortunates.

And within the area was Robin Hood.

Who was Robin Hood? Various theories have been advanced concerning his origin, some of which obviously cannot be taken seriously, but it seems quite clear that he was a man of valour who could control and lead outlaws. One source speaks of Robin as Earl of Huntingdon; another associates him with Loxley, a village north of the River Loxley. We can be certain that as an outlaw with his life at stake, 'Robin Hood' would be an assumed name.

We recall that after William conquered England in 1066 he pardoned Waltheof, lord of Hallam, and honoured him by making him Earl of Huntingdon and giving his niece Judith in marriage. It seems that Waltheof and Judith had a daughter, who was married to the King of Scots. After the 1074 rebellion Waltheof was beheaded at Winchester, and Judith was allowed to retain the manor of Hallam until she herself incurred William's displeasure and as punishment was dispossessed, the manor being given to her daughter's husband. But was Judith Waltheof's *second* wife? And had he a son by a former wife? History is silent on this point, but it is by no means beyond the bounds of possibility; and if this indeed was the case, such a descendant (being English) and never inheriting the estates which were given to the son-in-law of the Norman Judith, would probably consider himself to be the rightful Earl of Huntingdon. He would probably have Waltheof's courage, which in turn could be inherited by his sons and grandsons as they continued to dwell in the not too distant township of Loxley. And then, under the King of Scots the manor of Hallam had as tenants, after the powerful Roger de Busli, the milder de Lovetots and then the more warlike de Furnivals, who were favourites of King Richard I.

Sir Walter Scott evidently was interested by the stories of Robin Hood, and used the outlaws with their accurate archery in his

Sheffield University: one of the oldest parts
The City Hall

Ivanhoe, although the period of which he wrote may have been a little early for our Robin Hood.

Throughout a wide area around Sheffield there are references in place names to Robin Hood: there are several Robin Hood's Wells, Robin Hood's Cave, Robin Hood's Stride, Robin Hood's Larder, Robin Hood's Picking Rods, and there is even a hamlet overlooking the River Derwent called Robin Hood. And our conjecture regarding Robin's ancestry is by no means contradicted by what has been stated concerning his last illness, for it was then, accompanied by his faithful follower Little John, that he painfully made his way to Kirklees Priory near Brighouse, in Yorkshire, where his "sister or kinswoman" was prioress. There he died, and was buried by Little John.

It would appear that as living conditions became less harsh many of Robin's band had managed to find quiet places where they could make a home and live safely—although probably still on the verge of poverty—but there was no such retreat for their leader, Robin Hood, and only the faithful Little John remained with Robin to the end.

And who was Little John? Here we are on firm ground, for Little John, of taller than usual stature, was born in Hathersage, an ancient village over the high moors 10 miles west of Sheffield. Little John was a nail-maker, working at the ancient forge in the steep little valley below the church. To this day the families who have lived for generations in Hathersage will point out the site of Little John's cottage near the church; it was pulled down about a century ago and is known to have been a low, stone cottage with a thatched roof, and was very old when demolished.

Returning sadly to his Hathersage home, Little John dug his own grave under an old yew tree in the churchyard, near the Anglian preaching cross, and a short time after that he died. That he was held in affectionate esteem is shown by the fact that for centuries his cap of Lincoln green hung in the church alongside his bow. Some time ago both cap and bow were removed to Cannon Hall near Barnsley, in Yorkshire. The bow, more than 6 feet long, was made of spliced yew, horn-tipped, and required a pull of 160 pounds.

The grave was opened about the same time, and the remains interred there were seen to be those of a very tall man. Today, the grave is marked by a stone bearing the legend:

4

The Cutlers' Hall, Church Street

Here lies Buried
Little John
The Friend and Lieutenant of
Robin Hood.
He died in a Cottage (now destroyed)
To the East of the Churchyard
His grave is marked by the
Old Headstone and Footstone
And is underneath the Old Yew Tree.

Appropriately, the grave is maintained by the Ancient Order of Foresters.

How often Robin Hood and Little John must have passed through Escafeld and over the River Don crossing; and how respected Robin must have been by those who knew his sad story —a story common to many Englishmen of courage and hopeless desperation in the days of the Norman contempt for (and perhaps fear of) the 'Saxon dogs'.

IV

HARD TIMES

THE Free Tenants of Sheffield lost little time in getting together to
try to solve some of the town's more urgent problems—and
there must have been many. Little is known of their early efforts,
but they elected a chairman or leader and gave him the title of
Town Collector. For several hundred years the Town Collector
was regarded as Sheffield's leading citizen.

It is well to recall that when Thomas de Furnival was outlining
his famous charter in 1297, it was very timely, for twenty-two
years previously, in 1275, King Edward I, known as the Father
of the English Parliament, drew up his first Statute of West-
minster. This statute thoroughly reformed legal procedure, and
insisted that everyone, whether noble or peasant, should have the
protection of law. The King followed this by further reforms,
which had to be noted by the barons.

Thomas de Furnival, lord of Sheffield, died in 1332, and the
'inquisition' required to be held by an officer of the Shire following the death of a land-holder is a document which in this case
still survives. The details entered indicate that Hallamshire and
Sheffield were experiencing hard times, and suggest that the
population of the area had diminished. There was a corresponding
decline in trade and income, undoubtedly caused by the costly
Crusades which had needed men and money. And then, after a
period of years in which improvement should have been noted,
there was war with France and then with Scotland. Again our
area's isolated position saved it from the more serious consequences of these wars, but troubles there still were.

There are signs, however, that during those trying times more
attention was being paid to the area's hidden wealth, the iron-ore
and coal deposits. The 1332 'inquisition' records that the castle
was "frail"—which is difficult to understand as it had been rebuilt

in stone only about sixty years previously. A record of King Edward III's possessions in the Tower of London made in 1340, lists a knife made in Sheffield as well as several from Ashbourne. A few years later, in about 1380 one of Geoffrey Chaucer's *Canterbury Tales* mentions a "Sheffield thwitel". A 'thwitel' seems to have been an all-purpose knife; and to this day children in our area 'whittle' at pieces of wood with an ordinary small pocket-knife.

It has been suggested that the smiths had their forges chiefly in the villages removed from the centre of Sheffield, but that would be hard to accept entirely in view of the concentration of iron-works of various kinds which have existed along the streams joining the Don, and the Don itself in Sheffield, for many long years.

William de Furnival died in 1383, the last lord of his line, and the 'inquisition' of that date is in many ways the reverse of the earlier one. Sheffield and Hallamshire had made favourable progress; there were more free tenants and much more land had been brought under cultivation. One wonders whether, by that time, the dwellers in Sheffield had lost most of their crofts for the building of more houses and workshops. We do know, however, that the roads leading to and from Sheffield were narrow, stony, dangerous hill-tracks along which only pack-horses could carry goods, and the little lanes in the town were equally unattractive and probably dangerous.

One reason why the 'inquisition' following the death of the lord of the manor in 1382 indicates a decided social advance over that of 1332 was the unavoidable easement of several harsh feudal conditions after the havoc wrought by the terrible Black Death of 1348-9. By 1382 there had been over thirty years for the wounds to be healed.

It was following the so-called success of King Edward III's war in France, which culminated in the surrender of Calais in 1347 that the terrible pestilence known in England as the Black Death swept over from the East, and caused the deaths of more than one-third of the population. It is claimed that during the time this plague ravaged the country the population fell from about 4 million to little more than 2 million. Perhaps the Sheffield area, with its hills, its plentiful good water and its agricultural pursuits suffered less than many areas, but suffering there certainly was, and this, as elsewhere, resulted in a scarcity of labour. The workers eventually benefited, because in order to secure labour the old feudal villeinage began to disappear, and workers received wages. As would be expected, steps were taken at high level to try to compel men to stay in their manor, and the hated Statutes of Labourers was passed by Parliament, decreeing (1) that everyone must work for any employer who should require him to do so; (2) that wages should be the same as they were before the Black Death; and (3) that no one should leave the manor on which he was born. These statutes caused great discontent and the wages decree could not be enforced.

The fact that the 1383 inquisition indicated increased prosperity could suggest that our area was less badly affected by the plague than some areas, and that industrial activity was steadily increasing. The inquisition mentions that the

aforesaid castle within the manor is worth nothing yearly.... Also a certain deer park with deer living in the same together with hunting for the same and with parks woods and pastures in the same worth yearly sixteen pounds in silver yearly.... Also within the said park a certain fulling mill worth thirty shillings.... And there are two water mills worth yearly sixteen pounds.... Also a certain common bakehouse worth yearly thirty shillings.... Also a certain View of Frankpledge called the Sembly held every year on Tuesday in Easter week at Sheffield under the castle there, worth yearly forty shillings. Also a market held there each year in Tuesday in every week, and one fair held on Trinity Sunday in each year with the tolls belonging to the same market and fair worth yearly forty shillings.... And at Ollerton a certain water mill worth yearly fifty shillings.... And at Brightside a water mill worth yearly twenty shillings and not more, which is very frail and ruinous, and otherwise cannot be put to farm.... And at Wardsend a water mill very frail and ruinous worth nothing yearly.

The inquisition gives the names of the various villages in the manor, all of which adds up to the fact that this indeed was a very extensive, valuable possession.

We know little of the lords of Sheffield except their names. Joan, daughter of the last de Furnival, married Sir Thomas de Nevill, who became lord in her right, and their daughter Maud married a Talbot, a family who as lords of Sheffield and Hallamshire took great interest in their growth.

The national story was a sad one; there were wars, more wars, and peasant risings against the increasing oppression of the poor; and there was treachery. But although these events must have caused local repercussions and fluctuations in the area's trade, no events of a very serious nature occurred to dim our Portrait unduly.

The Talbots, who were Earls of Shrewsbury, were very much involved in various wars. It was about the year 1472 that The Wicker, at that time a wide, level stretch by the Don, beyond the castle, became important, for in that year during the tragic Wars of the Roses it was enacted that every man must have a bow of his own height and be able to draw it. The lord of the manor, or his steward, saw to the enforcement of this order, and wicker 'butts' were erected for bow-and-arrow practice. Dating from that period many hamlets in our area erected 'butts', and still have the site names Butt's Hill, The Butts etc. The Wicker has retained its name to this day, although it has also had other names, as we shall see.

The fourth Talbot to hold the lordship inherited the title when still a child, and it was then that Sheffield, towards the end of the fifteenth century, acquired fame. And the main factor behind this sudden rise to fame is claimed to have been the development of the use of water power.

The probable use of water-wheels by our early Anglian settlers is mentioned in Chapter II. Such a unique facet of our Portrait is provided by our wheels and the lovely streams which power them, that this demands further review.

History has shown that our Anglian settlers were essentially practical people—otherwise they could not have survived so noticeably in a new country. Their corn had to be grown, and ground. No doubt they used stone, rotary hand-querns, but as the land they brought into cultivation was extended it was deemed important to make the fullest possible use of any swiftly flowing stream in their vicinity. They were skilled users of timber, and to erect in a narrow stream a timber-built undershot wheel so that the rushing water would cause the horizontal specially aligned spars to turn the wheel, would not offer any great difficulty. The revolving wheel turned, connected to a grindstone, and ground the grain fed to it. In later years, when the manorial system had developed, this became the lord's mill, and throughout his manor all grain had to be ground at that mill, the dues being paid to the lord.

It is not surprising that those early English soon learned to adapt their wheels to work bellows for forges; and from that development, as the need arose, breast-shot and over-shot wheels were introduced, storage dams being made to ensure a constant supply of water as needed. And throughout the years their skill with this logical development of a natural resource was increasing steadily and reliably.

When, therefore, towards the end of the fifteenth century it was apparently realized that a stream which had long been utilized to turn a wheel to grind corn or work bellows could be used to turn grindstones to grind knives and cutting tools, Sheffield's name became widely known. Which other area in the country had such a profusion of rapidly flowing streams rushing down from the hills to join the main rivers? And where else could the needed materials be found—iron-ore, coal, wool for making cloth, gritstone from the moors for making grindstones, and the inherited skill of men?

In Domesday Book numbers of corn mills are mentioned, which indicates that long before the Norman Conquest water-driven corn mills were well known and valued. It has been claimed that during the long centuries when running water provided the only source of power, there was a greater concentration of water-mills in the Sheffield district than anywhere else in the country.

A subsidy roll of 1297 names only one cutler and one smith in Sheffield, and in Rotherham and Wath one smith in each. However, as in the case of the Domesday survey, the information given can be considered to be accurate as far as it goes, but it by no means tells the whole story. The subsidy roll lists a number of people for whom no trade is mentioned, and this number—the majority of names listed, in fact—may well have included names of smiths, cutlers, etc. whose trade is omitted.

The subsidy roll of 1378-9 indicates great advance in the metal-working trades; an area covering Sheffield, Rotherham, Ecclesfield, Handsworth, Kimberworth and Barnsley had forty smiths, three arrowsmiths, three cutlers, one locksmith and one ironmonger—and this, again, may well be an understatement. At that period the cutlers of the area had no higher standing than those of several other areas, but before the end of the sixteenth century Sheffield had earned a high reputation for its cutlery manufacture and was beginning to export.

It must be appreciated that this seemingly sudden development in the manufacture of cutlery and edge-tools took place under feudal conditions. George, the fourth Earl of Shrewsbury, lived in Sheffield Castle. The lord of the manor owned many of the grinding wheels, and the Hallamshire cutlers worked under the lord's control. In the first half of the sixteenth century there is written evidence for the existence of water-powered grinding wheels at Millsands, Ecclesfield, Greystones, Heeley, Lescar, Whitley, Little Sheffield, Wadsley Bridge, Rotherham and Wisewood.

The streams working the wheels were small and swift-flowing, hurrying down from the hills through beautiful valleys. In the Sheffield area are the Sheaf, the Porter, the Moss Brook, the Shire Brook, the Loxley, the Rivelin, the Blackburn and the Don itself. As the number of wheels increased dams were made, fed by a goit from the stream, and after turning the wheel the water escaped back again to the stream via the tail goit. Each building was of stone, usually referred to as a 'hull' though often just called the 'wheel', having an earth or a stone-flagged floor, with a maze of wheels and pulleys all of which were worked by the water-wheel outside. They were fascinating places, each in a lovely setting, and were worked by men who were craftsmen whether they knew it or not.

A description of the length of the little Porter Brook will aptly emphasize the importance of our wheels and the part they played in establishing Sheffield's world-wide reputation for cutlery and metal goods. In its comparatively short length of just over six miles the Porter had twenty water-mills.

The Porter Brook rises on the Hallam Moors at Brown Edge, the infant stream passing under a lane and through Clough Plantation before meeting its first tributary lower down the Mayfield Valley. This small tributary had already been harnessed, two wheels having been established at an early date, each being a flour mill and each with its own dam. Known locally as the Fulwood Upper and Lower Corn Mills, their origin is lost in the mists of time, but it is certain that they were associated with Fulwood Hall high on the hill to the north and overlooking the valley. Long before 1638 it was recorded that the Fox family of Fulwood Hall owned a "corn mill". Because they were so near the head of the stream both wheels were small, Upper Mill at one time had two pairs of stones and Lower Mill one pair. Now, alas, these ancient mills are no more. Both were working just over sixty years ago and both have now been demolished. The Upper Mill dam still exists although it is empty, and the Lower Mill dam is being filled in.

The Porter and its first tributary join just above Carr Bridge, continuing down the lovely valley to enter and fill the Forge Dam, which seems never to have powered a corn mill. At this secluded spot with its little group of ivy-covered buildings—always known as the Old Forge—were two water-wheels, the larger driving two tilt-hammers and the smaller driving the blower. But not since about 1888 has the thud of the tilts been heard, and today the wheels and some of their buildings have disappeared. Fortunately the dam is still there in its beautiful setting.

After flowing over the weir to leave the Forge Dam the Porter has cut for itself rather a deep valley, and high above it a long goit feeds the next dam, now known as the Wire-mill Dam. This is an historic site, for it was here in about 1743 that Thomas Boulsover built or adapted his rolling mill for the manufacture of the now famous Old Sheffield Plate. At that period the mill was known as Whiteley Wood Rolling Mill. Records show that after Boulsover's time the mill was used for grinding cutlery, edge-tools and saws. Fairbanks indicated in 1830 that there were then two dams and two great overshot wheels. By 1861 it seems that the two dams were joined (hence the present length of the dam) and one huge water-wheel was installed to replace the two former wheels, the premises then being used as a wire mill. By about 1875 the work was transferred elsewhere, and the great wheel was dismantled. Many people remember seeing the mysterious-looking massive masonry which once held the great wheel.

Thomas Boulsover lived at Whiteley Wood Hall on the hill to the south of the dam, and he had a factory at the Old Forge up-stream for silver-plating buttons and snuff boxes. It is claimed that during this same period one of the small Fulwood corn mills was used for buffing the buttons. Today, near the site of the wheel of Boulsover's rolling mill stands a memorial to his work. This so aptly sited tribute to Boulsover's memory was erected by the late Mr. David Flather, a former master cutler.

From the lovely Wire-mill Dam the water falls to the Porter in its valley, which gets shallower as it approaches the Whiteley Wood Bridge under which the brook passes before a short goit flows to the Leather Wheel Dam, also known as the Nether Wheel Dam. The bridge has been well known for many decades because of the unusual stone chairs at each end. This was a remarkably attractive spot. Writing in 1936 the late W. T. Miller says: "With the high wooded bank along one side, the footway on the other and the babbling stream below it, Leather Mill dam is one of the most picturesque on the Porter." So it was. Generations of small children crossed the brook via the weir to reach the pretty Bluebell Wood on the far side, and, happily, succeeding generations may follow in their footsteps, for the lovely wood is now saved from destruction. It is more than sixty years since the wheel was used, but both the water-wheel and grinding hull stood for several years more. Little seems to be known of its early history, but it was of great age and belonged to the Whiteley Wood Hall estate, for which probably it was the corn mill. In the later years of its working life the wheel was used for scythe and saw grinding, and some huge worn grindstones paved the ancient ford over which Dead Lane (now High Cliffe Road) crossed the Porter. Today, nearly forty years after Mr. Miller wrote of the beauty of this dam the visitor sees it dried out and filled with unsightly heaps of spoil!

The brook hastens past this sad sight to pass under Porter Bridge, a short goit leaving it to enter the dam of the Shepherd Wheel. Here again is a very ancient wheel, once known as the Porter Wheel, its original timber structure long ago replaced by metal spokes and wheel-rims. In its early days this wheel belonged to the estate of old Stumperlowe Hall (now know as Stumperlowe Cottage), one of the area's early Anglian cruck buildings (see Chapter II); it was once the corn mill for Stumperlowe. At a much later date—1584—"William Beighton of Stumper Lawe, cutler," bequeathed "To Thomas, Robte. and Hugh my sons all my interest term titles and possession which I have in and upon one Watter Whele called Potar Whele which I have of the grant of the said Earl [of Shrewsbury]." The Shepherd (Porter) Wheel, where two grinding hulls are powered by one overshot wheel was the last cutlery wheel on the Porter to be worked, and it was functioning until about forty years ago. For more than a century the smaller of the two hulls was worked by members of the Hinde family, the senior member being the 'Little Mester'. As well as being skilled craftsmen the Hindes were a musical family, several members having fine singing voices. At the turn of the century the Hindes, the Wildgooses and several other local families of craftsmen could have provided a choir of a quality hard to surpass.

A few yards in front of the hulls is the ford through the Porter, across which runs the ancient way which has come down from Stumperlowe and from The Wiggins high on the hill near the Roman Long Causeway as it passes the hamlet of Hallam; and the old track continues up the hill beyond the ford to pass alongside the fine Anglian cruck building at High Storrs (recently destroyed). The windows of the smaller hull are large unglazed openings closed by shutters overlooking the water-wheel and the meadows. An old fireplace in the wall between the windows always had a bright fire during working hours. It is heartening to know that after being closed and neglected during the war years (1939–45) the Shepherd Wheel has been restored to working condition by the Council for the Conservation of Sheffield Antiquities with the co-operation of the Sheffield City Council and others. This restored ancient wheel is an apt memorial to generations of 'Little Mester' cutlers and their workmen.

Below Shepherd Wheel a short goit carries the water to the dam of the Ibbotson Wheel (the Upper Spur-gear Wheel), the great wheel and hull of which have now been destroyed, though it was still intact in 1936 and was last used for file-grinding about 1910. This wheel also was of ancient origin, and was in the lordship of Ecclesall (one of the sub-manors). A document of 1587 refers to "a Wheele in Ecclesall near Greystone Cliffe and upon Porter Watter". The document refers to a lawsuit of that date, where evidence was given that the rent was paid, and war service with horse and armour rendered to the Earl of Shrewsbury for many years prior to 1587.

As for over a century a Hinde was Little Mester at Shepherd Wheel, so for at least a similar period an Ibbotson was Little Mester at the Ibbotson Wheel. The Ibbotson Wheel at Porter Glen was the last before the Porter leaves the delightful Whiteley Woods to pass under Rustlings Road to Endcliffe Woods, where a short goit takes water to the dam of the Nether Spur-gear or Greystones Wheel. This wheel was demolished many years ago and little of its story seems to have survived except that at one time it was used for knife-grinding. Today only the attractive duck pond survives.

The busy Porter hurries along in its little valley, a short goit soon leaving it to take water to the Endcliffe Boating Dam, which was the dam for the Holme Wheel. This was a knife-grinding wheel which ceased work about the year 1880. By 1936 the hull was in ruins and today, but for the fine dam, no trace of the mill remains.

Before leaving Endcliffe Woods the Porter fed one more dam, which worked the Endcliffe Wheel. By 1936 there was no trace of the hull, although in 1880 it was used for file-grinding. This was a secluded dam and before the turn of the century it was used as an outdoor swimming pool. It was quite a sight on a frosty Boxing Day morning to see stalwart enthusiasts diving in for a brisk swim. But by 1938 there was another generation; the dam was closed and filled in and is now a garden.

The Porter has now reached the end of Endcliffe Woods at Hunters Bar, and soon it passes under Ecclesall Road, continuing rather forlornly past the sites of several once fine dams and busy wheels, now completely obliterated. The Upper Lescar Wheel came first; it was mentioned in 1587: "a house and two wheels in Little Sheffield nether more" at "Lech Carr". It was a table-knife-grinding wheel. Nether Lescar Wheel was a matter of yards downstream, where at one time the dam powered a grinding wheel which later was used to work tilts or rolling mills.

And then, happily, the Snuff Mill is reached, where the dam still powers a great wheel which *works*. For near two centuries the Snuff Mill has worked economically and successfully, and long before that time the wheel was used for grinding cutlery. The Porter must be reluctant to leave this busy, well-maintained site, one surrounded by urbanization but retaining its old distinctive individuality and charming appeal. But the little brook must continue on its way, and passes the site of the now demolished Stalker or Stoke Wheel and its dam. Here, eleven trows once ground edge-tools and table-knives. Before the bottom of Ecclesall Road is reached there were three wheels in quick succession, each with its dam. They were Broomhall Wheel or Little Sheffield Grinding

Wheel, then the Broomhall Corn Mill which is said to have been built by William Jessop of Broom Hall before 1630. Next came the Norris Wheel, which rather unusually seems to have been an undershot wheel. Streets and houses have long ago covered these sites.

Passing under the road the Porter next powered Bennett's Wheel or Sheffield Moor Wheel, which ceased work about 1860. In 1794 this large mill had fifteen trows (a 'trow' being a crafts-man's work-place in the hull). Before this, in 1772, Mr. Edward Bennett paid land tax for his "wheel and sugar houses". By 1824 the wheel seems to have become a rolling mill, the dam being called the Vulcan Dam. Here the little Porter Brook is nearing the end of its journey, but before joining the Sheaf it supplied the dam of the Sylvester Wheel, which disappeared when Sylvester Street was widened. And then the brook supplied its twentieth—and last —dam, for Pond Corn Mill. This site originally was occupied by Sinderhill Wheel, a cutler's wheel. The New Mill erected in the eighteenth century was a water corn mill but it was pulled down in 1860 to be covered by Shoreham Street and St. Mary's Road.

Soon the little Porter joins the Sheaf, its twentieth mill, like its first, having been a water corn mill. Today, at the end of its journey the Porter is a tired, shockingly neglected little stream, the outstanding beauty of its upper reaches forgotten. And how busy it was when all its twenty mills were working, the same water turning wheel after wheel.

It was Sir Anthony Fitzherbert in 1523 who stated in his *Boke of surveyinge and of improvements*: "It is to be understande that ther be many maner of mylnes as . . . Fullyng mylnes, sythe mylnes, cutlers mylnes, smethy mylnes and all such other as the whele gothe by drifts of water. . . ."

The late W. T. Miller was probably the first person to under-take research into the story of our water-driven mills, and his *The Water-Mills of Sheffield* makes most interesting reading. He writes:

It is probably true that within a comparatively restricted area, and at the most intensive period of its development, our forebears made greater use of the water power available to them than in any other part of this kingdom, and yet there is no connected history of their achievements in this direction; moreover little appears to be known about those early engineers who, in this locality, were responsible for the utilization of this great source of energy for the various purposes of industry.

No doubt this is, in part, due to the fact that water power was the first of the great forces of nature to be harnessed in the service of man; its use in this country dates back to the eighth century, and the Domesday Survey contains many references to water-mills.

The application of the water-wheel, first to drive the stones for the grinding of corn, then for the fulling or dressing of woollen cloth, was recorded in this district more than 750 years ago, and its adaptation to the local trades would probably be a continuous and gradual process in the days when records were scanty. . . .

It is interesting to note that although the original water-powered mills built by the early Anglian settlers were for grinding corn, comparatively few of these mills continued solely for corn-grinding after the development of water-power for industrial purposes.

As elsewhere in the country, the monastic houses were very interested in securing water-mills; and the one abbey on the borders of Sheffield, Beauchief Abbey, gave its name to the Abbeydale section of the River Sheaf and owned several of the mills on that river. Included in his gifts of land to Beauchief Abbey which he founded in 1183 Robert Fitzranulph gave "the mill of Norton, with all its multure, its appurtenances and gearing, so that neither I nor my heirs shall build any other mill in the liberty of the said village nor permit this to be done by any man save the canons, but it shall be lawful for the canons themselves to erect other mills in the liberty of the same village". This may be the mill known as Bradway Mill, on the Sheaf.

The next mill on the Sheaf downstream was the Walk Mill, for fulling woollen cloth. This was destroyed by the building of the Midland Railway line over that section in about 1870. The Walk Mill was probably built by the canons of Beauchief Abbey, on whose granges much wool was produced. A grant of 1280 states that Sir Ralph de Ecclesall gave to the canons a piece of ground by the river Sheaf for the erection of a fulling mill, with leave to turn the river if necessary, he to have one-third of the profits and pay one-third of the expenses. Many hundred years later the Walk Mill became a grinding mill for sickles, then a paper mill and finally a saw-grinding mill.

The Abbeydale Works occupies the next mill-site downstream,

and happily this works has been restored and preserved. But there are no records that this mill ever belonged to the abbey, nor that it existed at all until the eighteenth century.

W. T. Miller reminds his readers that:

This is one of the most interesting and self-contained of all the works driven by water-power in the vicinity of Sheffield. Built round an open courtyard are the crucible steel-melting furnaces, the forge, the grinding wheel, the drilling and boring shed, and all the various small workshops concerned with the finishing of scythes, hay-knives, etc.; here also is the warehouse for storing the finished goods. It should be noted that all the firms mentioned in connection with this mill were scythemakers, so that the works specialized in that direction for 130 to 140 years. [In 1934 the great tilt] was then in fair order, with two wooden-helve hammers, complete with a massive main shaft of oak, driven by gearing from the large water-wheel, and with an independent wheel of smaller size for driving the blower; there were also two other water-wheels, one for driving the grinding wheel and the other the drilling machines for cutting the holes in the bodies and backs of the scythe blades.

The next wheel downstream, the Hutcliffe Wheel, a scythe and sickle grinding wheel, was destroyed in the railway building era. This wheel was owned and probably originally worked by the canons of Beauchief; it may have been the mill mentioned in a lease of February 1496 between "John, Abbat of Beucheff and convent and Roger Eyre. . . . Roger to have a bloom harth . . . and the Smethy Dam . . . with certain wodds, Hudclyff and the brood medowe abutt for cooll [charcoal] for ten years."

The next mill downstream was the Barton (or Barkin) Wheel, and then came Ecclesall Corn Mill, long known as Millhouses Corn Mill, which gave the name Millhouses to the surrounding hamlet. This mill also was a gift to Beauchief Abbey from Sir Ralph de Ecclesall in about 1280, and is one of the few water-driven corn mills in the Sheffield area which never changed its function.

The dissolution of the abbey in 1537, with the consequent change of ownership of the canons' water-mills, iron-ore granges and wool granges, had a noticeable effect on the area's industries.

According to W. T. Miller there were in the hey-day of water-mills no fewer than twenty-three water-mills worked by the River Sheaf and its small tributaries, and after its junction with its tributary the Porter there were four more mills before the junction with the Don. The Porter's twenty mills added gives a total of forty-seven water-mills on the Sheaf and its tributaries.

A very interesting fact in the story of water-mills on the Sheaf is mentioned by Miss R. Meredith, Archivist at Sheffield Central Library, in her pamphlet "The Water-mills of Abbeydale":

It is interesting to find that it was in fact at Beauchief that one of the earliest ventures in lead-smelting by water-power was carried out. The moving spirit was William Humfrey, goldsmith, assay master of the Royal Mint, and a leading member of the Company of Mineral and Battery Works, incorporated in 1568 for mining and working tin, lead, steel and iron. Under the patent granted in 1565, Humfrey was given protective rights for carrying out any "rare feats, practises and devices" in the working of mines and ores. About 1570 he set up his mill on the Sheaf near Beauchief Abbey for smelting lead by the new process. This process must have been successful for shortly afterwards the Earl of Shrewsbury brought men from the Mendips in Somerset to develop a similar smelting works for him at Chatsworth, and there was soon a number of imitators against whom Humfrey instituted proceedings for infringing his patent rights. At least one of his letters to the Earl survives, "wrytten at Beauchaff Abbay, the xiith of Aprill 1574," "touching the bringyng your ewer [ore] in to lead after amore easye rate then heretofore hathe bin." His process he believed left a much smaller proportion of metal in the slag than "common Boweling" i.e. smelting on the bole hills.

Another reference to "A lead-smelting-mill at Dore belonging to Edward Pegge" mentions the following tools there in 1671: "Tooles belonging to Mr. Burton att John Rotheram Smiltinge milne called Clyffe [Hutcliffe?] milne, about 3 or 4 years since.

"Two payre of Bellowes with other materiall belonginge to the said Bellowes, vizt. 4 swords, 4 hanks, 4 Iron sturrups, two beames (qr. the Cut), one weigh beame with Iron hankes to it, five great Iron Crowes, two Litle Iron Crowes, One Iron Lead Ladle, one Iron Trowell, one Lead Hatchett, two Iron pickes, one Iron walling hammer."

Twenty-three water-mills on the River Rivelin are listed by W. T. Miller: thirty on the River Loxley, eleven on the Blackburn Brook, twenty-five on the River Don between Oughtibridge and Lady's Bridge, and twelve between Lady's Bridge and Tinsley.

Sheffield Cathedral: the new extension at the west end

It would be unrealistic, perhaps, to close this important chapter without referring to the difficulty of transporting even locally obtained heavy materials such as iron-ore, lead-ore, grindstones, etc. to the water-mills in the valleys, and of carrying the finished products to sell at the various markets. Lead-ore smelted in the Sheaf Valley was carried on pack-horses, strings of which were driven by the 'jagger-lads' over barely passable tracks across the Pennines. To this day the ancient tracks can be seen, and many of the necessary road-markers are still in position; examples are the Wooden Pole where the track over Totley Moss turns across to the lead mines of the Eyam area; Stanage Pole, marking the line of the old Roman road to Hathersage with the huge stone Barncliff Stoop above the Rivelin Valley near the hamlet of Hallam; Lady's Cross marking a track over Big Moor; Ramsley Cross by the old track on Ramsley Moor; Shillito Cross and Wibberlsey Cross by tracks over Leash Fen.

All these and the tracks they marked—wild, windswept, dangerous ways—still have their historic, almost heroic place on the borders of our Portrait.

The corn mills, the fulling mills, the smelting mills, the grinding wheels, the paper mills, the forges, the tilts, the rolling mills, the wire mills, the scythe mills with all their appurtenances, powered by running water and fed by locally produced materials, had to depend to an appreciable extent on transport by pack-horse or, in fine summer weather within the town, on horse-drawn wagons.

5

Sheffield from Wincobank

V

THE BEGINNING OF SHEFFIELD CUTLERY

IT IS almost impossible to enumerate all the sites where iron-ore mining was carried on—and this also applies to the early, shallow coal pits, as it does to many of the lead mines on the western carboniferous-limestone fringe of the Sheffield area. There were dozens of small workings, for many of which there is no record of any kind. This fact was emphasized a year or so ago when the new stretch of the M1 motorway emerging to the north of Sheffield was being constructed. The *Sheffield Morning Telegraph* of 25th November, 1967 reports the county surveyor of the West Riding County Council as saying that it was still not certain that all the holes beneath that stretch had been filled. He explained that in the Blackburn area uncharted workings had to be filled in, and referred to the query which constantly presented itself: "Is there something you have missed because it is three or four feet below where you have dug?" The surveyor added that stringent precautions had to be taken to find out what was there.

In building the Sheffield section of the motorway 5,000 tons of usable coal were taken out and handed over to the National Coal Board. The surveyor stated: "We may have helped the fuel policy, but so far as we are concerned it has been a thundering nuisance", and he added that this "exercise into the unknown" had made the building of this section of the motorway particularly interesting. He mentioned that over 400 bell-pits had been found and filled in in the Thorpe Hesley area. How surprised the monks of Kirkstead Abbey would have been in the twelfth century if they had known that 800 years afterwards their industrious work on the hillside between the Blackburn Brook and Thorpe Common, and indeed throughout that whole area, would create "interesting problems" for highly trained engineers!

Lead production declined in importance in the area about a century ago, and appropriately it was the River Sheaf, on the west of the Don system and nearest to the lead mines of the Pennines, which had several water-powered lead works. Some time ago the local iron-mining industry declined, but the mining of coal grew to be extremely important. Today the coal-mining industry in the area around Sheffield is declining. It is not known at what date the mining of coal on a large scale was started, but *locally* coal was used in many places where mined; for example, the canons of Beauchief were mining and using coal in the thirteenth century. The use of wood and charcoal as fuel seems to have persisted, for this was a well-wooded region, although we learn from Leland who was journeying through these parts in the early sixteenth century, "betwixt Cawood and Rotherham be good plenti of wood, yet the people burn much yerth cole by cawse hit is plentifully found there and sold good chepe".

It was about Leland's time that it became apparent how quickly the forests were being used for fuel in certain areas, and that must have been very noticeable in this region of expanding heavy industry. The lords of Sheffield's manor knew there was plenty of coal to be mined, even in Sheffield Park; and money could be made.

George Talbot, fourth Earl of Shrewsbury, a very wealthy man, completed the building of a fine new residence on top of the hill in his park on the south side of the Don. This building, Manor Lodge, had been started by his guardian before the earl came of age. It was a great advance on the old castle down in the town, and was extravagantly furnished with elaborate Tournai tapestries, fine large fireplaces and beautifully moulded ceilings. The windows were wide, and glazed. The lovely Sheffield Park was extensive, stretching from the hilltop almost down to the river, and was famed for its herds of deer. The fashionable new Manor Lodge was built but 100 yards or so from The Laithes, the ancient building of early Anglian cruck construction which was the original manor house on that desirable site.

The new Manor Lodge in 1530 received as a visitor the ailing Cardinal Wolsey, where, on the orders of King Henry VIII, the lord of the manor detained him on his journey to London. The earl endeavoured to make the Cardinal as comfortable and welcome as possible in his two-week sojourn before he was arrested by the Constable of the Tower who came to escort him, a prisoner, to London. Wolsey died at Leicester Abbey on the journey south.

As the years passed the cutlery industry was steadily increasing, and by the mid-sixteenth century was so well recognized that regulations were issued in 1565 by the View of Frankpledge of the Manor of Sheffield, requiring local monopoly, official apprenticeship, and two 'stoppage' periods each year—two weeks in August and one month at Christmas. In 1590 further regulations were made, one of which insisted that cutlers must use only the 'marks' granted to them. In this document the cutlers were mentioned as "a whole fellowship and company", but the person in control was the lord of the manor.

It was not until 1624 that an Act of Parliament established the cutlers as a self-governing corporation with jurisdiction over Hallamshire and for 6 miles around it. From that date the Company of Cutlers in Hallamshire has played an important role in the story of our area. The company was incorporated "for the good order and government of the makers of Knives, Sickles, Shears, Scissors, and other Cutlery Wares in Hallamshire in the County of York and the parts adjoining".

In his *History of the Company of Cutlers in Hallamshire* R. E. Leader says that Hallamshire "in general language may be said to be that southern corner of the West Riding where Yorkshire ends, where Derbyshire begins, and of which Sheffield is the capital".

It was ordained that the company should be "One Body politic, perpetual and Incorporate of one Master, two Wardens, six Searchers, and twenty-four Assistants and Commonality".

The members of the Cutlers' Company were the more successful, wealthy industrialists of our region; but the hundreds of craftsmen working at their trows and benches, and tending their small plots of land, were an equally essential part of the organization.

The attitude of the company towards ensuring "the good order" of the Sheffield trades with which they are concerned has been adapted through the years to be in keeping with modern trends. In the early days the control of apprenticeships was considered necessary, as was control of those entering the trades. Some of the earlier references to apprentices give an idea of the hard conditions some of the lads had to tolerate: all were apprenticed for seven years, and until 1748 a boy could be apprenticed before he was 12 years of age. An apprentice had no money for himself, often had inadequate food and bedding, had to work long hours and could be thrashed at his master's whim, although it was stated that the chastisement should be "reasonable". Apprenticeship must be to a freeman of the company.

The story of the Cutlers' Company is long and interesting, and can be touched upon only briefly in the space available. The first Cutlers' Hall was built in 1638—a building of restricted accommodation but of stone, with a slate roof, a point worthy of mention in that it shows that new buildings in the town were being more sturdily built; on that site in Church Street (then Church Lane, a very narrow lane) there stands today the third hall, a suitably imposing structure.

From its earliest days the company has been ready to help members who were experiencing hard times, though it was not until after the lord of the manor ceased to be in control, in 1624, that the company was able to direct its own finances.

In 1860, in its fifth Act of Parliament, the company was empowered to admit to its freedom other manufacturers. This provided that "resident persons using or exercising the arts or trades of manufacturers of steel, and makers of saws, & edge-tools, and other articles of steel, or of steel and iron combined, having a cutting-edge" should be able to become freemen of the company. It was possible eventually for the company to be representative of all Sheffield's steel-using and steel-making industries.

Today, the importance of the office of master cutler is recognized nationally; and the company has become the active guardian of the "Made in Sheffield" reputation throughout the world. The company's most important social function is the annual Cutlers' Feast, which has long been recognized as one of the most outstanding social events of the North of England.

At this point, perhaps, mention should be made of the two branches of the metal industry which did not come under the jurisdiction of the Cutlers' Company; one was the ancient trade of nail-making, and the other was the manufacture of Old Sheffield Plate.

The manufacture of Old Sheffield Plate was achieved by a process of melting silver and fusing it with a copper alloy so that the two metals could be rolled together. Articles of many kinds, which previously had been made entirely of silver, could now be made of this much less expensive plate, and yet they looked just like silver articles. This process, invented by Thomas Boulsover in about 1742, was carried on in wheels in the lovely Whiteley Wood section of the Porter Brook, but as R. E. Wilson has pointed out (history of the Sheffield Smelting Company, *Two Hundred Precious Metal Years*), it was Boulsover's former apprentice J. Hancock who really extended this process to articles larger than Boulsover had made. Hancock seems to have established the Old Park Silver Rolling Mill on the Don opposite its confluence with the River Loxley about the year 1762. Other manufacturers took up this trade and a flourishing industry developed. Soon after 1840 Faraday's cheaper, more rapid electroplating was used for silver-plating, and Boulsover's invention went out of use. In the approximately 100 years during which Old Sheffield Plate was manufactured, many remarkably beautiful articles were made. These today are collectors' pieces.

In this isolated area (there were still no roads worthy of the name) local traditions were strong, and persisted. It is said that on the various village greens, including those in the town, May-games, sometimes known as Robin Hood's games, were held. Christmas was an important season. We have seen that from the middle of the sixteenth century the cutlers' work ceased for four weeks at Christmas, so it was natural that for several weeks previously hard work was done to try to earn extra money to see them over the stoppage period; in time the last three working weeks came to be known as the Calf, the Cow and the Bull Weeks. All the ends of candles used during the dark days were carefully saved; as much work as possible was done during the Calf Week (the first of the three busy weeks), extra efforts were made during the Cow Week, and when, in the Bull Week, the pre-Christmas tasks were accomplished all the candle-ends were lit and placed in the window of the cutler's 'shop' to indicate to the neighbours that he had 'got the Bull down'. The custom of going round to sing Christmas carols at a number of places was recorded several centuries ago.

Always there were the effects of foreign wars and internal strife; and the danger of outbreaks of pestilence was very real. (Many of the games which children played and sang a few decades ago spoke of those trying days. "Ring o' ring o' roses" recalls the ring of scarlet spots which proclaimed the plague; and the next line, "A pocket full of posies", recalls the herbs which were carried as a safeguard.) The free tenants under the leadership of the town collector dealt with innumerable problems to the best of their ability, but they still turned for help to the lord of the manor, who did his best and 'stood good lord' to them.

Francis, fifth Earl of Shrewsbury, became lord of the manor in 1538, and was lord through all the difficult days of the religious upheavals of the Reformation. The free tenants were then known as the burgery, and their slender resources had been increased from time to time by bequests from local people, several to be used specifically for religious purposes. When William de Lovetot had founded the Priory of Worksop and endowed it with one-third of the tithes of Sheffield, it was arranged that the canons should supply a priest to serve the Parish church. This arrangement had not proved wholly successful, so the burgery agreed to provide three priests to minister to the hamlets around the fringe of Sheffield's large parish. During the reign of the young Protestant King Edward VI this caused trouble, for by Act of Parliament colleges and chantries had been suppressed, and King Edward's commissioners decided that the priests were being employed contrary to the law. So out of the burgery's income of £27, £17 9s. 4d. was confiscated, leaving a slender sum to pay for all other needs.

When the Catholic Queen Mary ascended the throne the lord of the manor, himself a Catholic, supported a petition which the burgery presented asking the Queen for the return of the confiscated funds. Queen Mary reacted favourably, but decided to establish another body, called the Twelve Capital Burgesses and Commonality of the Town and Parish of Sheffield. A charter dated 8th June 1554 specified that the three priests be maintained as previously, and that any extra income should be devoted to the repair of bridges and highways, with any surplus being used for the relief of the poor.

Sheffield had now two bodies to watch over its interests, the free tenants and the less democratic body, the Twelve Capital Burgesses.

Earl Francis died in the reign of Queen Elizabeth I, in 1560, and his son George succeeded him. Poor Earl George was destined to carry out, on the orders of the Queen, a very exacting and onerous duty, as custodian of Mary Queen of Scots. And it was in 1560 that the Queen's Council paid further attention to the carrying out of the 'reforms' specified under the Reformation. For example, it was not until 1560 that the Twelve Capital Burgesses decided to remove the altars from the church; four years later they acquired a copy of Erasmus's paraphrase of the Bible; in 1566 they erected a plain communion table; in 1569 a big Bible from London was purchased; and in 1570 the lovely, ancient churchyard cross was removed.

In November 1970 the citizens of Sheffield were reminded of happenings 400 years ago, for on 28th November there was re-enacted Mary Queen of Scots's ride from Chatsworth, over the moors to Sheffield Castle, as a prisoner. Mary's escape from Lochleven Castle, the defeat of her army at Langside, her escape to Workington in May 1568, and her decision to put herself at the mercy of Queen Elizabeth is well known to history. And then came eighteen years of captivity, of which fourteen were spent in or near Sheffield. It was in 1569 that George Talbot, Earl of Shrewsbury and lord of the manor of Sheffield, was appointed Mary's custodian. All travel over the unmaintained trackways, which did duty for roads, was impossible in winter except on horseback or by litter. Mary was an excellent horsewoman, so on horseback she travelled south to the Earl's castle at Tutbury, where the countess, the famous Bess of Hardwick, had been hanging tapestries and trying to make the old castle more comfortable for Mary and her bevy of retainers. This journey was made during winter weather, and the party rested for three days in Rotherham.

In the spring Mary was moved to Wingfield Manor and then to the earl's great house at Chatsworth. Wherever she was Mary attracted admirers, and plots were hatched, all of which added to the serious task laid on the earl. In November 1570 Mary and her retinue were escorted from Chatsworth, up the moorland tracks leading to the hills on Sheffield's boundary, then down to the centre of the town, and the castle. From time to time Mary was taken up the southern hill to the earl's Manor Lodge with its lovely views over the park and the hills; it is said that a separate building, the Turret House, was built for her, so that from the flat roof she could watch the deer hunts in the Park, but her health gradually gave way under the strain of her captivity. And so did the health of poor Earl George, who eventually, in 1584, was released from his long task as Mary's custodian, and she was handed over to the care of Sir Ralph Sadler and Sir John Somers.

By this time the countess had quarrelled with her husband and they were separated, but the earl was fortunate in that his staff and his tenants never ceased to love and respect their lord, and they were grateful that in spite of his many serious problems he had always given as much attention as possible to the affairs of his manor. The earl died in 1590.

It is not known what the people of Sheffield really thought about Mary's presence at the castle and the manor, but the day by day difficulties to be dealt with and problems of the increasing and gradually changing industrial pattern must have pushed poor Mary's plight into the background.

In the sixteenth century the lord of the manor moved from the old Sheffield Castle by the River Don crossing to his fine new Manor Lodge overlooking Sheffield Park, with miles of magnificent views. New wheels were beginning to appear on the five rivers, and the long narrow strips of land in the town, each with its occupant's home at one end, were soon to have the craftsman's shop built beyond the dwelling, reducing the available garden area—but a shop in which superb, skilful work was quietly fashioned. The lord was still in complete control of his manor, but since 1297 "all Hallamshire" had its free tenants (by the sixteenth century, the burgery of Sheffield) to assist and be responsible for the people's own court (as distinct from the manorial court), known as the Court of Sembley Quest. In 1573 the free tenants actually went to law against their lord, Earl George, who was guilty of encroaching on the town waste.

Then and for many years to come salmon could be caught in the Don's clear waters just beyond the castle walls. And it is stated that in later years, during his visits to Sheffield Charles Wesley was fond of bathing in the Don at the Walk Mill (fulling mill) downstream from Lady's Bridge.

We know that the roads within the town were narrow, rutted ways, and that the tracks leading from the town were often impassable—this was one reason for Sheffield's isolation and probably a reason for the choice of the Earl of Shrewsbury, lord of Sheffield and Hallamshire, as custodian for Mary Queen of Scots.

But what of drinking-water supplies? All our hamlets originally were adequately supplied with springs and good wells, but a growing industrial centre presented problems. As early as the fifteenth century a pool had been constructed by a man called Barker, to supplement substantially the town's water supply from springs. Happily today there is still the name Barker's Pool designating the area formerly covered by the pool.

Accounts dating from the mid-sixteenth century remind us that the original duties of the petty constable, a manorial officer of centuries earlier, were now undertaken in a greatly expanded form by two constables who carried out many duties for the town burgery. Years previously the petty constable had been a very busy man, having to see that unwanted persons (vagrants) were sent or conveyed to the manor where they were born; receiving Sheffield manor's vagrants from other manors; rounding up and impounding straying animals in the pinfold (there is still Pinfold Street off Townhead Street) as well as a variety of other duties. By the sixteenth century the increasing duties of the *two* constables included collection of revenue such as the Defence Tax of 1581, and the apprehension of wrong-doers. The town burgesses of the period accepted responsibility for repairs to the pinfold, ducking-stool, pillory and gibbet; they also repaired the important Lady's Bridge as well as maintaining Barker's Pool, the Townfield gate, the Irish Cross, Townhead Cross and Market Cross, and the butts in the Wicker.

The town burgesses brought for trial to the people's court of Sembley Quest those who violated local regulations, such as failing to scour their ditches, or defiling wells; they provided the town 'waits' whose duties seem to have included being both watchmen and musicians. A very noteworthy point concerns the Twelve Capital Burgesses who had been established by Queen Mary in 1554, as we have noted earlier; for at some date before 1564 they founded a grammar school.

The large parish of Sheffield already had been divided into a number of townships—Sheffield, Brightside Bierlow, Ecclesall Bierlow, Upper Hallam and Nether Hallam, Attercliffe-cum-Darnall. Without doubt the lord, the town burgesses and the Twelve Capital Burgesses had many local administrative problems posed by the industrial growth of the area.

It was the monastic houses which had endeavoured as far as

possible to care for the aged and infirm poor, and the dissolution of the monasteries added this service to the growing responsibilities of the town. Earl George founded a charity to try to help the needy working handicraftsmen, but this could only touch the fringe of the problem of rapidly increasing poverty.

And on the tops of the highest hills of our area huge piles of combustibles were prepared for lighting—for the danger of Spanish invasion was imminent. Fortunately, the failure of the Spanish Armada in 1588 saved our country from invasion, and the beacon fires were not lit.

Poverty and vagrancy increased to such an extent that in 1601 Parliament passed the Poor Law Act, which remained in force until the nineteenth century; overseers of the poor were appointed in every parish, who were empowered to levy a Poor Rate on the inhabitants for use in trying to relieve the destitute who were born in the parish, and provide them with work.

By the turn of the century many of the wealthier citizens had gone to live beyond the town itself. The lord of the manor, Earl Gilbert, decided to make a definite contribution towards relieving the growing poverty, and in order to get precise information he instituted an enquiry, in January 1615. He learned that:

it appeareth that there are in the towne of Sheffield 2,207 people of which there are 725 which are not able to live without the charity of their neighbours. These are all begging poore. 100 householders which relieve others. These (though the beste sorte) are but poore artificers; among them is not one which can keepe a teame on his own land, and not above tenn who have grounds of their own that will keep a cow.

160 householders not able to relieve others. These are such (though they beg not) as are not able to abide the storme of one fortnight's sickness, but would be thereby driven to beggary.

1,222 children and servants of the said householders; the greatest part of which are such as live of small wages, and are constrained to work sore, to provide them necessaries.

Revealing as this report is concerning the hard lives of a section of Sheffield's people, it can be regarded as being very much in line with most of the other growing centres of industry in the country, at that time.

Arising from this report the lord provided in his will for the founding of a hospital: "I will and appoint an hospital to be founded at Sheffielde for the perpetual maintenance of twentie poore persones, and to be called the Hospitall of Gilbert Earle of Shrewsbury; and the same to be endowed with such revenues as possessions as my executors should think fitt, not beinge under two hundred poundes a yeare."

In fact, it was not until 1665 that steps were taken to found the hospital. Earl Gilbert died in 1616, his successor being his brother Edward, who died eight months later. Edward's death brought to an end the succession of Talbots, Earls of Shrewsbury, who had been lords of the manor.

By 1666 the earl's almshouses were being built on land later known as Broad Street. This was near the junction of the Rivers Sheaf and Don, on part of the former castle orchard. By 1673 the almshouses were opened, under the Trusteeship of Francis Jessop of Broom Hall, esquire; Thomas Chappell senior, lawyer; William Spencer of Attercliffe, gentleman; and Cuthbert Browne of Handsworth, clerk.

The Talbots had taken great interest in their local estates, and had lived here. All this was now to change. Although the estates descended through Lady Alethea Talbot's husband Thomas, Earl of Arundel and Surrey, to the Duke of Norfolk, none of the succeeding lords were so interested in Sheffield. And now, by the turn of the century, in our isolated area which still had no satisfactory communication routes with the rest of the country, various bodies, including the free tenants (the burgery), the church burgesses (the Twelve Capital Burgesses), the oversees of the poor, and the constables had increasing control of its affairs.

VI

THE TOWN AT WAR

THROUGHOUT the first quarter of the seventeenth century national events were becoming ominous, and in 1642 Civil War broke out. Sheffield's lord no longer lived in the area, and the Puritan and Parliamentary sympathies of well-known local families such as the Brights of Carbrook, the Jessops of Broom Hall and the Spencers of Attercliffe were more or less representative of Sheffield's leanings. The Jessops had the right to present two in every three vicars of Sheffield, and they chose men with a bias towards Puritanism.

But despite the national upheavals the Sheffield workers continued at their trades, isolated by their beautiful surrounding hills —roadless, except for one ill-maintained road to Bawtry on the River Idle, a tributary of the Trent, and a much used water-highway.

In 1637 the lord of the manor employed John Harrison to make a survey and his resulting map reveals the town's small size, but also that it was a small town with houses still not unduly crowded together, many houses still having gardens and orchards. As Miss M. Walton points out in her *Sheffield, Its Story and its Achievements*, even the workhouse which had been built of timber by the burgesses in 1628, in West Bar, had its own little croft. Harrison's map shows a number of narrow lanes, some of which he names (Blind Lane, Church Lane, Greene Lane, Hallam Lane, Townfield Lane, New Lane, Broom Hall Lane, Balme Lane and Mill Sands), but shows only two streets, High Street and Market Street.

The outbreak of Civil War made little local impact at first, although the capable young John Bright of Carbrook enthusiastically supported the Parliamentary cause and recruited a regiment from the area. At the beginning of hostilities Sir John Gell of Hopton Hall in Derbyshire, a general on the side of Parliament,

77

marched to Sheffield and took possession of the castle, meeting
with no opposition. He left a small force as garrison. In 1643 the
Earl of Newcastle approached with a contingent of Royalist
troops, on his way south. The small garrison knew they were
greatly outnumbered by the approaching force, so lost no time
in evacuating the castle before Newcastle arrived. For the second
time the castle was occupied without recourse to fighting.

It has been stated that during their occupation the Royalist
forces took advantage of Sheffield's heavy industry facilities, and
had weapons made. W. T. Miller* mentions the claim that the
first wrought cannon made in Sheffield were forged at the Clay
Wheels, situated on the Don in the vicinity of Wadsley Bridge.
Miller also mentions that below Clay Wheels "is what we may
call Niagara Weir, and from this weir runs a long goit which must
be very old, older probably than most people realize, for this
waterway served the ancient Shrewsbury furnaces and forges
which were active in the period 1560 to 1600".

The Royalist dislike of the Puritans was evidenced during
Newcastle's occupation of the castle when the vicar, John Bright,
died. Instead of allowing the appointment of either Toller or
Rawson, who were assistant ministers also with Puritan leanings,
by some influence a Royalist supporter, Edward Browne was
appointed vicar. It will be noted that at this period two John
Brights—the vicar and the young Parliamentary colonel, were
playing their parts in Sheffield's story. Both were members of the
Carbrook family.

Newcastle installed Sir William Savile as governor of the castle,
and he was soon followed by Major Thomas Beaumont, Lady
Savile remaining at the castle when her husband was moved on
to York. The young Parliamentarian supporter, John Bright,
was at that time a colonel with Fairfax's army, and his regiment
probably fought at Marston Moor in July 1644, the battle which
resulted in the defeat of the Royalist cause in the area. Various
small Royalist groups still held out, including Beaumont's force
in Sheffield Castle, and steps were taken to overcome them. In
August 1644 Major-General Crawford and Colonel Bright were
sent with a small detachment to Sheffield, and having viewed the
castle the two officers differed in their opinions as to its strength.
Bright felt it could be taken without too much difficulty. Accounts,

* *The Water-mills of Sheffield.*

evidently written by an eye-witness, appear in a pamphlet published in 1644, "for Hugh Perry" and entitled "A journal for a true and exact relation of each day's passage ... from the first of August to the end of the same month. ... Purposely set forth for the honour of that party". This account of the "army under the command of the ever-honoured Major-General Craford" is in the Bodleian Library and a photostat copy is in Sheffield Central Library, "When the Major-General had viewed it, he found it to be a very considerable strength, both for natural situation, being in a triangle with two rivers, the water deep in the east and west sides of the castle, flackered on all sides, a strong fort before the gate pallisado'd within the trench, between it and the castle." Whatever was the strength or otherwise of the castle Major Beaumont refused to surrender, and in this he was staunchly supported by Lady Savile.

The attackers' efforts to drain the deep, river-fed moat failed, and the colliers detailed to mine under the castle were defeated by the hard rock on which it stood. This was the hard rock which ages previously had compelled the River Don to make a sharp turn to the north-east. Eventually big new cannon were trained on the walls, a few shots from these convincing Beaumont that resistance was useless, and after some deliberation terms for surrender were agreed.

It was an honourable surrender, with no reprisals. Major Beaumont and Lady Savile (who was recently widowed) with her new-born child were given honourable safe conduct, and the garrison, on the laying down of arms, was permitted to disperse freely. The date of the surrender was 11th August. Colonel John Bright was established as new governor of the castle.

Other small pockets of resistance in the area were at Staveley Hall, Bolsover Castle and Wingfield Manor, but these were soon overcome by Crawford.

Four years later, in 1648, following a Parliamentary decree, most inland castles were 'slighted'. This included Sheffield's castle which had dominated the small settlement and the growing town since it was built by de Lovetot in the twelfth century. The townspeople began to remove the stone of the castle's ancient walls for their own use, and many of the narrow lanes paved with "grindlecowkes" now saw the erection of stone-walled buildings.

Today, just the foundations of one of the great bastions and a few flanking walls remain, buried deep under the foundations of the fine Castle Market. The moat has disappeared, but the River Don continues along its important course, deflected by the hard rock formation which has supported notable buildings from the Anglian cruck building of the sixth century to today's modern, busy market.

It was in the mid-seventeenth century, as noted above, that religious trends in Sheffield had become increasingly puritanical. There were several sincere, excellent preachers who held the offices of vicar and assistant ministers, including Thomas Toller who became vicar in 1598, a nominee of the Jessops of Broom Hall, and his three assistants, who were the successors of the three priests of pre-Dissolution days. It was Toller who in 1622 re-opened Ralph de Ecclesall's chapel at Ecclesall, which had been served until the Dissolution of the Monasteries by the canons of Beauchief Abbey. Toller also established a chapel at Attercliffe in 1629 with Stanley Gower in charge. Gower, a most capable minister, had been one of Toller's assistant ministers at the parish church. In 1635 Toller decided to become an assistant, after being vicar for some 37 years, and John Bright was promoted to vicar in his place. The calibre of many of the Sheffield clergy of that date makes it clear that when, during the Stuart restoration, the 'dissenting' clergy were discouraged, these men whose sincerity had made such an impression on their Sheffield congregations would not easily be forgotten.

In spite of its protective isolation, Sheffield had its share of religious difficulties, and several of her clergy suffered imprisonment.

In the reign of Charles II, in 1662, Parliament authorized the use of the Old Prayer Book with a few alterations. By the Act of Uniformity all persons were to attend the services of the Church, all clergymen were to adopt the Prayer Book, and repudiate the Covenant. About 2,000 clergymen refused to conform and left their livings. Such was the beginning of the Nonconformists or Dissenters. In 1665 the Five Mile Act was passed forbidding all Nonconformist ministers who would not take an oath of loyalty to Church and State from coming within 5 miles of any town.

The vicar, James Fisher, was greatly respected, and he was one

Long Causeway, the Roman road

of those ejected in 1662 from his living. He suffered several spells of imprisonment. When he died in 1666 his congregation chose Robert Durant, and converted a house at New Hall for their services. Durant died in 1681, and his congregation chose Timothy Jollie as minister. Gradually after 1688 the religious restrictions were relaxed, and Jollie, who was a very zealous worker, was able to see his Sheffield congregation build a church in 1700 on land later known as Norfolk Street, lying between Pepper Alley (off Fargate) and Alsop Fields. This building was known as Upper Chapel, and was the first of the really substantial Nonconformist places of worship to be built.

It was during 1665 that a tragic happening occurred in a village on the hills some 12 miles to the south-west of Sheffield—a happening which, but for the heroic action taken by the village people under the leadership of the Reverend Mompesson and the Reverend T. Stanley could well have had most disastrous consequences in Sheffield. The village was Eyam.

In that year London had experienced a completely rainless four months, which resulted in appallingly insanitary conditions, and a terrible outbreak of the plague. One-fifth of London's population died, and many outbreaks occurred in the provinces. In September a package of cloth-samples sent from London to a tailor in Eyam carried the epidemic to the unsuspecting village, and as the 'ring o' roses' on the chest betrayed the nature of the pestilence, the wealthier folk fled from the stricken village.

Three years earlier, in 1662, the vicar, the Reverend T. Stanley, had been evicted from his living because he refused to accept the Act of Uniformity, and his place was taken by the Reverend William Mompesson. Stanley still lived in the village, and when Mompesson took heroic action to isolate it from contact with nearby villages, it was Stanley who became his staunchest helper. By October 1666 the survivors realized that the pestilence had run its course. Two hundred and fifty nine adults and 59 children had died out of a population of 350 souls.

And Sheffield? Our small town could have suffered a similar fate, for at the beginning of the outbreak at least two people fled over the hills and down the narrow trackways to friends in Sheffield. Perhaps in the early days the danger to Sheffield was not realized; but as soon as it was known that the pestilence was raging

6

The Anglian cruck timbers in Stumperlowe cottage
The shaft of the Sheffield Cross

in Eyam just over a dozen miles away, the burgery and the constables carefully watched for "comers", and any contacts were forcibly detained in their homes.

It was earlier, just after the turn of the century that the burgery's firm action similarly had prevented an outbreak of the plague in Sheffield, when Chesterfield, 12 miles away to the south, was badly affected. Thus it was that the control by the town trustees together with the heroism of the people of Eyam saved the area from tragedy.

Mention must be made of an event enacted in 1688 not in Sheffield, but in a village some 10 miles to the south. This event, which was the planning of the Glorious Revolution of 1688, heralded conditions which had much to do with the easing of the religious difficulties mentioned above, as well as having far-reaching effects at national level.

The Stuart dynasty had proved to be difficult and very unpopular with the ordinary people who were longing for more freedom—freedom of worship being not the least of the reforms they sought. It became obvious that there must be a change, or disaster could follow. Discussions evidently had been taking place secretly between representatives of well-known aristocratic families, including at least two in our area. It is claimed that William, fourth Earl of Devonshire, of Chatsworth, met his friend Danby at the village of Old Whittington near Chesterfield to take part in a hunt on Whittington Moor; but later in the day they repaired to an inn in the village, the 'Cock and Pynot', where without interruption they were able to take needed refreshment —and talk over plans for revolution. Devonshire and Danby were two of the seven persons who on 30th June, 1688, signed the invitation to William of Orange, the husband of Mary, daughter of King James II, to come to England with a view to accepting the throne. No one knew how this invitation would work out, and very many things could go wrong; but in spite of all difficulties the revolution was successful and bloodshed was avoided. The old, thatched 'Cock and Pynot' is now restored and preserved, and is known as the Revolution House. After William and his wife Mary had become joint rulers, the earl was created the first Duke of Devonshire.

Before closing this chapter mention must be made of the brave efforts made in the seventeenth century towards providing formal education for certain sections of the folk in our area. As there was no monastic establishment within the manor, it is unlikely that educational facilities were available to any but the children of the wealthier citizens. But at some date before 1604 (which seems to be the date of its charter) the grammar school was founded. Perhaps the earliest building was on Townhead Street, near to or on the site of the later building erected in 1649, largely using stone removed from the 'slighted' castle. It was in 1603 that one Thomas Smith made a bequest of £30 a year to pay two learned men to act as schoolmaster and usher at the free grammar school. The school had been established already by the church burgesses (the Twelve Capital Burgesses). The endowment land at Leverington in Cambridge was augmented in 1670 by land at Wadsley.

The growing Nonconformist group in the town were not happy about the school being controlled by the church burgesses, particularly after 1660, and it was a Nonconformist minister, Richard Frankland, who succeeded in establishing an academy at Attercliffe Hall, made available by the Nonconformist family, the Spencers. The academy was established in 1686 and was remarkably successful. Timothy Jollie succeeded Frankland as schoolmaster at Christ's College as it was called, and during the time it functioned (it was closed in 1718, four years after Jollie's death) among its pupils were a number of future ordained ministers, a Fellow of the Royal Society and Professor of Mathematics at Cambridge, a Chancellor of Ireland, and an Archbishop of Canterbury. Attercliffe Hall was by no means a young building when it became Christ's College, but like so many of the area's interesting buildings which were the homes of leading families in the sixteenth and seventeenth centuries, it became shockingly neglected later. "William Spencer of Attercliffe, gentleman" was living at Attercliffe Hall in 1673, but evidently the Spencers had left the hall by 1686 when the academy was established.

In *The Story of Old Attercliffe* G. R. Vine says:

With diamond panes a low building stood behind the 'Golden Ball Inn'. I was led to the stone roofed edifice below the main road next door but one to the Golden Ball. To my great surprise I found upstairs ceilings and a space of two feet down the walls one beautiful display of relief work in white plaster; some of it is most elaborate, comparing remarkably with the famous relief decorations on the ceilings of Queen Mary's room in the Manor Lodge, or that of the famous historical room in Carbrook Hall. . . . This building was demolished in March 1934.

Certain features of this fine old building, such as stone mullioned windows and carved doorways, were rescued and used in the restoration of other buildings of similar date. Among the treasures saved from Attercliffe Hall was a text executed in good plaster-work lettering, which had been mounted over a fireplace. This reads: "Whatsoever thou dost take in hande thinke of the ende and seldom so shalt thou ofend." Happily this was carefully removed and now appears mounted on the wall over a fireplace in the parlour of the ancient Cartledge Hall in the village of Holmesfield, situated on a significant hill site some 8 miles to the south-west of Sheffield.

The same text appeared in at least one other now-demolished hall near Sheffield, and whereas its origin is not actually known, attention has been called to the Apocrypha, Ecclesiasticus 7, verse 36: "Whatsoever thou takest in hand, remember the end, and thou shalt never do amiss."

Mr. Doncaster mentions that on one occasion a small boy scout who was visiting Cartledge Hall carefully read the text aloud, and after some thought interpreted its meaning as: "If you are going to pinch anything, remember that you may be caught."

A reminder of the ancient settlements, and of their early origin and fine sites is proclaimed by the wealth of old halls which existed, some of which still stand. As in the case of our Anglian cruck aulas, each significantly sited, the halls, most of them showing Tudor work in addition to later additions, stand proudly. Many of them are near a still-existing or recently demolished cruck building.

We here mention just a few of these recently demolished halls: Lees Hall, on a hill above the Meers Brook to the south of Sheffield; Whiteley Wood Hall, on a hill above the Porter Brook to the south-west of the town; Crowder House or Winskley House to the north-east, in Ecclesfield; Owlerton Hall, above the junction of the Loxley and the Don; Walkley Hall, overlooking the Loxley Valley; Darnall Old Hall, on a hill to the south; Attercliffe Old Hall, in the former manor of Attercliffe.

But during the seventeenth century these buildings were bravely standing. In that period our still-isolated area showed an increase of population, a gradual extension of building beginning along the ridges and radiating out from the early township; a decided increase in religious enthusiasm and a practical approach towards the establishment of a system of education. The town's industries both in type and volume also showed definite advance. But the isolation due to lack of means of communication for conveying goods remained a problem to be solved.

At this time the area's exceptionally beautiful setting was still unspoiled. Hills climbed from the Don Valley to distant skylines to the north, the west and the south; lovely streams cascaded down from the heights, turning busy, picturesque wheels and filling attractive dams on the way. Ancient ways and footpaths, beloved then as now by Sheffield's citizens, provided countless beautiful walks; and patches of densely wooded valley and hill-slopes displayed a range of delightful colours throughout the year, and a fascinating pattern of tree-shapes against winter skies. Blue-bells, primroses, foxgloves, moonpennies and buttercups clothed woodland and valley dells, giving way to the purple heather and ling of the moors. Pussy-willows and catkins spoke of spring, and the rich profusion of sloes, hips, haws, blackberries and rowans ushered in the autumn.

VII

RELIGION AND EDUCATION

APART from the Parish Church of Sheffield which was founded by William de Lovetot in the twelfth century, no doubt on the site of the early Christian church of the seventh century, no further churches were founded in the large parish until Ralph de Ecclesall, lord of the sub-manor of Ecclesall in the thirteenth century, founded a chapel at Ecclesall to be served by the Canons of Beauchief; and later the Chapel of Jesus was founded by the Reverend Thomas Toller in Attercliffe.

The Act of Uniformity of 1662 hastened the growth of the Nonconformist movement, the first Nonconformist chapel being built in 1700 in Norfolk Street (at that time just a narrow country lane), and since known as Upper Chapel. In the reign of Queen Anne Upper Chapel had more than 1,000 members. Nether Chapel was opened in 1720 and Queen Street Chapel in 1783.

A document concerning Queen Street Chapel shows the steps which had to be taken officially to open a new Nonconformist place of worship. It reads:

To the Right Worshipfull the Justices of the Peace at the Sessions at Doncaster Jany 21st. 1784.

We hereby apply to you to register our Chapel situate in Queen Street Sheffield in the Diocess of York for the Worship of Almighty God according to the Discipline common among Protestant Dissenters

Cornelius Wildbore	John Smith
Thos. Fennor	Saml. Ostliffe
John Read	Saml. Glossop
W^m. Smith	

Doncaster Sessions 21st. January 1784

West Riding of Yorkshire } I do hereby certify that a Chapel situate in Queen Street, Sheffield in the said West Riding is certified to this Sessions by John Smith, Sam[l]. Ostliffe, & Sam[l]. Glossop to be a Place for the Worship of Almighty God according to the Discipline common among Protestant Dissenters, and is recorded as such at the said Sessions pursuant to the Statute in that Case provided. Given under my hand at the said Sessions

Rich[d]. Fenton

Clerk of the Peace for the said County

Another document applying to Queen Street Chapel, dated 1830, reads:

West Riding of Yorkshire   I Lamphugh Hird, One of His Majesty's Justices of the Peace for the West Riding of the County of York, do hereby certify that John H. Muir of Idle this day appeared before me, and did make and take and subscribe the several Oaths and declarations specified in an Act made in the 52[d]. of Geo. III intitled, 'an Act to repeal certain Acts and amend other Acts relating to religious Worship and Assemblies and persons teaching and preaching therein'.

Witness my Hand this Eleventh Day of November, One Thousand, Eight Hundred, and Thirty.

L. Hird

Another Queen Street Chapel document, of April 1870, outlines in detail the duties of the chapel keeper, giving evidence of the comfortable furnishing of the building (there were carpets on floors and in the pews) and that there was a vestry and well-maintained school.

The Society of Friends never included a very large group in Sheffield, but in 1660 they had a meeting house at Woodhouse. George Fox was visiting the area in 1654 but it is not known that he actually visited Sheffield. A meeting house was established in Meeting House Lane in 1709, not far from the parish church and Queen Street Chapel. In 1739 Joseph Broadbent built a new meeting house in Hartshead on land that was then an orchard (Orchard Street is not far away). The original meeting house, No. 3 Meeting House Lane, has long been known as The Cottage, and regrettably is due to be demolished in one of the devastating 'clearance' schemes being carried out today. Enemy bombing in 1940 wrecked the meeting house and it was not until some twenty years later that a new building was erected; it was opened in 1964, on the opposite side of Hartshead.

Between the years 1754 and 1805 the Reverend James Wilkinson was Vicar of Sheffield, and it has been said that he virtually ruled the town, for he was resident magistrate for the West and North Ridings, as well as vicar and squire. A wealthy man, he lived at Broom Hall, then to the west of the town, and never at the vicarage. This was a period of population growth, and during his time as vicar the population of the parish increased from about 20,000 to nearly 50,000. Wilkinson had no sympathy whatever with Methodism and there is no doubt that growth of the various branches of the 'Protestant Dissenters' during his years as vicar was partly occasioned by his somewhat harsh, dictatorial attitude.

John Wesley began his visits to Sheffield to preach in 1743. His early preaching was received badly. In July 1779 he preached in the stylish Paradise Square, speaking from the top of a flight of stone steps, "to the largest congregation I ever saw on a week day". Later, in 1788, writing of Sheffield and Hull he described, "the largest morning congregations I have seen in the kingdom". The various branches of the Methodist movement went from strength to strength, and several fine new buildings were erected.

The Church of England expansion began somewhat later. In 1800 a start was made in rebuilding the nave of the parish church, and this was completed in 1805. By that date two other churches had been built—St. Paul's on Pinstone Street in 1720 and St. James's Church built just outside the gates of the old church in 1789. Both these churches have now been demolished, and on the site of St. Paul's, bounded by the town hall, Norfolk Street, St. Paul's Parade and Pinstone Street is a delightful public garden with walks and seats.

An important development began in 1785, when the Sunday school movement was started. These schools were chiefly to teach reading and writing, but religious instruction was included. Almost all the area's charitable institutions grew from the Sunday school movement. For example, workshops for the blind, provided by the Misses Harrison, arose from the work of an adult Sunday school started by James Howarth in 1850. In 1861 work was started for the deaf and dumb. The first Hospital

Sunday was held in September 1798; Earl Fitzwilliam's chaplain, John Lowe, preached in the parish church, St. James's and St. Paul's, and useful collections were taken. A little later collections were added from Norfolk Street, Scotland Street and Howard Street chapels. Thus the hospital movement and many other charitable works originated in the churches of all denominations.

The Roman Catholic Church movement developed from the mid-eighteenth century when the Duke of Norfolk made available for worship a large room in Fargate, in 1767, and paid the stipend of the priest. Later a chapel was built in Norfolk Row (in 1815), and the large St. Marie's Church was built there in 1850.

The remarkable growth of the town's religious institutions which began about the beginning of the eighteenth century was conducive to both educational development and voluntary welfare services.

Undoubtedly it was the success of the Attercliffe Academy which awakened interest in education; here was an institution, in little, isolated Sheffield which even produced an Archbishop of Canterbury! Before the academy closed in 1718 several charity schools were established, the first being built by public subscription, in the north-east corner of the churchyard of the parish church. It was in 1706 that the vicar, the Reverend Drake and his assistant the Reverend Terrie began their efforts towards this end and in 1710 the school was established. An undermaster of the grammar school, James Hill, left land at Gilberthorpe Hill for his school, and in 1709 a house for the headmaster was built. Charity schools were established at Fulwood and Crookes in 1724, at Wadsley in 1712, at Broad Oak Green in 1729, at Sharrow in 1782, at Grimesthorpe in 1793 and at Upper Heeley in 1801.

One William Birley established a charity for a free writing school, built in Townhead Street in 1721, near the grammar school. In the second half of the eighteenth century the famous mathematician John Eadon (he wrote, among other works, the *Arithmetician's Guide* in 1766) followed Gosling as master of the free writing school, and it is known he taught both there and at the grammar school.

Sheffield's population was growing apace, and so was the determination to secure good educational facilities, especially in scientific subjects. The newly established Sunday schools were certainly playing their part.

One of the first Sunday schools was established in 1785 in West Street; and after the turn of the century a Nonconformist-inspired Sunday School Union was founded, with James Montgomery as secretary. By 1820 there were 8,000 pupils attending Nonconformist Sunday schools and 3,000 attending church schools. An important event was the visit to Sheffield in 1809 of Joseph Lancaster. He has been called the 'apostle of the monitorial system'. Money was collected, an old rolling mill bought and a Lancastrian school opened. In 1812 this school was attended by about 700 boys.

By about 1815 a number of Jewish people who had landed at Hull, fleeing from troubles in Europe, began to make their slow way across country to Manchester, many coming by way of Sheffield. They had travelled along the trackways following the river valleys from the Humber, and having reached Sheffield soon realized that to continue to Manchester they would have to climb by hazardous routes over the Pennines. Many of them pressed forward, but a number who had noted the cutlery and silver-plating industries of our small town decided to try to get work and settle here. It was only a small community which stayed here in the first quarter of the nineteenth century, but by 1837 they were able to establish a synagogue. In 1872 this was followed by a second. Today, the Jewish community of Sheffield numbers about 1,400, and it has also played its part in educational development.

The growing enthusiasm shown in founding schools reflected the whole country's awareness of educational needs; and Sheffield's achievement between the early eighteenth and mid-nineteenth centuries can arouse only admiration.

The next step on the educational ladder was the establishment of secondary education, and the Church of England was to the fore in this, founding the Sheffield Collegiate School on Ecclesall Road in August 1836. Next year, on Clarkehouse Road, the Nonconformists opened the Wesley College (known at first as the Wesleyan Proprietary Grammar School). Both these schools had difficulties in their early days, but both had the advantage of having very good headmasters, H. M. Shera at Wesley College and the Reverend G. B. Atkinson at the Collegiate School being outstanding. Atkinson realized the essential value of technical education to a town such as Sheffield, and tried hard to advance this. A little earlier, in 1823, the free grammar school had been moved from its original site in Townhead Street to Broad Lane, opposite the then new St. George's Church.

The education of girls was by no means overlooked. The Girls Public Day School Trust opened a high school for girls in the old music hall in Surrey Street, transferring it in 1884 to a new building in Rutland Park, off Clarkehouse Road.

Dr. Arnold of Rugby wrote a number of articles in 1831 for the *Sheffield Courant*, and in one of them he emphasized his opinion of the lack of concern about their workers' *minds* shown by many employers. He wrote: "Our great manufacturing towns have risen solely with a view to this relation of employers and employed. The very name shows this, that they are places where men have assembled together, not for the purposes of social life, but to make calicoes or hardware or broadcloth. A man sets up a factory and *wants hands*; I beseech you, Sir, to observe the very expressions that are used, for they are all significant. What he wants of his fellow creatures is the loan of their hands; *of their heads and hearts* he thinks nothing."

This paragraph written by a man of acute perception throws interesting light on the thoughts of an outsider viewing the struggle of many people of the town working for the furtherence of *real* educational facilities. Perhaps Arnold failed to realize the struggles which many of the employers had experienced; and that at that period, although the former narrow gap between 'mesters' and men was widening to an unfortunate extent, the town's welfare depended to a large extent on the hard work of the 'hands' for, in most cases, hard-working employers. There were many who were openly suspicious of the possible result (from their own point of view) of improved educational facilities, and no doubt this had been noted by Arnold.

A great step was taken in 1823 by a group of promoters who formed a "Library for the use of Mechanics and Apprentices", to gratify "the strong desire for indulging in the recreation of useful reading at a time when the laborious classes can be spared from their occupations". The "useful reading" envisaged did not permit the use of Sir Walter Scott's novels! In 1832 a Mechanics Institute was founded, and to reassure suspicious citizens the promoters stated that there was "no danger that the increase of knowledge will cause those who possess it to show want of respect to their superiors or to disobey their masters . . . the best and most orderly servants have invariably been those that received the best education".

One particularly broadminded secretary of the Mechanics Institute became very unpopular because he allowed 'subversive' books to be used in the library. Nothing daunted, this man, Isaac Ironside, took an active part in the founding of a Hall of Science in Rockingham Street, which provided a wide range of adult education. This undertaking was the first of its kind in the country, and was in type an Owenite centre, having been inspired by the views of Robert Owen, who first visited Sheffield in December 1833.

It was the work of the Hall of Science which was responsible for the determination shown by the various demoninations towards furthering adult education. The Unitarians opened an Adult school in the Hollis Hospital; the Society of Friends opened one in 1845, and the Church of England opened an educational institute in 1853. In 1842 the efforts of the Reverend R. S. Bayley were rewarded by the foundation of the People's College, an institution for the liberal education of working men, the first of its kind in the country, and which was so successful that it led to the founding of similar educational institutions in Nottingham, Leicester and London.

A number of private schools were opened during this period of educational growth, for the children of somewhat wealthier parents, and several of these were of decidedly high standing.

It is said that John Roebuck, a pupil of the grammar school during the eighteenth century was a pioneer of the Industrial Revolution, his work being directed towards stimulating interest in scientific instruction. It was an age of scientific exploration, which led to the founding of the Society for the Improvement of Mechanical Knowledge, which met at the coffee house in Howard Street, and the Sheffield Society for the Promotion of Useful Knowledge. Charles Sylvester, Dr. Davis, John Waltire and Samuel Catlow were notable lecturers in scientific subjects.

One rather amazing fact is that this admirable, dedicated work towards educational development in the expanding town was taking place throughout the period of the tragic American War of Independence, the French Revolutionary War, the Napoleonic War, and trouble in India. It was a period when considerable sums of money were expended in the support of our armies abroad.

A glance round our area at the beginning of the eighteenth century when religious and educational stirrings were beginning to be noticed, would be of interest. From the heights of Sky Edge in the extensive Manor Park it is noticed that the recently deserted, poorly maintained great Manor Lodge crowns the hilltop immediately to the east. There were previously fine stands of timber and acres of pasture land stretching away through the immense park, and many tiny streams babbled down the slopes. But in 1706 Thomas, the eighth Duke of Norfolk, had allowed the Lodge to become ruinous and partly dismantled. The great trees were felled and much of the park divided into farms. Attention was then given to other areas of the manor, and the famous tree-clothed slopes of Fulwood and Rivelin had most of their great trees felled.

Round the horizon the hilltops, both near and distant, rise to the sky; but to the north-east the River Don has created an area of lower, wider marshland. Except on the distant high moors to the west, a hamlet appears on every suitable site, each connected to its nearest neighbours by narrow, rutted trackways. From the west strings of packhorses can be seen making their way down to the small town beyond the foot of Sky Edge, and other strings are slowly, wearily climbing the long hills leaving the town. In the town itself, where the river has made a sharp right-angled turn to avoid the hard rock of the southern hill-slopes, a bridge crosses the river, leading to a wide area near which archery butts stand. Just a few ruins on a small hill between the Don and its tributary the Sheaf mark the site of the 'slighted' Sheffield Castle. Two somewhat wider streets can be seen paved with grindle-cowkes (the worn-down centres of grindstones); the rest of the roads in the town appear from this distance to be narrow alleys, often unpaved and lined with houses, though it can be seen that many houses have a garden stretching behind them, and many have smoke issuing from the shop behind the house, where a cutlery craftsman is at work.

There is the parish church standing on a slight eminence which slopes steeply to the north to the river, and a new building can be seen at the south-east corner of the churchyard. This is the new town hall built in 1700 to replace an older manorial property which probably stood on another site. This new town hall was erected jointly by the Duke of Norfolk and the town trustees, to be used to hold courts, as a gaol when necessary, and as a place for holding public meetings.

On the five rivers and their small tributaries groups of low stone buildings can be seen, each the site of a wheel powered by water coming over a weir or from a lovely dam.

From Sky Edge only few of the town's buildings can be identified; but the Upper Chapel can be noted as it stands on a narrow way above Alsop Fields; and Broom Hall is seen, standing in its park beyond the western bounds of the township.

The extraordinary beauty of the town's site at the foot of its guardian hills is striking; but also there is another impression—that this small town is isolated.

The time is coming when steps will be taken to overcome that isolation.

VIII

SCIENTIFIC SOLUTIONS

ONE concern of the growing population in the eighteenth century was adequate good-water supply. In the past wells and springs had been considered adequate, but improvement was now essential. As long ago as 1610 a mercer called Rollinson had arranged conditions with his tenants for the use of Plumtree Well, which he had made in Figtree Lane. A fence was to be erected round it and kept in repair, and a door made which could be kept locked at night. The tenants agreed to pay a charge of a farthing a year, and it was stipulated that "cloaths and calfes heades" should not be washed there. Other privately owned wells were sunk but still the problem of water supply was acute.

At an earlier date Rollinson had taken steps to improve the Barker's Pool, which continued to be well maintained by the lord of the manor and the free tenants. Eventually, in about 1712 a reservoir was made at Upperthorpe, near White House. This was small but successful, and the makers, Goodwin, Littlewood and Matthewman as a further private venture gained permission from the lord of the manor for the construction of a series of dams, five in all, on the Crookesmoor. Of these the Godfrey Dam, the New Dam and the Old Great Dam were of considerable size and certainly solved the water-supply problem for the time being.

It has been noted in an earlier chapter that Gilbert, Earl of Shrewsbury, made provision for a hospital, which eventually was established in 1673. In 1703 Thomas Hollis founded an almshouse for sixteen elderly women, the widows of cutlers or other Sheffield manufacturers. Both these charities exist today.

It is rather surprising that in the small town at the foot of the hills, served only by rough trackways, with a water-supply only recently made adequate, and, where poverty among the working classes was rife, there was actually a number of people interested in books. Miss Walton's *Sheffield, Its Story and its Achievements* (1948) mentions that only one book written in Sheffield before 1692, survives. This was written by James Fisher. It is known however that Francis Jessop's *Propositiones Hydrostatical* was published in 1687.

In 1692 Nevil Simmons auctioned in Sheffield a collection of books (written elsewhere); and he lived in Sheffield, continuing to sell and publish books, the books he published being printed in London. He actually published works of two Sheffield writers, the vicar, the Reverend N. Drake and Timothy Jollie the minister of Upper Chapel. So there must obviously have been a small reading public in Sheffield's area before the eighteenth century, perhaps chiefly amongst those who had been able to afford some sort of education. Miss Walton reminds her readers that what is probably the earliest authentic picture of Sheffield life was written in an autobiography by Samuel Roberts, who was a child after the second half of the eighteenth century. He wrote of the ill-paved, almost unlit narrow streets, where as in other towns and villages the sports of all classes were apt to be brutal.

Francis Jessop (1638–1691) of Broom Hall, whose ancestors for at least five generations had lived in Sheffield, was a remarkable scientist, whose observations on the problem of firedamp in coalmines were published in 1675 in the *Philosophical Transactions* of the Royal Society. Jessop studied the firedamp problem at first hand in one of the Earl of Shrewsbury's coalmines in Sheffield Park; he recorded cases of explosions caused by firedamp, which he discussed with William Croone and John Ray. With Francis Willughby be discussed biological subjects. Jessop also had dealings with Martin Lister, the physician.

Jessop's interest in the firedamp problem seems to have been first aroused on reading Sir Robert Moray's publication of 1665, *A Relation of Persons killed by Subterraneous Damps*. In about 1682 Jessop secured the services of William Ronksley, a young man who had been a schoolmaster at Hathersage and at Bakewell. In Bakewell Ronksley had written and published his *Regiae Grammaticae Clavis*. Ronksley was an outstanding schoolmaster; it was he who endowed a school at Fulwood in 1724, to be controlled by Francis Jessop's heirs; if this line failed it was to revert to the town burgesses.

Francis Jessop was assisted in his chemical experiments by two

Castle Market, on the site of the Norman castle

sons of the vicar, James Fisher, ejected from the parish church in 1662. Of the sons, Samuel and John, one was a surgeon and one a physician. Unfortunately, just 100 years after Francis Jessop died in 1691, Broom Hall, then the home of the wealthy vicar, James Wilkinson, was burnt by an angry mob and the fine library destroyed.

It cannot be denied that from the time of Francis Jessop in the seventeenth century—and perhaps earlier—sons of the same isolated town of Sheffield played a noteworthy part in the growth of scientific knowledge in the area, and indeed in the country.

A well-known medical author was Dr. Thomas Short who came to live in Sheffield in about 1728. In addition to keeping a detailed record over a certain period of Sheffield's weather—temperatures, pressures, wind-directions, etc.—he was interested in the waters of the spas of England, particularly in the composition and effect of their waters. One of his published works was *Natural, experimental and medicinal history of the mineral waters of Derbyshire, Lincolnshire and Yorkshire*.

And at the village of Sprotbrough alongside the River Don some 16 miles north-east of Sheffield there lived another eminent landowner-scientist, Sir Godfrey Copley (1653–1709), to whom Sheffield owes a great deal. He was a Fellow of the Royal Society, a reader of the *Philosophical Transactions* and extremely interested in the works of the water engineer George Sorocold. It was Copley who first made a practical approach, in 1697, towards making the River Don, then navigable to Doncaster, similarly navigable right up to the growing industrial town of Sheffield. It was many years before his far-seeing plans succeeded.

It was whilst living in Sheffield at Hartshead, in the house later occupied by James Montgomery, that Dr. Buchan wrote his widely read *Domestic Medicine*. This was published in 1769, quickly ran to nineteen editions and was translated into every European language.

The fame of many of the Sheffield Grammar School pupils of the eighteenth century, though largely unsung, should add significantly to our Portrait. The famous Fairbanks family belong to this period, William (*c.* 1688–1759), his son, grandsons and great-grandsons. The first William and William his son were schoolmasters who made a remarkably accurate survey of the

7

View down the Don Valley to the east

town and surrounding area, work which was continued by their descendants. At this time also lived Charles Sylvester, a pioneer in the field of magnetism and electricity; he was said to have invented galvanized iron—iron coated with zinc.

Another local pioneering feat of this prolific century was the application of John Curr's cast-iron narrow-gauge railroad with L-shaped rails to underground use in collieries. Curr had invented this in about 1775, and it was to be used for the next seventy years. The Earl of Arundel and Surrey, lord of the manor, employed Curr as manager of his Arbourthorne Colliery.

It has been noted that the dingy cutlery town was on the threshold of a rousing awakening. The cutlers were hampered by lack of trading facilities; and, even though the excellence of their wares was well known throughout the country, they still depended upon transport for their goods and raw materials by owners of packhorse trains or using the water-route from Bawtry to the coast. It is claimed that Field Sylvester, a member of the Upper Chapel congregation, was actually the first Sheffield merchant. Somehow, despite difficulties, trade in cutlery was established with the Continent and with America.

By the beginning of the eighteenth century the number of manufacturers owning marks included, in addition to the long-established cutlers, "sheresmyths" (sicklesmiths and woolshearsmiths), scissors-smiths, filesmiths, awl-bladesmiths and scythesmiths. By the mid-eighteenth century coal was being mined more extensively, and more iron and steel were needed for the increasing manufacture of cutlery, scythes, files, saws, and all kinds of edge-tools. Many of the surrounding villages had their wheels and forges, and some of these villages at a later date were absorbed by the growing township.

An event which occurred in about 1740 has been described as Sheffield's "first contribution to the Industrial Revolution". At about that date a Lincolnshire-born Quaker, Benjamin Huntsman, moved to the village of Handsworth to the east of Sheffield, from Doncaster. He was a clock-maker, and was interested in getting a really suitable steel for clock-springs. Steel was produced in Sheffield before this period, but Newcastle was better known for steel production—which was made by what is known as the cementation process. This was a lengthy, not wholly reliable process, producing a steel known from its appearance as blister-steel. By further refining, shear-steel could be produced.

This steel did not meet Huntsman's requirements for clock-springs, so at Handsworth he steadily experimented, hoping to produce the steel he wanted. He had failure after failure, and quietly he buried these. He heated blister- and shear-steels in clay crucibles together with a flux, the composition of which he kept secret. One difficulty was to obtain a clay which would withstand the very high temperatures needed. In the Handsworth area he found the heat-resisting clay required, and at last succeeded in producing the steel he needed—a very hard steel suitable for clock-springs, razors, knives, and for many other purposes. The 'teeming' of this melted steel was, and still is, a fascinating sight; the white-hot metal from the heated crucible was teemed into the mould at the right moment, carefully and precisely, a hand-operation requiring accuracy, strength and skill.* Sheffield steel-workers still claim that crucible steel is always wholly reliable. How satisfied the quiet, unassuming Huntsman must have been with his eventual success, though he would never accept any honours for his remarkable discovery.

The hard crucible steel was not immediately popular with the Sheffield cutlers, but it was eagerly bought by French cutlers.

At some date before 1763 he built a works at Attercliffe, and it was not very long before French competition compelled the Sheffield cutlers to sit up and take notice, and Huntsman's crucible steel became widely used. Huntsman did not patent his process and it was soon imitated by at least seven other firms; but none of them produced a steel as hard as that made by Huntsman and his descendants.

It has been noted that as early as 1697 Sir Godfrey Copley of Sprotbrough realized the importance of getting the River Don made fully navigable right up to Sheffield. He was an educated, widely travelled man and was aware of the important contribution made to the economy of other countries by well-developed inland waterways. Even before the last quarter of the seventeenth century transport by water was the cheapest and most practical route available to the Sheffield manufacturers. It was a tedious

* In September 1971 a demonstration of 'teeming' was given at the Abbeydale Industrial Hamlet.

journey, involving as it did carriage by packhorse to Bawtry on the River Idle some 20 miles away, transference of the goods to small boats which proceeded to Stockwith on the River Trent and then transhipment to larger vessels for carriage to Hull. Unless Sheffield was to remain a small isolated town her home and overseas markets must be catered for—and good water transport supplied much of the answer. In 1697 Sir Godfrey Copley presented a Bill in Parliament (he was the Member for Thirsk) to secure powers to make the River Don navigable up to Sheffield. The Bill was opposed by Bawtry and Doncaster, and was unsuccessful. Seven years later Doncaster had a change of heart and presented a similar Bill; this also was unsuccessful. Nearly thirty years were to pass after Sir Godfrey's unsuccessful effort before common sense won the day. In the meantime the dreary journey by packhorse to and from Bawtry continued.

With its headstreams on high ground north, west and south of Sheffield the River Don, a tributary of the River Ouse, was liable to sudden, serious flooding, and there is evidence that in its lower reaches this sudden flooding had caused the river to change its course several times. It was to try to devise a plan to overcome the disastrous flooding of the lower, marshy regions, particularly in the region of Thorne and Hatfield, that the great Dutch Engineer Cornelius Vermuyden was consulted, about the year 1600. The draining of the vast area of marshland was a task presenting enormous difficulties, but Vermuyden eventually solved them by making a cut from the Don near Stainforth to the River Ouse at Goole, a length still known as the 'Dutch River'.

It is thought that it was Vermuyden's success in overcoming great difficulties and draining much of the marshland which first aroused Sir Godfrey Copley's interest in the possibility of making the Don navigable right up to Sheffield. We have seen that Copley's Bill to this effect presented in 1697 was unsuccessful, but even at that date the Cutlers' Company was interested.

The first reference to the Don (or Dun) Navigation is to be found in the Cutler's Company accounts for 1697:

1697–8 At a meeting with Rotherham men about
     ye river   00. 03. 08.
     charges about addressing his Maiesty   01. 01. 08.

Traffic to and from Hull continued to be shipped via Bawtry.

The importance of Bawtry as an inland port was described by Daniel Defoe, who made a journey through Derbyshire and Sheffield and on to Bawtry some time before 1726. The account of his tour was published in 1726, and says:

> The Town of *Bautry* becomes the Center of all the Exportation of this Part of the Country, especially for heavy Goods, which they bring down hither from all the adjacent Counties, such as *Lead*, from the Lead Mines and Smelting-Houses in *Derbyshire*, wrought Iron and Edge-Tools, of all Sorts, from the Forges at *Sheffield*, and from the Country call'd *Hallamshire*, being adjacent to the Towns of Sheffield and Rotherham, where an innumerable Number of People are employed . . . Also Millstones and Grindstones, in very great Quantities, are brought down and shipped off here, and so carry'd by Sea to *Hull*, and *London*, and even to Holland also. This makes Bautry Wharf be famous all over the South Part of the West Riding of *Yorkshire*, for it is the Place whether all their heavy Goods are carried, to be embarked and Shipped off.

Except in times of drought the River Don was navigable up to Doncaster, but in the seventeenth century much of the river above Doncaster was interrupted by weirs for the supply of water-power to turn wheels. There were weirs near The Wicker, at Attercliffe, Rotherham, Thrybergh, Kilnhurst, Conisbrough and Sprotbrough.

By 1722 the Company of Cutlers realized that something must be done, and they supported a proposal to make a series of cuts to bypass the weirs and dams on the Don. Eight such cuts were planned, but the scheme was opposed by the then Duke of Norfolk and by those whose weirs would have to be bypassed. It was therefore decided that the terminal basin must be made at Tinsley, because there the river was outside the Duke's manor. Fortunately, Doncaster strongly supported this Bill and so did the town trustees. When the Bill was presented in Parliament the Company of Cutlers was represented by John Smith and George Steer, and the town trustees by Samuel Shore; the Bill passed the Commons on 14th April and the Lords on 6th May. The Cutlers' Company was given the sole responsibility "for making the river Dun navigable from Holmstile in Doncaster up to the utmost extent of Tinsley westwards", for levying rates and duties, and for improving and keeping in repair the highway from Sheffield to Tinsley.

The successful passing of this Bill in 1726 led to scenes of re-
joicing. The town trustees granted £10 for a feast. An item in the
accounts of the Cutlers' Company reads: "1726. 30 Aug. Paid
Wm. Moore for glasses which he said was broak at the Navigation Feast   .   .   .   .   3s. 9d."

The road journey from Sheffield to Tinsley was a serious dis-
advantage and a suggestion was made that a cut should be made
through Brightside, thus avoiding the weirs between Tinsley and
Sheffield. This plan was not adopted, and for almost 100 years the
advantage of having the Basin right in Sheffield was missed.

The Cutlers' Company floated a company in 1729 to raise
sufficient money to carry out this interesting project, calling it
The River Dun Company, and after amalgamation with Doncaster supporters the company in 1732 became The Company of
Proprietors of the Navigation of the River Dun. As soon as the
waterway was made navigable to Tinsley Sheffield traders
benefited by this new, economical transport facility. The company paid its first dividend in 1732, of £1 16s. 4d. In 1762 the
Cutlers' Company's own seven shares earned £242. In 1826 one
share was sold for £2,300.

This was a fine water-highway, one of the most highly viable
waterways in the country. From 1762 when the great canal
engineer James Brindley was consulted, such engineers as John
Smeaton, William Jessop, Robert Mylne, Robert Whitworth,
Benjamin Outram and Thomas Telford were consulted.

But the story of this remarkable water-highway to the sea
must be continued in a later chapter.

Our Portrait up to the early eighteenth century shows the trackways which were the small towns' communication routes, along
which packhorse trains carried raw materials and finished products.
For Doncaster, Worksop, Tickhill and Bawtry the route crossed
the Don by Lady's Bridge just below the site of the castle, all
these routes crossing the wide Wicker Common. For Doncaster
the route climbed Spital Hill, re-crossed the Don at Washford
Bridge continuing near the line of the former Roman road to
Rotherham and Doncaster. For Worksop a track branched to the
east at Attercliffe, and for Tickhill and the river port of Bawtry a
track branched north-east from Tinsley. Some 6 miles east of
Sheffield the great north–south post road passed between Mans-

field and Barnsley, and the three trackways from Sheffield crossed this road.

A fourth road from Sheffield ran along the north bank of the Don to Bridgehouses, climbed steeply up Pye bank to Pitmoor, and on to Barnsley and York.

The trackways leaving Sheffield for the west and south had to negotiate very difficult country. For Derby and Mansfield the route left Sheffield by way of Fargate and Coal Pit Lane, across the open Sheffield Moor, over the Porter Brook at the hamlet of Little Sheffield and over the Sheaf at Heeley, then up a steep hill via Newfield Green, which even in 1692 was described as "a very ancient way, being worne very deep". Because of the gradients two alternative routes were made but they also were steep and difficult.

The western route began with a long climb from the town up Western Bank, Lydgate Lane and the Roman Long Causeway via Stanage across the moors, then came the steep descent to the Derwent Valley, to Hope, then up again through the wild Winnat's Pass from Castleton and down the long slope to Chapel-en-le-Frith. Another westerly route lay over Sheffield Moor and up to Ringinglow where it turned left to cross a section of the moors by a track which led down to the Derwent Valley to Grindleford, or on to Hathersage.

Our Portrait is about to have new roads added—the turnpikes, which, with their necessary attractive little tollhouses, began to appear after 1756.

Turnpike trusts were formed by a group who put up the capital needed to turnpike a section of road, and an Act of Parliament was sought to authorize the work. Once completed and in use money for maintenance was collected from actual road-users at the gates across the road by the tollhouses. Fortunately a number of picturesque tollhouses still exist in our area, though a number already have been demolished in the interests of 'modernization'. It is difficult today to envisage the enormous amount of work required to turnpike a road; dozens of horses and carts were used to bring stone quarried from sites as near as possible. The roads in the limestone districts were all made of limestone, and limestone seems also to have been used in other areas. Even at the beginning of the twentieth century these roads were a mass of white dust in summer and sticky with white mud in winter.

It is surprising that Sheffield, a town of heavy industries, should have been rather late in taking up the turnpike road idea; but once started in 1756 the Sheffield promoters pushed ahead, and by 1821 ten main roads were turnpiked. The Fairbanks family surveyed the route for the early Sheffield turnpikes. In 1756 the important Sheffield–Chesterfield (via the steep Derbyshire Lane) –Derby road was turnpiked, and it is of interest that during 1970 heavy traffic has been stopped from going *down* the steepest part following several serious accidents, when heavy lorries careered down out of control. How did the poor horses drag heavy wagons and coaches up, and hold them back down such hills? For many years boys from poor homes would earn a few coppers by having a 'shoe'—a hollowed-out piece of iron the width of a wheel and fastened at the end of a long pole—which at a sign from the driver they pushed under one of the rear wheels during an ascent, to hold the vehicle while the panting horses had a brief breather. The last of the difficult local roads was turnpiked in 1821; this was the road to Glossop. The gradients were appalling, and even today the road's modern successor is usually closed several times each winter because of impossible weather conditions.

Our Portrait must now show the Angel Inn in the centre of Sheffield, at the head of Angel Street, where the landlord Samuel Glanville in 1760 started the first stage-coach service from Sheffield to London, Leeds, Wakefield, Chesterfield, Mansfield and Nottingham. At first the Sheffield–London journey took three days; but by 1787 it had been amazingly reduced to twenty-six hours. This suggests that further efforts had been made to improve the road surfaces, and that at each post house the horses were standing ready to replace the tired team when the coach with horn sounding and whip cracking drove into the inn yard. Glanville was succeeded by Samuel Peech, and the 'Angel's coaching service continued to be well patronized.

In 1785 the Tontine Inn was built on a site between Dixon Lane and Castle Folds. This inn had ample accommodation for guests and extensive stables. In 1838, with horses ready for harnessing day and night, thirteen coaches left daily.

The stage-coach service eventually was displaced by the less picturesque railways. But well into the twentieth century carriers' carts used the "Tontine" yard as their headquarters; it was there that country people on certain days of the week could buy a seat on the open cart drawn by one horse going to or through their village. Goods and parcels of all kinds would be taken by the carrier to his village customers.

Wagons were able, at any rate in good weather, to carry quantities of raw or finished products to and from the town, and trade prospered accordingly.

It is appropriate, during this period of the town's rapid expansion of communications and trade, to look at the effect on the towns-people. As wealth increased, so class distinction became more evident—an almost new state of affairs in homely Sheffield. There was a tendency for the newly wealthy to move to the west, north and south of Sheffield, a tendency which quickened in the nine-teenth century.

Our Portrait clearly shows the developments of the eighteenth century: the new places of worship of all denominations; the newly formed charitable institutions; the schools and colleges; the growing, fine water-highway to the sea; the new turnpikes; the expanding trade arising largely from Huntsman's invention of crucible steel; the new reservoirs for water supply; the improved roads and lighting (still oil lamps and candles) in the town. And now mention must be made of social life.

Sheffield has long had a high reputation for music and drama, and many of her people inherit good singing voices as well as a love of music. We shall see that social life grew apace despite the serious repercussions caused by a long period of dreadful wars. A start had been made for people to get together for card-playing and dancing at the charity school on certain evenings, and on such occasions the resident pupils were unable to go to bed until the festivities were over. A large room at the 'Angel' was used for social festivities and also for presenting plays. A building called, aptly, the Assembly Rooms was opened in Norfolk Street in 1762. A building called the Theatre provided better accommodation for plays than the 'Angel', so such activities were carried on at the new building, which in 1763 became known as the Theatre Royal. Famous stage personalities of the period played to crowded audiences—Mrs. Siddons, Mrs. Jordon, the Macreadys, the Kembles, Edmund Kean, and others. There was an orchestra at the theatre, the leader being the Joseph Taylor who helped to inaugurate Sheffield's first musical festival in 1769.

This was indeed a festival of music. There was sacred music in St. Paul's Church, musical concerts in the theatre, and a ball at the close of the festival. The *Messiah* was sung—and it must have been sung many times in Sheffield every Christmas since that date. Sheffield people *love* the *Messiah*, and many of them know it by heart. Perhaps it is not out of place here to mention the experience of a couple from the south coast who attended a performance of the *Messiah* in the Victoria Hall in Norfolk Street about the year 1952. They soon were aware that probably they were the only members of the audience not armed with the complete musical score; and that at the tap of his baton every eye was on the conductor until at the first note attention was transferred to, and remained on the score. Every head nodded slightly in rhythm with the conductor's beat! The visitors wondered what *would* have happened if any member of the choir or orchestra sounded a wrong note! It did not happen. It would be hard to envisage such a thing happening in Sheffield. The visitors appreciated that every member of the crowded audience, loved, and knew, the *Messiah*.

Sheffield's love of music included grand opera, the comic operas and music-hall singing. More than one music-hall artist of the nineteenth century (and perhaps earlier) has been known to admit that really he did not *need* to sing to a Sheffield audience, except, the first verse and the chorus; after that all he had to do was beat time—his gallery audience did all the singing for him, at the top of their voices.

In his book, *Here's a How-de-do*, published about 1952, Martyn Green a well-known principal singer with the D'Oyly Carte Opera Company mentions the embarrassment if one fluffed a line at a performance in Sheffield—at once came a prompt from the audience!

Choral singing has long been very popular in Sheffield, and a world-renowned conductor, Sir Henry Coward, was born and lived in Sheffield. In the early twentieth century his Sheffield Choir toured the world. During the first quarter of the twentieth century choral singing, to a high standard, was taught in many council schools.

The fine musician Sir William Sterndale Bennett was a son of Sheffield, and so was the actor Sir Henry Ainley.

Sheffield's isolation and its preoccupation with hard work and the growth of the steel industries may have been mainly the reasons why the development of a reading public lagged behind that of certain other towns in the North of England. But the eighteenth century with its remarkable progress saw efforts made to provide a library for public use. In 1771 a group of people succeeded in establishing a subscription library known as the Sheffield Library, in the much-used music hall. This was a brave beginning, the forerunner of today's excellent public libraries in Sheffield.

It was in the eighteenth century that efforts were made to produce a Sheffield newspaper, an undertaking which, once under way, had to weather many storms. The first newspaper seems to have been Lister's *Sheffield Weekly Journal*, which functioned for a few years from 1754. The next journalistic effort started in 1760 and was Ward's *Sheffield Public Advertiser*, which later went into partnership with the *Courant* about the year 1793. The *Sheffield Register* was started by Joseph Gales in 1789, and for the first time a Sheffield newspaper actually tried to reflect local opinion, which for nearly two centuries had been increasingly radical. Gales soon became unpopular with the authorities, and eventually he left for America, leaving his clerk, James Montgomery, to edit the newspaper. Perhaps for reasons of policy the name was changed to the *Sheffield Iris*. During the next century—the nineteenth—James Montgomery was able to play a notable part in continuing, indeed in furthering, Sheffield's development.

During that century of remarkable developments the fine arts were not neglected. The great sculptor Francis Chantrey was born in 1781, the son of a farmer at Jordanthorpe Farm in the historic village of Norton, on the hill to the south of Sheffield. At first Chantrey worked at a small shop in Sheffield, but soon he became apprenticed to a carver and gilder, Robert Ramsey of High Street. Chantrey was now in his element; he quickly learned the trade, and there also he met J. Raphael Smith, a mezzotint engraver. A fortunate fact is that through relatives who worked in London he met their employer Mrs. D'Oyley, who was a grand-daughter of Sir Hans Sloane. Chantrey rented a building in Paradise Square, where he painted portraits. When he again visited his relatives in London in 1802 Mrs. D'Oyley helped him to become a student at the Royal Academy. Sir Francis Chantrey, R.A., made his name as a fine sculptor in marble.

A painter of repute was T. C. Hofland, who painted many scenes at Meersbrook and other areas in the south of Sheffield. He was born in Worksop in 1777, married a Sheffield lady and lived here until his death in 1843. That excellent designer, Alfred Stevens, taught for two years at the school of art, which had been founded in 1843, following an inspiring lecture to the Literary and Philosophical Society by Benjamin Haydon. Stevens's work was quite outstanding, and his work at the school of art from 1850 to 1852 set a very high standard of design. It is not surprising that in Sheffield, with its fine tradition of Sheffield Plate designing, Stevens should find that many of his pupils became prize-winning designers and artists.

An outstanding sculptor of a later date was Charles Jagger, well known for his 'big gun' Royal Artillery Memorial at Hyde Park Corner. Like Stevens, Jagger's work was very fine, and his work was widely commissioned. Another noteworthy sculptor was Edwin Smith, who has been claimed as a rival of Chantrey. He was born in 1820, and among his works is the statue of Montgomery which he completed in 1843. It was Samuel Roberts, one of Sheffield's sons, both practical and far-seeing, who arranged for Montgomery to sit for Edwin Smith.

Sheffield produced several very good engravers, of whom the first known was Elisha Kirkall, born about 1682. His work was very popular in the eighteenth century.

Godfrey Sykes studied in Sheffield under Alfred Stevens, and one example of his work in Sheffield is the Weston Park gates, which he designed. He also designed the decorations on the South Kensington Museum (now the Victoria and Albert Museum). Both Sykes and Stevens executed work for H. E. Hoole of the Green Lane Works in the early part of the town near the river.

Another disciple of Stevens was Charles Green, who designed the lovely font in Sheffield Cathedral (the former parish church). Stevens's influence on Sheffield artists of his day was profound. One of his portraits in the National Gallery was described by Sir John Rothenstein as one of the finest portraits painted by an English artist.

Hugh Stannus, a son of the minister of Upper Chapel, Norfolk Street, worked with Stevens (as his assistant) on the Wellington Memorial in St. Paul's. Stannus designed the decorations for the large banqueting hall in the Cutlers' Hall; his designs for this work were discovered in the Victoria and Albert Museum and were lent to the Cutlers' Company when the decorations were restored some years ago. Stannus became the professor of achitecture at the Royal College of Art. One of his works of art in Sheffield is the processional staff of the Cutlers' Company, bearing the company's coat of arms.

A famous son of Sheffield, and her only R.A., was Thomas Creswick, born in Ecclesall in 1811. He exhibited in the Royal Academy when only 17 years old, and his paintings are in the collections of a number of famous galleries.

T. B. Hardy, born in Sheffield in 1842, was a famous painter of sea-scapes.

The portrait painter Ernest Moore, who had a studio in Church Street, had many famous subjects, including the Duke of Norfolk and Alderman Marsh; this latter portrait was exhibited in the Royal Academy in 1903 and was praised by Sir John Millais.

A famous horse painter, William Malbon, lived in Pear Street in the last quarter of the nineteenth century, and has been claimed as one of the best horse painters known in this country.

John Mastin was born in 1865; his paintings were so fine that he was invited to exhibit in the fine art section of the Paris Exhibition.

Other artists whose names are associated with Sheffield include the painter John Thomas Cook, the sculptor Rossi, the painter Nathaniel Tucker, and Needham, who was painting portraits in the mid-eighteenth century. And there was the famous woodcarver Arthur Hayball, who lived 1822–87. There are many others, sons of this town of craftsmen.

The development of banking in the last quarter of the eighteenth century was an essential outcome of, and contribution to, the small town's rapid growth. As firms extended their business dealings the question of loans was bound to arise. By the beginning of the nineteenth century there were about 46,000 people living in the large parish, compared with about 20,000 in the mid-eighteenth century. It was realized before the end of the eighteenth century that banking facilities were needed, and it was some of the merchants themselves who became bankers.

Benjamin Roebuck's Bank was founded in 1770, Thomas

Broadbent's Sheffield Bank in 1771, John Shore's Bank in 1774 and Mrs. Hazlehurst's Sheffield Old Bank in about 1782. There was much financial instability, largely due to the continuous wars, and of the four banks established only Shore's survived after 1785. After being joined by two other well-financed banking concerns Shore's Bank was able to weather the financial storms which affected so many banking firms throughout the country. An important local bank, the Sheffield Savings Bank, was founded in 1819, instituted by James Montgomery and other philanthropists, to encourage saving by "industrious mechanics and labourers". This bank is a flourishing concern today.

Another feature of the eighteenth century growth was the beginning of the Trade Union movement. Early in the century a number of trades formed friendly benefit societies, but it soon became evident that they would do well to try to look after the industrial interests and working conditions of their members. Records exist of the Tailors' Society, formed in 1720, which at once took action to shorten the long working hours. At that period the average life of Sheffield citizens was twenty-four years—a higher average than that of several other growing towns, but still a serious reminder of conditions, including working conditions.

The Tailors' Society stated: "Whereas we usually work about at peoples' houses from six o'clock in the morning to eight o'clock in the evening for a day's work, and we now find the same prejudicial to us, and do all of us think it is too long confinement for the wage we receive for a day's work, therefore be it mutually covenanted. . . . That we will not at any time hereafter work abroad for any person whatsoever in their houses longer than six o'clock in the evening, nor begin before six o'clock in the morning."

By the end of the century there were some forty such societies, of which about ten, confined to the skilled trades, had become definite trade unions.

Strictly, the formation of these trade unions was contrary to the law of the time; but as growth of trade together with fluctuating markets had suggested that the masters should combine to provide for themselves a stronger financial position, so the hard working conditions and long hours of the employed had led to the formation of unions for needed protection. In 1777, 1787, 1790 and 1796 the unions of the file, table-knife, scissors and spring-knife trades had staged strikes for better wages. The first two were fairly successful; but by 1796 the country was again at war, and a nervous government revived old laws which permitted the strike leaders to be imprisoned despite the shocking living conditions of the workers. The basic soundness of the Sheffield craftsmen was severely tried, and among some of them less worthy standards were fostered.

From A. W. L. Seaman's article "Reform Politics at Sheffield, 1791–97" which appeared in *The Transactions of the Hunter Archaeological Society*, a good idea is obtained of the efforts being made among the Sheffield workers towards constitutional reform. The Sheffield Society for Constitutional Reform was established towards the end of 1791, its stated object being the disseminating of useful political knowledge among the mass of the people. Seaman wrote:

It began humbly with "an assembly of some five or six mechanicks" and from its inception had opposition from the "people of consequence and property"—and the Society's aims were deliberately misrepresented. To try to counteract malicious rumours the Society inserted a notice in the "Sheffield Register" on December 2nd., 1791 assuring the local people that its intentions were peaceable and that they were not, as had wrongly been claimed, a "dangerous mob". On December 28th. the lawyer James Wheat wrote to the Marchioness of Rockingham's chaplain that the "associators" comprised principally "the lower class of manufacturers", and in January 1792 the Vicar of Sheffield, the Rev. J. Wilkinson described the Society as being almost entirely composed of "the inferior sort of manufacturers and workers".

The Society agreed that they were workers; a petition for reform was sponsored by the Society in April 1793 in which the signatories described themselves as "tradesmen and artificers unpossessed of free-hold land and consequently have no voice in choosing members to sit in Parliament".

Membership of the society steadily increased, and always at their frequent meetings the members were reminded that the gathering must conduct itself in an "orderly and peaceable fashion, thereby frustrating the wishes of all party and designing men". And the society continued to work steadily towards reforms of various kinds.

Their efforts were strenuously opposed, and they appeared to make little headway towards the reforms they sought. But their unremitting work of enlightenment was by no means wholly in vain. As Mr. Seaman says in his article: "The failure of the Sheffield reformers, even the impracticability of their hopes, should not be allowed to obscure the impressive integrity and steadfastness of purpose which marked their actions. Posterity can judge them more kindly than did their contemporaries, and perhaps more fairly." This illustration of steady, unspectacular integrity is typical of most of the early Sheffield people and their efforts.

By the second half of the century no longer did many of the town's houses have a garden remaining, and the areas of West Bar, Gibraltar Street and up to Upperthorpe were being built on. Beyond the Townhead Cross new buildings appeared, which spread over Carver Fields and Backfields. An interesting group of good buildings was started by Thomas Broadbent in Paradise Square in 1771. To the south-east of the town Alsop Fields were being covered with buildings, some residential and some factory buildings. This project was planned for Vincent Eyre by William Fairbanks between 1776 and 1793. Beginning in 1790 buildings and streets were soon to cover Park Hill.

By the date of parliamentary Enclosures there were no longer either commons or open fields left in the township of Sheffield, but the manor's surrounding townships were the subject of Acts for Enclosure. Ecclesall was enclosed between 1779 and 1788, Brightside between 1788 and 1795, Upper Hallam, Nether Hallam and Heeley between 1791 and 1805, and Attercliffe between 1810 and 1819. All these were within the ancient Parish of Sheffield.

After 1779 buildings, with the necessary roads, began to invade the gorse-grown Sheffield Moor. In 1795 the Assembly Green beyond the Don was enclosed, and the road we know as The Wicker laid across it. This heralded the building of houses on both sides.

This population and building expansion should have brought increased income from the Poor Rate assessment, to be used for increasing poor relief. But a letter written in November 1781 by Benjamin Blonk, a scissorsmith, to the lawyer James Wheat emphasizes the need for the building of a much-needed new

The two 'hulls' of Shepherd Wheel in Whiteley Woods

poorhouse. He wrote: "And the great obstruction thereto in this town I may safely affirm to be the present poorhouse, a place where most people whose assistance is to be wished dread to enter thinking with too much reason that contagion and disease reign there."

The conditions there were highly insanitary, and overcrowding was appalling, so no wonder it was impossible to get "most people whose assistance is to be wished" to visit the place to see for themselves. The assessing of the Poor Rate was unpractical, and the overseer of the poor was quite inadequately supported in his onerous, unpaid work. In 1789 a committee was formed to arrange for the building of a new workhouse in Broad Lane, but this plan came to nothing.

On the other hand, subscriptions were raised, under the leadership of Dr. John Brown, for the building of a new hospital, and in 1792 the building of the infirmary began.

All the eighteenth-century developments in our area had been contained in the context of our country's development, and certain aspects of the national development require brief mention.

The Union of England and Scotland took place in 1707. George I ceased to attend the meetings of his ministers, as he could neither speak nor understand English; this led eventually to a more democratic form of control. There was a fortunate, much-needed period of peace until 1739.

Agriculture benefited enormously by the introduction of the turnip and other root crops, for this made it possible to have a four-year rotation of crops without leaving land uncultivated for one year in three, as had been the custom. Also the growth of root crops provided food for cattle and sheep during the winter. This gave more manure and therefore greater land fertility.

At the same time the iron industry, as we have seen, was developing significantly. In about 1760 the use of charcoal for smelting iron gave way to the improved use of the blast, which would permit coke and coal to be used instead of charcoal. This had the advantage of boosting the coal industry as well as arresting the destruction of our valuable forests. Henry Cort invented new methods of rolling and puddling iron.

Shortly after 1740 Benjamin Huntsman succeeded in inventing a method of manufacturing hard, crucible steel. In 1769 James

8

The Abbeydale Industrial Hamlet

Watt produced the first practical steam-engine, used mainly at first for pumping water.

In 1777 the first iron bridge was erected; this was built over the River Severn, and is still there. In 1790 the first iron vessel was launched.

In 1761 James Brindley's fine Bridgewater Canal was opened, from the Worsley Collieries to near Manchester; this at once halved the price of coal to Manchester consumers. This project was followed eventually by a network of canals connecting the large cities and centres of industry, thus providing for the cheap, safe, efficient transport of goods.

The turnpike-road system was developed at this time, of value chiefly for passenger transport.

It was within this national context that our area's remarkable developments took place.

IX

THE IMPORTANCE OF TRADE

As the page of time turned to the nineteenth century our armies were still fighting in France. The long Napoleonic War dealt hard blows on the newly developing Sheffield. Napoleon's successes robbed England—and Sheffield—of her European markets, and eventually all foreign trade was lost. Writing of the early nineteenth century Leader says: "The town presented the sad spectacle of landlords seizing goods in lieu of rent, of their stripped tenants clamouring for bread ... and of artisans perishing for lack of work."

Even hastily increased poor rates were quite inadequate. As usual in the past, voluntary subscriptions were generously given. At the beginning of the century Dr. John Browne's Corn Committee was selling grain at low prices, and at the same time a miller of Attercliffe, called Hartopp, was selling flour he had ground at half the market price.

Somehow, the town's affairs were carried on; a new poorhouse was built by Brightside Bierlow in 1801; new bells were hung in the parish church in 1799; a new reservoir was built on Crookes Moor in 1802. In 1807 a new newspaper, the *Sheffield Mercury* was published by W. Todd.

Sheffield's growing interest in scientific knowledge was coming very much to the fore. Already in 1794 the Society of Friends of Literature had been founded, with John Pye-Smith as president. For his geological work, Pye-Smith was elected a Fellow of the Royal Society. In 1804 the Society for the Promotion of Useful Knowledge was founded, its real instigator being Dr. David Daniel Davis (1778–1844). He was a distinguished obstetrician, being elected a physician at the Sheffield Infirmary in 1804. His name and work were so well esteemed that he was chosen to attend the Duchess of Kent when the future Queen Victoria was born. He became the first professor of midwifery at University College, London.

During the first quarter of the nineteenth century Sheffield's medical men were the town's leading scientific group. A private anatomical museum was established by Dr. Overend and his son, and this later became a medical school. Dr. Arnold Knight was interested in founding the Medical Book Society in 1816, the Medical and Surgical Society in 1819, and the Sheffield Medical School in 1828. Small, 'backward' Sheffield had a wealth of leading scientists and medical men.

In 1822 Arnold Knight with Thomas Asline Ward founded the Sheffield Literary and Philosophical Society. Together they wrote the society's preliminary address, in which they said:

The Utility of Science is everywhere visible. She is no longer a recluse in the cell of the monk or the closet of the student. . . . As social intercourse and free discussion on literary and philosophical subjects are conducive to the development of truth, the correction of error and the advancement of science, it is proposed that these shall form a principal part of the business of this Society, and since lectures accompanied by experiment may be regarded as bringing all theory to the test of fact and reality, such means of improvement will constitute another most important feature in the intended plan.

The society grew apace, having a membership of 179 at the end of its first year. A museum was established, for botany, entomology and zoology, minerology and geology, antiquities, philosophic research and books. What an undertaking!

From 1829 to 1888 the Sheffield School of Medicine functioned in its new building in Surrey Street, with the motto "*Ars longa Vita brevis*" carved over the entrance.

The year 1831 was notable. Dr. Holland, a pioneer of social medicine, gave the first lecture towards the formation of the Mechanics Institute; the Sheffield Banking Company was formed in that year, and a Board of Health set up. In that year also J. H. Abraham, who had been awarded the gold medal of the Society of Arts in 1822 for the invention of a magnetic device to prevent dry grinders from inhaling steel dust, represented the Sheffield Literary and Philosophical Society at York, the occasion being the founding of the British Association. In 1842 a Congregational minister, the Reverend R. S. Bayley organized the

People's College—the first college of this type in the country.

The dreadful Napoleonic Wars ended in 1815, and then after a time the distress which inevitably follows war, affected the whole country—and Sheffield certainly had its share. The years 1818 to 1850 were notorious. By the 1830s Sheffield's trade with Europe and America was practically at a standstill. It was the canal which saved the day, by making coal-transport cheap and practical.

The lord of the manor, the eleventh Duke of Norfolk, had let his collieries in and near the great Sheffield Park to the Sheffield Coal Company, and they had almost a monopoly in supplying Sheffield consumers.

The Cutlers' Company still considered the possibility of continuing the canal right into Sheffield, thus making the town an important inland port. By 1814 their plans were made and the next year they succeeded in obtaining an Act to continue the navigation from Tinsley to Sheffield "with a branch to Greenland Engine towards the valuable collieries and Beds of Coal and Ironstone which abound in that direction". Powers were granted to take water from the Sheaf, from the mines at Greenland Engine and at Crookes Croft, and to make reservoirs on the Darnall Brook and Acres Hill Dyke.

Four years were needed for the construction of this cut, in which nine locks were built to lift the navigation from the original terminal basin in the township of Tinsley to the fine new basin in Sheffield, the cost for this important extension and ancillary works being £104,719. Although the various sources of water-supply named in the Act were legally available, it was realized that when fully working there might be a water shortage. It was therefore agreed to build a pump-house at Tinsley capable of pumping water from the Don up to summit level as and when required.

The new terminal basin in the heart of Sheffield covered several acres, with fine warehouses, extensive wharves, several mobile cranes, weigh-bridges, storage and stable facilities. On 22nd February 1819 the Sheffield Canal was formally opened, the *Industry* of Thorne leading six other vessels to berth in the Sheffield Basin. Surely no other navigation in this country has such a history of frustration and success; nor has any other navigation so amply justified its construction. One hundred and twenty-two years after Sir Godfrey Copley's first unsuccessful Bill to make the Don navigable to Sheffield, his aim was achieved, and it was possible to sail a Humber keel from tidal waters into the busy heart of Sheffield.

During February 1819 there was considerable distress and unrest in many parts of the country, largely the result of the recent wars; but there is ample evidence that the timely completion of the canal into Sheffield, by making available cheaper transport of goods with the resulting increase in trade, did much to save the district from experiencing the bitterest effects of the national unrest. As soon as the canal was opened into Sheffield Earl Fitzwilliam opened a colliery at the Tinsley end, so that coal from there could be carried to Sheffield by water and could compete favourably with the coal from the Duke of Norfolk's collieries which hitherto had enjoyed a monopoly.

The Sheffield Basin, within hailing distance of the castle site, presented scenes of welcome activity, a practical lesson in economics not overlooked by go-ahead manufacturers who, in the eighteen-twenties, were already looking forward and evolving schemes for further navigable waterways to link the town with the busy Lancashire and Midland canals. A link with the former would place the town and its environs in direct water communication with Liverpool, and with the latter would ensure a route for the direct supply of crucible clay and iron, and an outlet to the Midland regions for Sheffield's steel and manufactured goods.

Back in 1751 when the River Don (Dun) Navigation was opened to Tinsley there was a considerable upsurge in Sheffield's trade, including a spectacular rise in the timber trade. In 1792, 1802 and 1813 various plans were proposed—and thwarted—for continuing the canal to Sheffield, and for connecting the Don Navigation with the Chesterfield Canal (from West Stockwith, on the River Trent to Chesterfield, built by James Brindley and opened in 1777), and the Peak Forest Canal (from Buxworth near Chinley to the Ashton Canal at Dukinfield, built by Benjamin Outram). Progressive citizens remembered these plans, and in 1820 the famous engineer Thomas Telford was consulted.

Telford planned a canal from Kelham Wheel to Wortley, thence climbing to Penistone through long flights of locks, tunnelling under the moors at Woodhead, then descending the valley of the River Etherow by flights of locks through Mottram to Hyde, to join the fine Ashton Canal. The estimated cost of this stupendous project was of the order of half a million pounds.

The Sheffield–Midlands scheme proposed to connect Sheffield to Chesterfield via the Sheaf and Drone Valleys, then along the Rother Valley via Clay Cross to the Amber Valley to join the Cromford Canal at Buckland Hollow. A tunnel would be needed under the Sheaf–Drone watershed and one under the Rother–Amber watershed. The estimated cost of this canal was £365,769. The Chesterfield Canal Company was quite ready to join in this scheme, and especially in the various branches envisaged, the value of such a waterway for the transport of coal, ironstone, lime and limestone being fully appreciated. Unfortunately, coming at this time of serious national unrest, both these schemes were laid aside.

However, plans to improve the River Don Navigation were carried out, new cuts being made at Arksey, Ings, Barnby Dun and Mexborough.

By 1830 the new Railway Age had arrived, and the railway promoters naturally were interested in the mineral wealth surrounding the Don and its tributaries. It was deemed expedient to reduce canal tolls, and in 1844 the River Don Navigation Company bought up the busy Dearne and Dove Canal running from the Don Navigation at Swinton to the busy Barnsley Canal at Barnsley. The company reduced the tolls on coal on the Dearne and Dove Canal to ½d. per ton/mile.

Fearing canal competition the Manchester, Sheffield and Lincolnshire Railway in 1864 bought up the navigation, and from that date the canal was poorly maintained. This danger to the canal's efficiency—and therefore to Sheffield's trade—was recognized by both the Sheffield Corporation and manufacturers, and in 1889 a Bill was introduced for the compulsory purchase from the Great Central Railway Company of the 57 miles of navigation so vital to Sheffield, by the newly incorporated Sheffield and South Yorkshire Navigation Company. Because of the Railway Company's neglect, the new Navigation Company had to face annual bills of between £10,000 and £14,000 to catch up with arrears of maintenance. The Railway Company had put up powerful resistance to this compulsory purchase, and it was considered necessary to effect a compromise whereby the Railway Company kept control on the board of directors. So the difficulties under which

this important trade route operated continued. In the twentieth
century it will be seen that the navigation's difficulties were
substantially and deliberately increased.

At the beginning of the nineteenth century three children were
born who were to become railway engineers of outstanding merit;
they were Robert Stephenson (son of George Stephenson) born
in 1803, Joseph Locke born in 1805 and Isambard Kingdom Brunel
born in 1806. Of these three, Locke was a son of Sheffield; he
was born in a cottage on Attercliffe Common, his father William
Locke being manager of a colliery nearby. The family left
Attercliffe when Joseph was still a child and eventually moved
to Barnsley, where Joseph attended the grammar school. In 1823
when he was eighteen he was sent to work under his father's
friend George Stephenson at Newcastle, and from that time his
application and knowledge took him to the top of his profession.
Later, he succeeded Charles Vignoles as Engineer-in-Chief of
the new Sheffield, Ashton-under-Lyne and Manchester Railway,
which followed a route not so far removed from the canal route
planned by Telford in 1820—a plan which was abandoned at the
time, as we have seen, because of the prevailing national unrest.
Another quarter of a century was to pass before the railway was
built—but this we will refer to later.

In his book *Great Engineers*, L. T. C. Rolt points out that Locke,
like the great canal engineer William Jessop, was essentially a
quiet man, and says: "His greatest achievement was to set the civil
engineering profession new standards of accuracy, order and
discipline. For this the world owes him a debt which is seldom
acknowledged."

After the Napoleonic Wars distress and poverty in Sheffield, as
elsewhere, mounted. There were brief periods of trade recovery,
followed by lengthy periods of distress. Towards the end of the
eighteenth century and early in the nineteenth century several
public-spirited citizens had founded charities for some specific
cause, but the desperate problem of growing poverty and sickness
was practically untouched.

Sanitary arrangements in many parts of the town were appalling; and in 1832 the dreaded Asiatic cholera reached Sheffield,
having entered England, it is claimed, via London and Hull. No

remedy was known at the time; it was not even suspected that open drains were largely responsible for the spread of the epidemic. Over 400 people died in Sheffield, one of the victims being John Blake, the master cutler. Near Norfolk Park, the last area of the former great Sheffield Park to be retained as a park by the Duke of Norfolk, a 60-foot-high monument to "402 victims in 1832" was erected.

In 1841 the Duke gave the citizens of Sheffield permission to walk in the park, but in 1883 the public was denied access to the Cholera Monument Grounds. However, when approached in 1899 the Duke agreed to lease the grounds to the corporation for twenty-one years at the nominal rent of two shillings per year. In 1909 the Duke formally presented Norfolk Park to the corporation for use as a park in perpetuity, and in 1929 he formally gave to the city the Monument Grounds with the tall Cholera Monument.

The Sheffield and South Yorkshire Navigation had proved to be of tremendous value to the people of Sheffield after its opening in 1819, the safer, cheaper carriage of goods benefiting the industrialists and the workers alike. But a new worry was facing Sheffield; other manufacturing areas were served, in addition to their water connections, by the new railways. Sheffield's approach gradients were considered a deterrent, engineers such as George Stephenson preferring to avoid the hills. Sheffield became concerned about the possibility of being bypassed by the new railway companies.

The town trustees took such action as they thought desirable to encourage the building of a railway to Sheffield, and they were supported by the Cutlers' Company. In March 1830 it was agreed to support a petition concerning a Parliamentary Bill for making a railroad from Manchester to Whaley Bridge, with a view to its later extension to the town of Sheffield, "opening communications with the mineral district of Derbyshire and the port of Liverpool . . .".

In the following year they supported a petition for a line between Manchester and Sheffield. The prospectus for this proposed venture points out that: "A large proportion of the manufactures of Sheffield is consumed in Manchester or exported from Liverpool, and there is no other way of transporting this merchandise than by horse and cart over the mountains of

Derbyshire which is very expensive; or by the circuitous route of ninety miles through the Yorkshire Canals, which is scarcely less expensive. . . ."

This Bill was passed but the scheme was abandoned, partly because another plan was proposed, to bring the North Midland line through Sheffield. The Town Trust in January and April 1836 passed resolutions to make financial grants towards bringing the North Midland Railway through Sheffield. George Stephenson pointed out that such a route, because of the ridge of high land between Chesterfield and Sheffield, would need cuttings of 90 to 100 feet. His suggested route from London to pass through Birmingham, Derby and Rotherham to York was adopted in the North Midland Railway Act of 1836. The line was opened in 1840.

A further Act of 1836 authorized the building of a branch line from Sheffield to the North Midland route at Rotherham. This connection was strongly opposed by the Duke of Norfolk, who feared it would damage his lucrative Sheffield coal trade; it was opposed by the Canal Company and by "120 respectable people of Rotherham" who were afraid that the railway would have the effect "of causing the idle, drunken and dissolute portion of the Sheffield community to flock to Rotherham". Nevertheless this plan was carried out and the branch opened in October 1838. The station was built in The Wicker, the journey from there to Rotherham taking about sixteen minutes, and the fare was 6d. This line, constructed on the north side of the River Don was until 1870 Sheffield's only connection with the North Midland Railway. Although this connection was only a branch line, Sheffield had the satisfaction of being served by a water-highway to the sea, a system of turnpike roads and a railway.

The Cutlers' Company still entertained the idea of direct rail connection with Manchester, the opinion no doubt being held that if a canal could be built from Sheffield to Manchester, as planned by Telford in 1820, surely a railway could follow a similar line. The Cutlers' Company renewed their agitation for a Sheffield–Manchester railroad, and were supported by the Duke of Norfolk and Lord Wharncliffe. They succeeded in getting a Bill through Parliament in 1837, before the Rotherham–Sheffield branch line was completed.

The new line was to be known as the Sheffield, Ashton-under-Lyne and Manchester Railway, and eventually (following Charles

Vignoles's withdrawal) the Sheffield-born Joseph Locke became engineer for the project. It was a tremendous undertaking, requiring the building of the summit-level tunnel at Woodhead, through the Pennines. The tunnel penetrated the hard gritstone, but Locke insisted that the tunnel must nevertheless be lined throughout, the estimated cost of this being £98,467. Most of the 3-mile tunnel was lined with local stone. Woodhead Tunnel took six years to build, and was completed in December 1845; it was a fine engineering feat and was the longest tunnel constructed up to that time. The tunnel took a single-line track. When this was opened the company decided they wanted a second line through the tunnel. A second bore therefore was made parallel to the first, and opened in 1852.

The Sheffield station for this line was at Bridgehouses, but when two years later the line was extended to Lincoln, it was decided to build another station, and the new Victoria Station was opened in 1851. Through various amalgamations the Sheffield, Ashton-under-Lyne and Manchester Railway became the Manchester, Sheffield and Lincolnshire Railway, then the Great Central Railway and finally the London and North Eastern Railway. Between Sheffield and Manchester this line was electrified in 1954: and a new tunnel of much larger bore was constructed. By 1970 all passenger trains on this fine route were withdrawn and the Victoria Station closed. Considerable goods traffic still uses the route.

Determination still persisted to have direct rail connection between Sheffield and London via Chesterfield, but there was a great deal of opposition. It was not until 25th July 1864 that the Bill was finally passed and received the Royal Assent. Work started in July 1865.

The most difficult section of this route was the ridge between Sheffield and Chesterfield, through which the Bradway Tunnel was made, 2,024 yards in length. This bore caused a lot of trouble; it passed through both hard rock and shale, the shale sections having to be very firmly lined with brick. Many springs were encountered, and considerable efforts had to be made to overcome this serious water problem. Eventually the water was channelled from the tunnel and used for various railway purposes several miles nearer to Sheffield. The station in Sheffield (today's rather attractive Midland Railway Station, although since amalgamation it has been the London, Midland and Scottish Railway

Station) was built 'in the Ponds', actually right over the River Sheaf. The *Independent* of 3rd November, 1866 reported: "The selection of the Ponds as the site of the station has involved great labour and difficulty in dealing with the River Sheaf on the one hand, and the overhanging cliff beneath which it runs on the other. Large numbers of men have been engaged in constructing long rows of arches, built lengthwise to the course of the stream, upon which the station and the line will be built. When the arches are covered in, the rest of the work will be comparatively easy." The Sheffield–Chesterfield length of the North Midland Railway was opened on 1st February 1870.

This completed work certainly put Sheffield in direct rail communication with London and with the valuable coal deposits round Dronfield and district; but the vast mineral deposits of various kinds in that part of Derbyshire between Sheffield and Chinley could still be transported only over hilly roads. Competition between the various railway companies was very keen and at times bitter, but eventually consent was obtained in July 1884 for the building of a line from the North Midland Railway at Sheffield which would be a second trans-Pennine route to Manchester.

This was to be a remarkable engineering feat, occupying the years 1884–93. The new line branched to the west at Dore and Totley Station on the Sheffield–London line, and climbed to pass under the high land of Totley Moors via the Totley Tunnel, 3 miles 950 yards long, emerging at Grindleford. The line continued up the valley of the River Derwent and its tributary the Noe, having to tunnel again beyond Edale through Cowburn Tunnel to the valley of the Blackbrook, a tributary of the River Goyt on the west side of the Pennines.

Thus, by the end of the nineteenth century Sheffield had added to its Portrait serviceable communications—a fine navigation leading from the heart of Sheffield to the port of Hull, a direct railway line to London, and two remarkably engineered routes across the Pennines to Manchester—because of the hills one of these routes leaving Sheffield to the north and the other to the south.

X

REFORMS

IT HAS been noted that although during the eighteenth century and into the nineteenth Sheffield's population was growing, and that during the bad periods of trade fluctuations there was considerable and appalling poverty, the collection of the Poor Rate was totally unrealistic. Just before the turn of the century Benjamin Blonk suggested in a letter to James Wheat, the lawyer, that application be made to Parliament to borrow money in order to build a new poorhouse and also to enable the town to be better supplied with water and better cleaned and lighted. He stated—with reason—that half the property in the growing town was not rated at all. A report from a Mr. Staniland concerning conditions at the existing poorhouse was positively alarming. In 1789 a committee was set up to arrange for the building of a workhouse. Their efforts came to nothing.

The improved transport facilities, by providing cheaper and better communication, gradually helped the manufacturers and the workers, but the collapse of the bank of Parker, Shore & Co. shook the investors badly. It was realized that the joint-stock banking system was more reliable than the previously trusted private banks, and most firms accepted the new system, though they regarded it as less friendly.

By the mid-nineteenth century it was found that infant mortality in Sheffield was very high; scarlet fever was a persistent scourge, and in the grinding trades tuberculosis was rife. It was probably the cholera outbreak in 1832 which hastened the founding of the public dispensary, afterwards to become the Royal Hospital. Sheffield's medical men and scientists of that time were, perhaps unknown even to themselves, establishing a medical and scientific tradition which in years to come would be second to none in the country.

The many 'good works' initiated by different groups in aid of a number of causes is an indication that there were not a few citizens who were concerned about the recurring poverty with all the accompanying tragedy; but four men stand out as indefatigable workers towards social improvement. They were James Montgomery of the *Sheffield Iris*, who had already been imprisoned for his opinions; Thomas Asline Ward, a cutlery merchant; Samuel Roberts, a silverplater; and Rowland Hodgson, gentleman. To these should be added a fifth name, that of Ebenezer Elliott, iron-founder, who moved with his family to Sheffield from Rotherham when his works went bankrupt. He was a remarkable man, with clear vision and sensitive nature, which was completely revolted by the cruelties he saw around him. He saw men flogged, and starving people unable to buy bread. Like Montgomery, he loved to express his views in verse. He fought long and hard for the repeal of the dreadful Corn Laws, and shared the opinions of Bright and Cobden. In 1846 the Corn Laws at last were repealed, and the poor once again could afford bread.

During the first quarter of the nineteenth century Joseph Hunter wrote his monumental work, *Hallamshire*, a history of the parish of Sheffield and the neighbouring townships; and some ten years later appeared his *History of the Deanery of Doncaster*. About this time there lived also Ebenezer Rhodes, editor of the *Sheffield and Rotherham Independent*, published as a weekly in 1819. Later, when controlled by the Leader family, this paper set a fine example. Rhodes loved the countryside. By trade he was a cutler, though obviously he was much more interested in writing. Between 1818 and 1824 he published his *Peak Scenery*, containing a collection of engravings by his friends Francis Chantrey, Hofland, Blore and Thompson.

Despite all the praiseworthy attempts we have noted—educational, social, scientific, religious, charitable—Sheffield still had no centralized local government. There were the Town Trustees, who undertook as much street improvement as they could afford, and in 1808 built a new town hall (later used as the court house); the county magistrates who actually controlled the town (and lived away from it); the Cutlers' Company who had limited powers; and the lord of the manor's manorial courts of Sheffield and Ecclesall, which dealt with debtors. The dreadful manorial gaol in King Street had been replaced by a better one in Scotland Street, and the Ecclesall manorial gaol was in Thomas Street. But change was imminent. In 1818 two Bills were presented in Parliament, and passed without opposition—one for lighting, 'watching' and cleansing the streets, the other for "lighting the streets with gas". It was in 1818 that two towns, many miles apart, had a gas company founded. The towns were Sheffield and Brighton. On 6th October 1819 Prince Leopold of Saxe-Coburg (Queen Victoria's uncle) visited Sheffield, and on that day gas was used for the first time for lighting the streets of the town.

By the Improvement Act, commissioners (ninety-eight in number) were appointed with power to levy a rate, appoint watchmen and remove nuisances and obstructions. Alas, very little of this was actually carried out, but the gas company had installed some street lights, for which they charged a good price. A police force was assembled by the commissioners, with control only over the built-up area which was estimated to house about 68,000 people, the police force having sixteen day men and fifty-six night watchmen.

The mid-nineteenth century witnessed great activity in the erection on the outskirts of the town of some good dwellings and well-laid-out, tree-lined streets. The estate surrounding the dignified Broom Hall was made available for the building of good houses; Kenwood, George Wolstenholm's large house in Sharrow, had wide streets set out in the vicinity to accommodate new houses; the grounds at Broom Hill were made available for good buildings. In the town itself the lord of the manor, the twelfth Duke of Norfolk, sold part of his land to the town; he built a Corn Exchange in 1830, and this was replaced by a quite striking building in 1881. In the twentieth century this building unfortunately was burnt down, and never restored. In 1827 the Duke arranged for the inmates of the old Shrewsbury Hospital to be moved to larger, more pleasant premises in Shrewsbury Road. In almost every village on the north, west and south of the town it was evident that new building was gradually creeping towards them from the town itself.

To the east, along the Don Valley, and near the canal and railways spread the town's heavy industries, accompanied by the building of rows of brick houses for the workers.

The Parliament of the day was slowly getting round to repealing several laws which had caused much unfortunate discrimination and suffering; in 1828 the Test Act was repealed, which had been in force since 1673 and required all persons holding any military or civil office to take the Sacrament and the oath of supremacy and sign a declaration against transubstantiation. In 1828 the Corporation Act (requiring every member of a town corporation to take the Sacrament according to the rites of the Established Church) was repealed; and in 1829 the Catholic Emancipation Act was passed. These Parliamentary measures eased a frustrating religious situation and were a prelude to greater reforms.

It has been noted that the year 1830 was a period of recurring national distress, very evident in towns like Sheffield. In some parts of the country a desperate working class resorted to rioting, rick-burning and machine-smashing. The position of the trade unions was somewhat strengthened by the Act passed early in 1825 which legalized them, but the much-needed reforms were slow of achievement. At last it was realized that drastic methods must be used to focus attention on the desperate conditions of the workers.

In Sheffield the machine-damaging, called 'rattening', was aimed particularly at the tool-grinding trades. It is not known exactly when this was started, or by whom; an amazing system of secrecy was faithfully maintained throughout. Rattening was taking place in 1820, and by 1860 became very serious. At first, rattening seems to have been directed towards strengthening the unions by making non-members join, and by making members who had not paid their union dues, pay up. By secretly removing some essential item of a grinder's machinery such as a wheelband which would immobilize all that it controlled, a defaulter could be 'persuaded' to toe the line, and as soon as he satisfied union requirements his machinery would be restored to working order —again secretly. It has been claimed that most of the members of a particular trade union would be aware of action being taken, but no one ever divulged the name of the person or persons who dismantled, and restored, the machinery.

Parliamentary reform, including the removal of members who represented 'rotten' boroughs and 'pocket' boroughs and allowing the growing industrial areas to be represented, was now essential.

The Tilt Hammer 'Shop' at the Abbeydale Industrial Hamlet
An example of Old Sheffield Plate

Lord John Russell introduced the Reform Bill in March 1831, seeking the disenfranchisement of sixty small boroughs, giving thirty-four seats to large towns as yet unrepresented, and giving other seats to London and certain counties. The conditions included in the Bill showed that the middle classes would be enfranchised, but not the lower classes.

The Bill did not pass. The rattening continued.

There was a general election under the existing conditions, and a new Parliament. Hopes ran high. In September the Commons passed the second Reform Bill. It was thrown out by the Lords. There was frustration throughout the country, and further unrest. Meetings of the popular 'political unions' in large towns were now forbidden.

In March 1832 the Reform Bill was introduced into the Commons for the third time, and it was feared that again the Lords would defeat it. The situation became extremely serious. Eventually the king, William IV, took action, and privately asked a group of well-known anti-reform members of the House of Lords to refrain from voting. This timely, though unusual action, was effective, and the Bill became Law. It has been said that the passing of the Reform Bill in 1832 ended the greatest crisis since the Revolution of 1688.

Sheffield was delighted when two members were allocated to the town—for the first time in the town's history. In December the voters chose as their two members John Parker and James Buckingham. Feeling still ran high, and the unenfranchised citizens made it evident that their choice would have been Thomas Asline Ward, whose broad outlook and vision were well known. During the evening, when the successful parties were celebrating at the Tontine Inn, a crowd gathered there, and some of the wilder spirits threw stones and broke windows. The situation got out of hand, the reading of the Riot Act being ignored by the crowd. Perhaps because the successful party was feeling *very* successful, and realizing that the small police force probably could not deal with a large, unruly mob, the army was called in. At last the order was given to fire into the crowd, and five people were killed. Two magistrates who were present at once stopped the firing—but tragedy had occurred. The coroner's verdict was 'justifiable homicide'. It was a grim reminder that Parliamentary Reform still had a long way to go.

9

Grindstones lying unused below Burbage Edge

A total of about 3,500 citizens of Sheffield now had the right to vote by virtue of the £10 qualification.

We have seen that the new Act enfranchised only the middle classes, and that the working classes who so desperately needed representation, were not yet enfranchised.

Against this national and local background, how very tragic it was that five people lost their lives when Sheffield's first Members were elected. But reforms were on the way—slowly and clumsily perhaps—but our town was beginning to take its affairs very seriously, despite the sad periods of recurring depression.

The fact must not be overlooked that as long as sixty years earlier a number of enlightened Sheffield people desired Parliamentary reform. The vicar, the Reverend James Wilkinson, and others were interested in the work of the Reverend Christopher Wyvell in his *Yorkshire Association*. A few years later the Sheffield Society for Constitutional Information was founded and in 1793 a petition was presented to the House of Commons asking for the parliamentary system to be replaced by one of representation based on population. The year 1832 saw the introduction of the first of the desired reforms.

One of the first Acts passed by the new Parliament was the Act for the Abolition of Slavery (1833). In Sheffield a determined group led by Montgomery had worked for many years to bring this about. In 1834 the new Poor Law Act was passed, establishing workhouses to be managed by Boards of Guardians. Instead of getting 'outdoor relief' paupers now had to enter the workhouse, a system that was by no means well received in Sheffield. In 1835 another step forward was taken, by the Municipal Corporation Act.

The system of poor-relief was in need of drastic reform despite the fact that a succession of overseers of the poor had done their best to cope with difficulties. But the 1834 Poor Law Amendment Act solved some difficulties and created others. One step taken was the setting up of a number of larger unions throughout the country to replace the great number of small parish and township poor-relief units. The new larger unions in some cases disregarded parish boundaries, and this happened in Sheffield.

The elected guardians of the two new unions established in Sheffield in 1837 had to carry out the recommendations in the

Act as soon as possible; they had to establish workhouses and reduce the payment of 'out-relief'. Samuel Roberts wrote and spoke in a most dedicated way against the implementation in Sheffield of the Act's insistence on the provision of workhouses, but to no avail. Sheffield citizens of all classes hated the thought of poor paupers being herded into workhouses.

The two unions set up in Sheffield in 1837, were the Sheffield Union and the Ecclesall Union, the former including the townships of Sheffield, Brightside, Attercliffe and Handsworth, and the latter the townships of Ecclesall, Upper and Nether Hallam, Totley, Dore, Beauchief and Norton. The Sheffield Guardians found they had two poorhouses which must become workhouses, the Sheffield poorhouse established in 1829 by altering the old Kelham cotton mill and the Brightside poorhouse in Rock Street. The Ecclesall Guardians had one poorhouse in Psalter Lane and one at Crookes. They built a large new workhouse at Nether Edge. Many abuses crept into this new workhouse system, none of which helped to popularize it with the people.

Rather surprisingly, the 1835 Municipal Corporation Act was not at first welcome to many Sheffield people. The town was entitled to apply for a charter under the terms of the new Act, to become a borough and be controlled by its own elected council. All householders, provided they had occupied property for three years and paid the requisite poor rate, were entitled to vote. Certainly Sheffield, with its lack of a controlling body, needed municipal reform, particularly as if granted borough status a Commission of the Peace and a Court of Quarter Sessions could be applied for, in addition to several other desirable innovations.

A number of householders signed a petition desiring that the charter should be applied for, but a larger number of the wealthier citizens produced a counter-petition against it, their objection being that a charter would definitely mean the paying of higher rates. The counter-petitioners were successful. This group was soon to be rudely awakened and made to realize that the lack of a properly constituted ruling body in the town could lead to serious consequences. It was the People's Charter and its supporters the Chartists which alarmed them.

Under a leader, Feargus O'Connor, throughout the country voteless people supported a People's Charter embodying six points:

Manhood suffrage.
Vote by ballot.
Annual Parliaments.
Payment of Members of Parliament.
Abolition of the property qualification of members.
Equal electoral districts.

Such far-seeing reforms (most of which we enjoy today) were opposed by the Government. As no headway could therefore be made by peaceable means this resulted in several serious riots, which were easily suppressed. Agitation continued and Sheffield, which would not even apply for the charter to which it was entitled, had many supporters of the People's Charter. So had the surrounding districts. Sir Charles Napier as military commander in the North managed to prevent riots in Sheffield in 1839; but in 1840 events took a more serious turn. In Sheffield, the local headquarters, a plan was drawn up whereby at a certain time the Tontine Inn and several other points would be seized, and at the same time the homes of known opposers of the Charter would be set on fire to draw military action away from the town centre. Supporters from Eckington, Handsworth, Rotherham, Grenoside, Ecclesfield, Chapeltown and Kimberworth were to help. Although by this time people in all walks of life were aware of the near hopelessness of many working-class people, the thought of violent action was unacceptable even to many of the Chartists themselves.

Fortunately, Rotherham's Chief Constable, John Bland, became suspicious about the actions of James Allen, who was the leader of the Rotherham Chartists, and he managed to uncover details of the plans. These he made known to the Sheffield Police Surveyor, Thomas Raynor. The Sheffield Chartists leader, Samuel Holberry, was arrested at his home, and hidden arms were found. Without Holberry the plans for the rising collapsed. Holberry and several other leaders were sentenced to three years in gaol, and Allen was "sent abroad".

Realization of how serious this planned rising could have been, largely because of lack of central control in the town, prompted the citizens to raise again the question of another petition for a charter, but even then it was not certain that there would not be opposition. In the meantime an Act was passed in 1839 giving counties authority to establish police forces on lines similar to the metropolitan police force which had been successfully launched by Robert Peel. As Sheffield was still not a borough it would have to be county controlled as far as provision for a police force and several other matters were concerned. Such a possibility alarmed even the no-charter supporters; a second petition was quickly arranged and duly presented.

Royal Assent was given on 31st August 1843 and the historic charter was read at the town hall on 13th September. The first municipal election was held on 1st November, the wards represented being St. Peter's, St. Philip's, St. George's, Ecclesall, Upper Hallam, Nether Hallam, Brightside, Park and Attercliffe. The new council had a total of fifty-six councillors and aldermen. The mayor was William Jeffcock and the town clerk was Edward Bramley. Many of the members of the new council were engaged in industry. A number of formidable tasks were to present themselves.

XI

A GROWING POPULATION

BY THE date of the passing of the Reform Act, 1832, Sheffield's population had grown enormously, the rate of growth being higher than the national average. Although, officially, the first population statistics became available in 1801, the year the census of population was taken, Sheffield has figures for earlier dates. In 1615 an estimate of the population was prepared by "twenty-four of the most sufficient inhabitants"; in 1736 there was a house-to-house survey; there were the Poll Tax returns of 1692, and the parish registers.

Sheffield was an extensive parish, including the small original township and several villages and hamlets. From a combination of the various sources mentioned above it has been estimated that at the beginning of the seventeenth century the population of the parish was about 3,000, of whom perhaps 2,200 lived in the crowded area surrounding the castle. By the end of that century estimates suggest a parish population of about 5,000, and of this number maybe about 3,500 lived in the crowded little township. In view of the various national crises during that period the increase in population was noteworthy, probably being attributable largely to the steady development of local industries. Better conditions of employment provided more food, less poverty and less sickness, combined with longer life.

The eighteenth-century population growth escalated. The 1736 survey estimated a population of about 10,000 in the township; by 1750 there were about 20,000 in the parish as a whole. Thus, within the sixty years from the 1692 assessment the population had quadrupled, and in the fifty years up to 1801 had more than doubled again, there being almost 46,000 in the parish, of whom about 31,500 lived in the township.

It has been stated that from outlying districts beyond the parish boundaries immigrants were moving to Sheffield, attracted by its industries.

By the mid-nineteenth century when the town was incorporated the population had grown to 135,000, some 120,000 of this total living in the central area. Yet until 1843 Sheffield had no central civic control, what control there was being shared by several bodies—the oldest being the town trustees or burgery, founded by the lord of the manor's charter of 1297, which still functions today; there were also the Twelve Capital Burgesses and Commonality of the Town and Parish of Sheffield, founded by Queen Mary in 1554, known as the church burgesses because of their church commitments, which also exist today. Officially, the town trustees with their elected town collector are chosen by the town's freeholders; over the years their income (expended on highway repairs, bridge maintenance, town lighting, etc.) has fluctuated. In 1681 a decree in Chancery required the burgery to consist of thirteen trustees, with the need to bring the number up to thirteen again when three had died, election to be by "the greater part of the inhabitants". This arrangement was not satisfactory and in 1817 a second decree stated that the right of election was still the prerogative of the freeholders. The town trustees therefore could be elected by only a limited section of the community. But their record, considering the difficulties with which they had to contend, was quite remarkable; together with the Cutlers' Company and Doncaster Corporation they worked for the improvement of the River Dun Navigation up to Tinsley in 1726; they assisted with the turnpike schemes, and in 1814 pressed for the extension of the navigation from Tinsley to Sheffield, taking shares in the new canal company. In 1734 they provided oil-lamps for lighting the township, and in 1818 supported the move which secured the Act setting up commissioners for the improved lighting, cleansing and policing of the town. The newly appointed commissioners became the third of the controlling bodies. The Cutlers' Company from time to time helped towards highway work, poor relief, etc.; and a fifth organization, a parochial vestry body, also gave assistance. The lord of the manor controlled the market, had authority to hold a court leet, to appoint constables, searchers of bread and ale, etc., and every three weeks to hold a manorial court to deal with debtors.

There were thus five organizations, plus the lord of the manor to control the town. Yet, despite their frequent co-operation, many urgent matters were outside their jurisdiction, and there were serious conditions which demanded attention.

The death-rate was very high; parts of the town still had no sewers; water, in many sections, could be obtained only from shared outside stand-pipes on three days a week. Around the densely crowded Castle Green area overcrowding and lack of sanitation were appalling—although the conditions were no worse than those existing in a number of towns.

At last, as we have noted, in 1835 the Municipal Corporations Reforms Act was passed, and this entitled Sheffield to apply for a charter granting borough status. This was granted in August 1843.

Its members duly elected and a mayor and town clerk appointed, the new corporation began its formidable task. A health committee was established in 1846, but, although the health problem was long overdue for attention, the committee made slow progress until a Medical Officer of Health was appointed in 1872. One of the causes of overcrowding was the building of 'back-to-back' houses; in 1875 under the Public Health Act the corporation was empowered to prohibit further building of this type of dwelling.

A police force was organized, and a bench of magistrates set up in 1848.

With the rapidly growing population and expanding industries the water-supply problem was acute. The corporation decided that it was essential to control four of the then privately owned services—water, gas, electricity and transport.

The story of Sheffield's water undertaking goes back to the fifteenth century, when the first artificial pool was made where we still have the name, Barker's Pool. This was maintained by various individuals and organizations, but the pool was seen to be inadequate to meet increasing demands. In 1713 two men, Goodwin and Littlewood, were given permission by the lord of the manor to lay pipes in the roadways from springs near White House, and in 1737 a reservoir (now demolished) was built there. In 1782 the lord of the manor permitted the construction of reservoirs on Crookes Moor. Five service reservoirs where built between 1785 and 1829, and the two largest, Godfrey and Old Dam Reservoirs, were in use until recently.

A new company, the Sheffield Waterworks Company, was incorporated in 1830; this company bought up the property of the former owners and the Act gave permission for the construction of two storage reservoirs at Redmires, near the Roman Long Causeway, the upper reservoir being built actually *over* the Causeway, a new road to replace it having to be made on the north alongside the reservoir. These reservoirs are still in use. The company also was permitted to build the Hadfield Reservoir at Crookes, which is still in use though now completely covered over. A conduit (no longer used) was built from Redmires to Crookes.

The Waterworks Company certainly appear to have tried to keep up with the increasing rate of water consumption; in 1845 they obtained a further Act permitting the building of the third reservoir at Redmires and two 'compensation reservoirs' at Rivelin.

The question of compensation water was important in this area where so much industry depended upon water-powered wheels, and in addition the River Don Navigation required adequate water-flow from its headstreams and tributaries in order to remain navigable. In 1853 another Act was obtained permitting the construction of reservoirs in the Loxley Valley—Strines, Dale Dyke, Agden and Damflask. Of these the first to be built was the Dale Dyke Reservoir, where construction began in 1859. This reservoir at Low Bradfield was completed early in 1864, and by the beginning of March was nearly full.

And then disaster struck.

On 11th March, following a day of unusually high winds blowing straight down the valley, the water of the huge new reservoir burst its impounding dam and over 114,000,000 cubic feet of water, in a gigantic wave rushed down the Loxley Valley.

Not surprisingly, the extraordinarily strong wind made the company's resident engineer decide to inspect the retaining dam during the afternoon. He was definitely concerned about the force of the water crashing on the dam, but eventually decided that there was no need for undue alarm, and went home. At about five o'clock a workman on his way home crossed the valley via the top of the dam, and it was then that he noticed what seemed to be a tiny crack running down the embankment. In view of the still

increasing violence of the wind he informed several of his neighbours, and they agreed that the water company officials should be
alerted, but it was more than an hour later before a horseman was
found who could gallop to Sheffield to see the resident engineer.
The impression is gained that the messenger himself was not
unduly alarmed, and in making a brief stop at Damflask further
downstream his report to the villagers was not serious enough to
alarm all of them, although some were quite worried.

The water company's staff reached the reservoir as soon as
possible and although they took all available precautions, such as
trying to force open the safety valves, and even attempting to
blow a breach with gunpowder just upstream of the dam (un-
successfully, for the torrential rain had damped the gunpowder),
they still had faith in the strength of the dam. And the gale, which
was felt all the way down the valley, increased.

The resident engineer spent more than an hour making a close
inspection by lantern light, with waves lashing over the top. Just
before midnight those inspecting the top of the dam realized that
the structure was about to give way. The engineer was at the foot
of the dam, and above the screech of wind and roar of waves just
managed to catch a frenzied yell from his men; he made a rapid
dash to safety as the centre of the dam, with deafening noise
suddenly gave way, releasing millions of gallons of water in a
hideous monstrosity of sound, to take swift death and destruction
down the valley to Sheffield.

The village of Malin Bridge felt the worst of the flood's fury, for
there the river was narrowed by higher banks and two bridges;
here the Loxley is joined by the Rivelin, and some of the angry
flood-water surged into the Rivelin Valley, some sweeping over
the lower meadow land at Owlerton. The main volume of water
poured into the Don, tearing along to destroy buildings and
gardens. In Sheffield the flood, with its grim flotsam and jetsam of
wrecked buildings, corpses, mud, trees and struggling survivors
blocked the arches of Lady's Bridge, swept over the parapets and
on through The Wicker to Brightside. Here the valley is wider
and the raging torrent lost height as it surged over the land, its
fury well-nigh spent.

The flood struck and passed in just over forty minutes. Dale
Dyke reservoir was empty.

The people were stunned by the speed, the confusion and the

tragedy of the catastrophe. Dozens of injured, half-drowned people and animals was found feebly moving in the shallows as the flood raged on.

Long before dawn the valley was being searched for survivors; every house in the district was thrown open to feed, clothe and shelter the sufferers. It is know that 240 people lost their lives, nearly 700 animals were drowned, more than 100 buildings and fifteen bridges were wrecked, and over 4,000 buildings were flooded, much of their contents, including craftsmen's tools, being damaged or lost.

The small police force was quickly on the scene collecting the dead and rescuing the injured and bewildered. The mayor hastened to the scene of the tragedy; the board of guardians threw to the winds their limiting 'out-relief' regulations and ordered that help must be given at once to all in need. A relief committee was set up and a relief fund opened a few days later. Generous donations poured in, many hundreds of workmen donating a day's wages.

On 23rd and 24th March the coroner and his jury held their official investigation, at which one important witness was the engineer who had inspected the damaged structure on behalf of the Government. The coroner's investigation must have been a great strain for the water company's engineers and especially for the man responsible for designing the dam. In their verdict the jury recorded that "there had not been that engineering skill and attention in the construction of the works which their magnitude and importance demanded".

Perhaps the verdict was a fair one; but there still exists a second professional opinion which holds that the choice of that particular site for building the embankment was wrong, and that the embankment itself was well constructed.

The water company accepted liability and introduced a Parliamentary Bill seeking permission to raise extra capital of £400,000 and to increase water charges for a period of five years to enable their liabilities to be met. The Bill was passed.

The corporation never slackened its efforts to buy up the water company, but another twenty years passed before permission was gained, in 1887.

Having secured the desired control, the corporation had reason to be satisfied with their subsequent successful efforts to keep ahead of the town's increasing water requirements. A fair price was paid to the water company, the purchase including nine impounding reservoirs (the Upper, Middle and Lower Redmires Reservoirs, the Upper and Lower Rivelin Reservoirs, and the Strines, Agden, Dale Dyke and Damflask Reservoirs in the Loxley Valley). By 1887 the original Dale Dyke embankment had been replaced by a new one some 400 yards upstream, the reservoir itself being smaller. The purchase also included the Crookes service reservoirs and many miles of conduits, in addition to the site for the Broomhead and Morehall Reservoirs in the Ewden Valley, and the permission granted by an Act in 1867 to build impounding reservoirs at Langsett and Underbank in the Little Don Valley.

The purchase price paid by the council was of the order of £2,000,000.

From about 1852 several small firms had operated a horse-bus service, first to Heeley and then to Attercliffe, the Barracks, the Botanical Gardens and Broomhill—the last two routes involving quite a climb from the town centre. The corporation began to take an interest in the possibility of establishing an adequate system of horse-drawn tramways, and before 1871 was considering the question. But the borough surveyor felt that a combination of steep gradients and winding narrow streets made the problem of laying tramlines too difficult, although it might be feasible in the more level sections.

Eventually agreement was reached between the corporation and a private company, the corporation to construct the tramlines and then lease the working of the tramways system to the company for twenty-five years. The first horse-drawn tram ran from Lady's Bridge to the Golden Ball Hotel at Attercliffe on 6th October 1873. This route was extended to Tinsley at a later date, and in 1875 trams were running from the Twelve O'Clock Hotel in Savile Street to Brightside. Further tramline routes were constructed from Snig Hill to Hillsborough Bridge, Owlerton, and from Moorhead to Heeley and Nether Edge. There was a good deal of friction between the corporation and the company, the former claiming that the tracks were ill-maintained by the latter.

In January 1877 steam-trams were tried out in Sheffield.

The tramway company applied for a provisional order to use

mechanical power for the tramways, but in February 1877 the council declined to adopt the highways committee's recommendation that this be approved. As the time approached in 1896 for the expiry of the tramways company's lease, arguments and discussions caused many changes of opinion as to whether or not the council should itself take over and operate the tramways. Eventually the corporation decided on a take-over; the tramways company agreed, after the corporation had deposited £20,000, that on 10th July at midnight the change-over should be carried out. The corporation acquired from the company 310 horses, 44 tramcars, 4 omnibuses, 182 employees and 9 miles of tramlines.

The corporation's efforts to get control of the gas company were not successful. The Sheffield United Gas Company was established by the Act of 1844, by merging two rival companies which had existed for nine years. From 1818 to 1835 Sheffield's original gas company had functioned.

Still unsuccessful in gaining control, the corporation made a final attempt in 1919, and again the attempt failed. By that date the Sheffield and District Gas Company was operating very efficiently, giving a good service at a very reasonable charge, a satisfactory state of affairs which continued until the gas undertakings were nationalized on 1st May 1949.

As early as 1888 the Electric Lighting Act, a general Act, was passed. Shortly afterwards two private companies in Sheffield sought permission to supply electricity, but this was refused on the grounds that the council itself might seek the necessary powers to undertake this supply. However, in October 1891 the council agreed to the Sheffield Telephone Exchange and Electric Light Company's plan to seek a provisional order to supply electricity, including in the order powers enabling the corporation to purchase the undertaking at a later date if such action was considered desirable.

In April 1897 the council decided that the time had come to take over the company (by that time it had become the Sheffield Electric Lighting and Power Company Limited), and gave notice of their intention. As in the case of each of the other take-overs it was preceded by a good deal of fierce argument. At last, in February 1898, the company's claims were met and the corporation assumed control.

Another matter which engaged the attention of the council at this time was the question of market rights. Markets play an important role in the life of every town and city—as indeed has been the case for many centuries. As early as 1296, in the reign of King Edward I, the market rights of Sheffield were granted by charter to the lord of the manor, and continued as one of the lord's prerogatives.

In August 1874 Sheffield Council decided to make approaches to the lord of the manor, the Duke of Norfolk, with a view to purchasing the market rights and the markets themselves. Negotiations were opened with the duke's agent, and the sum of £267,450 was suggested as payment; but after a time, because of several differences of opinion between the duke and council, negotiations broke down.

It happened that in 1887 a Royal Commission was sitting on the question of market rights, and as it was seen that Sheffield was the only town with a population of more than 100,000 which still had the market rights privately owned or held by the lord of the manor, the council requested that the commissioners' enquiries should be extended to include Sheffield. This was agreed, and in August 1888 the visiting commissioner made his report on eight markets in Sheffield—Fitzalan Market, Norfolk Market Hall, Castle Folds Market, Sheaf Market, Corn Exchange, Smithfield Market, Wholesale Fish Market and the Slaughter Houses—the total income being estimated at £15,081 10s. 2½d. Until 1898 nothing further was done about the proposal to acquire the market rights, but in October of that year the Lord Mayor, Alderman Franklin, took up the matter with the duke and negotiations were again opened, with the result that eventually terms were agreed for the council's purchase of the Sheffield Market and market rights from the Duke. A Bill was promoted and in August 1899 received the Royal Assent. The purchase price was £526,000.

At this point it may be well to mention several other happenings which indicate a lessening of manorial control. In an earlier chapter mention has been made of the sub-manor of Ecclesall, the only one of the sub-manors which still continued to exist until the year in which all manors were discontinued officially. In 1866, in view of the growing powers and acceptance of responsibility by the new Borough Council of Sheffield, Ecclesall's lord of the manor, Earl Fitzwilliam, decided to cease holding his manorial court of Ecclesall, at the same time handing over to the council the standard weights and measures of his court.

In 1909 Earl Fitzwilliam donated to the city part of the area which is now known as Millhouses Park, consisting of some 32 level acres alongside the River Sheaf.

Sheffield's lord of the manor, the Duke of Norfolk, made several much appreciated gifts of land for public parks and recreation grounds in the last quarter of the nineteenth and first quarter of the twentieth centuries, including Attercliffe Recreation Ground, in 1878, and Parkwood Springs Recreation Ground in the same year; Burngreave Recreation Ground and Nottingham Cliffe Recreation Ground in 1887; Roe Wood, Pitsmoor (which includes a Brigantian site) in 1897; Wincobank (including the famous hill-fort, which the duke hoped the Council would preserve and maintain) in 1904; Norfolk Park in 1909 and the Monument Ground in 1929. These land gifts cover some 150 acres.

Sheffield's amazing acreage of lovely parks, woods and fine recreation grounds—more than those of any other city in the country—will be mentioned in another chapter.

In an earlier chapter the use of rattening was mentioned. It began before the year 1830 and was continued at intervals until the tragic happenings in 1859 and 1861. The conspiracy of silence was maintained throughout.

Some of the rattenings had been quite serious, but usually when the person against whom action was being taken 'toe'd the line' the interference which had immobilized his machinery was put right. Rightly or wrongly people began to attribute blame to the trade-union movement, although nothing against the unions was officially proved. Gradually action became more desperate, and threatening letters signed "Mary Ann" were sent to many industrialists.

Small charges of gunpowder were being increasingly used, hidden in chimney stacks and even in grinding machinery. Men were shot at, and some had their farm animals killed—the amazing thing being that few people, if indeed any, were actually injured. But a reign of terror began, and in 1859 there was a tragedy, a man called James Linley being shot dead by an air gun. It has never been proved that this dreadful affair was anything other than the result of action meant to terrify—not injure—the poor victim. And still there was silence. This serious affair would have been expected to put an end to further violence; but after a pause the rattenings continued, and in 1861 a charge of gunpowder placed in the house of a man called George Wastnidge caused the death of a woman who lodged there, and Mrs. Wastnidge who tried to rescue her was herself burnt so badly that she was very ill indeed. At last it was realized that the trouble was still going on, and effort should be made to break through the cloak of secrecy to unmask the ringleaders. But still there was silence.

In 1864 William C. Leng came to Sheffield as part proprietor of the *Sheffield Telegraph*. He found the rattening and the conspiracy of silence offered a challenge, and investigated the matter in his own way. He soon began to suspect a certain person as ringleader; but nothing could be proved. Partly as a result of Leng's persistence, a Royal Commission was appointed "to enquire into the organization and rules of trade unions, with power to investigate any recent acts of intimidation, outrage or wrong alleged to have been promoted, encouraged, or connived at by such trade unions". Three local examiners were appointed, and their investigations began on 3rd June 1867. It was soon found that no one would speak unless he was granted absolute immunity, and eventually evidence began to point to the man whom Leng had suspected to be the ringleader. It was considered prudent to have Leng guarded constantly by the police. Nothing about this dreadful affair commands respect. In an action which speaks of the strongest bullying the weakest, an unhappy little man of the name of Hallam was chosen as the right man to be threatened, cajoled, brow-beaten, and patted until after several spells of fainting and complete collapse he eventually told all he knew. His evidence implicated William Broadhead, a sawgrinder, and treasurer of the Associated Trades of Sheffield. In his defence Broadhead implicated no one else. It transpired that Hallam and one Samuel Crookes had been jointly responsible for James Linley's death, however unintentionally.

There is no doubt, judging from the carefully written report of the commissioners, which was accompanied also by a minority report, that most of the trade unionists were not implicated in the more serious aspects of the rattening. Broadhead was deported to the United States, being allowed to return some years later.

Although the years before 1873 had been years of industrial

The Iron Wharf on the Sheffield and South Yorkshire Navigation in about 1880
Part of the Sheffield Basin in 1961

expansion, the working classes, who were without any vote or voice in the Government, and who still lived and worked under appallingly unhealthy conditions, must have wondered what action they could take to call attention to their grievances. It was a sad episode.

One significant outcome of the minority report was perhaps the passing of the Trade Union Act in 1871 which legalized the unions. But there were bad times for industry lasting almost to the end of the century. It was a period calling for initiative and reorganization, and inevitably there was a certain amount of confusion. Foreign-produced cutlery and metal goods were beginning to get ahead of the Sheffield trades. The trade unions were still small and numerous, and it was not until the turn of the century that many of them gained strength by joining the Federated Trades Council. It was a period causing considerable worry to both masters and men.

From the second half of the eighteenth century the pace of our town's industrial growth was accelerating, although rather quietly. We have already noted the importance of Huntsman's invention of crucible steel about the year 1742, an advance on the former cementation process for steel for certain uses. Although Sheffield industrialists were at first rather slow in using Huntsman's crucible steel, by 1787 there were probably as many as eleven firms making steel by this process.

Sheffield's industries were still, in the main, carried on by a number of small firms, usually in confined space. It is claimed that in 1856 there were 135 steel-making firms in Sheffield, but from this date, except in the case of some of the long-established cutlery firms, expansion and amalgamation to form larger organizations was about to begin.

An invention which had a great effect on steel-making was introduced by Sir Henry Bessemer. At the Cheltenham meeting of the British Association in 1856 Bessemer read his famous paper on "The Manufacture of Iron without Fuel"— a title which could be misleading, as in fact it meant without the fuel used in puddling iron or in melting crucible steel, the methods in use at that time. Bessemer found that by blowing air at great pressure through molten pig-iron the impurities would be burnt out. His successful early experiments used iron with a relatively low phosphorus

10

content, such as the west Cumberland haematite ores, or ores from Spain. With our local ores his method was less successful. His method used a 'converter', and for some time iron-masters did not favour it. In 1858 Bessemer decided to open a works in Sheffield himself, and from this venture he made a fortune.

John Brown at his Atlas Works in Brightside was the first Sheffield iron-master to use Bessemer's process. His firm became a limited company, employed a rapidly increasing labour force, and became an integrated organization with coalmines in England and iron-ore mines in Spain. In 1899 the firm acquired the Clyde-bank Engineering and Shipbuilding Company, and in 1902 bought a substantial proportion of Thomas Firth and Sons' ordinary shares. Several other firms followed a similar pattern—one which is continuing today.

An earlier invention which contributed to the growth of the steel industry was Nasmyth's steam-hammer, which was intro-duced in England in 1843, and six years later was being used by the firm of Thos. Firth and Sons. In 1860 steam-powered tilt-hammers were being used to forge steel at Sandersons' steel works in Attercliffe. At the old-established firm of Daniel Doncaster, Sheffield's only remaining cementation furnace, which was built about 1830, was used until 1951.

In 1870 R. F. Mushet made a further valuable contribution to the steel industry, patenting a self-hardening steel containing manganese, silicon and some tungsten. At first Mushet's steel had little success, but after the turn of the century his steel began to be widely used for turning tools.

Over the years many people, in special ways, contributed to the development of the industry. It was Smeaton (1724–92) who improved the efficiency of the water-wheel to such an extent that water power continued in use long after the introduction of the steam engine. Arising from James Watt's work in replacing water power by his rotative-motion steam engine in 1781, water power slowly went out of use.

Dr. Henry Clifton Sorby, a remarkably gifted son of Sheffield, carried out work in metallography which established modern ferrous metallurgy; and it was the work of Sir Robert Hadfield, who was an outstanding scientist and the chairman of a very large firm, whose research into the effects of alloys led to his invention of manganese steel.

Firth College was opened in 1879, an institution which in time supplied many of the men who were to work in the research laboratories newly set up by the large steel firms. J. O. Arnold, who became Professor of Metallurgy at Sheffield University (founded in 1905), was an authority on the use of vanadium.

In 1913 a discovery was made which proved to be of great importance in the steel industry. This was Harry Brearley's invention of stainless steel. Sheffield born, of working-class parents Brearley was a genius and a philosopher with amazing powers of observation and deduction. One of his books, *Steel-makers*, gives fascinating insight concerning the workers, the bosses, the research chemists and the organization of a steel-works.

An earlier important invention was patented in 1861 by William Siemens: a method of making steel in a regenerative gas furnace. Like the earlier inventions, this new method was adopted very slowly by the large firms. As Bessemer had done earlier, Siemens decided to set up his own works and train workmen in his new process. He established his works in Birmingham, with success. By 1867 John Brown's firm, and in 1876 the Admiralty were his customers. His invention made possible the manufacture of a very reliable mild steel. By the year 1880 he experimented with the use of an electric furnace, and succeeded in establishing an electric-arc furnace.

The change-over from dozens of small specialist firms to the large firms formed by amalgamation and the adoption of new processes, was gaining momentum.

Space was needed for the newly expanding firms, and level ground—and that was available only by building down the Don Valley, through Attercliffe, Brightside and Tinsley, towards Rotherham. High chimneys towered over new works premises, and a pall of smoke and fumes cloaked the area. The outlines of our Portrait were expanding along the river, the canal and the railway, to the east. To the west also there were additions to our picture, as the increasingly wealthy heads of the growing firms moved up the hills away from the centre of the town to build elaborate new homes. The quiet, country suburb of Ranmoor, overlooking Endcliffe and the Porter Valley witnessed the erection of affluent homes in spacious grounds. Industrial magnates such as Sir John Brown, the Firths, Mappins, Stephensons, Jessops, Wilsons and others from about 1860 onwards moved to this

district between Broomhill, Tapton and Fulwood, far removed
from the smoke pall of the east-end heavy industries.

It has been stated that in about 1888 the age of iron ended,
giving way to the new steel age—a change which was not accomplished without many struggles and disappointments. It was
perhaps Sir John Brown and his partner J. D. Ellis at their Atlas
Works who were to the fore in this change-over. Before 1860
both France and the United States had iron-plated battleships. By
1867 the Admiralty was adopting the iron-clad technique, and at
least three-quarters of the necessary plates were fashioned at the
Atlas Works. By 1888 all-steel armour-plate was used.

By the turn of the century four large firms specialized in the
armament industry: Firth's made guns, gun parts and projectiles,
for which they erected special works; Vickers' also specialized in
guns; Brown's and Cammell's specialized in armour for armour-
plating, and in this field 'Era' armour made by Hadfields was an
important addition. When war broke out in 1914 Sheffield's role
as the country's chief producer of naval armaments was recognized. But the armament industry was only part of the story;
almost every steel-made requirement, from the tiniest tool to the
most enormous piece of equipment, was made in Sheffield.

In order to view the rapid growth of large industrial firms in
the right perspective it must be noted that dozens of small undertakings which had functioned for many years could now be found
operating as part of, or contributary to, the organization of one of
the industrial giants. In 1910 a distinguished son of Sheffield,
Professor Ripper, emphasized that "Sheffield affords a striking
illustration of the tendency of the special type of engineering in
which it is engaged to concentrate into large business units consisting of separate but related processes under one administration".

It would seem that this new growth would remove the role
played for centuries by the 'Little Mester'. But not yet! Their
numbers decreased, but even in the mid-twentieth century some
of these respected craftsmen still functioned.

Inevitably, therefore, by the first quarter of the twentieth century
our Portrait shows the development of world-famous large steel
industries of various types; and all have grown from those small
cutlery, tool and iron industries which arose from the use,
through the centuries, of the area's hidden wealth—the ironstone
deposits in the coal measures, the lead-ore in the carboniferous

limestone of the Peak District, the charcoal made from former extensive woodlands, the coal from the coalfields, the millstone grit from the western hills, the fire-clays from the coal measures, the water power from the many swift-flowing streams, and the skill of the craftsmen.

XII

FESTIVAL DAYS

THERE are colours of a different hue waiting to be added to our Portrait, and they must not be overlooked. Despite the poverty, the crowded, unhealthy conditions in the built-up part of the town, the poor health and high death-rate, the people of that time were great lovers of outdoor pursuits. They loved walking to the hills whenever they could; they played various ball games even in the crowded alleys; they had clubs for cross-country running, and hurdling. Long before 1826 cricket was very popular, even three-day matches were being played against an 'all-England' team. There were rambling clubs, and there were choral societies. It is quite obvious that then, as now, Sheffield people were very interested in a number of outdoor pursuits. Wrestling and boxing (without gloves) appealed to many of them.

In an earlier chapter reference has been made to the pre-Christmas Bull Week, which persisted for a long time in the village of Wadsley.

In most manors the lord had an annual feast day, by the king's favour. In Sheffield Feast Day was Trinity Sunday.

One of the most popular customs, dating back "beyond the memory of man" was the celebration of May Day. This day heralded the coming of the summer, and the season of growth for crops and animals. Different localities had their special form of May Day celebration, and Addy quotes a writer in Hone's *Everyday Book* who gives details of the celebration held by the people of Scotland Street on 29th May. This was called locally the Scotland Feast. On the eve of 29th May parties of Scotland Street folk walked out to the surrounding country, particularly to Walkley Bank which was well known for its profuse growth of birch trees. During the night the people felled and carried to Scotland Street from sixteen to twenty trees which they planted alongside the kerbstones on each side of the narrow road. Branches were used to decorate every door and window of the houses, and by dawn on the morning of the 29th Scotland Street resembled a grove. Ropes were stretched across between the trees, suspending a number of garlands of wreathed foliage and flowers with coloured ribbons fluttering, rustling with asidew (a thin, bright golden-brass leaf) and gay with silver tankards, pint pots and watches. Among the branches was an effigy of Charles II. There is no doubt that the May Day ceremony existed long before the time of Charles II. Birch trees were used traditionally for the maypoles around which the people danced.

A custom of a different kind may well be peculiar to Sheffield. When presented with the gift of a knife in Sheffield, the recipient must give the donor a penny; otherwise friendship would be severed. This custom is strictly observed today.

A delightful happening to which reference must be made—although hardly old enough to be called a custom—is the children's annual Whitsuntide 'sing' in certain of Sheffield's many fine parks. This seems to have been introduced towards the end of the nineteenth century, reached its peak around the nineteen-twenties and now, alas, appears to be declining somewhat. For several weeks prior to Whitsuntide the children attending the Sunday schools run by the Nonconformist churches had practised specially written Whitsuntide hymns, being supported by the excellent choir of their church (or chapel, as they were usually called in Sheffield).

Whitsuntide always seemed to be warm and sunny we are told, and at each Sunday school the children assembled, every girl wearing a new white dress and every boy a new cap. Endcliffe Woods was one of the lovely parks in which a 'sing' was held. A large grassy area had a conductor's platform erected in the centre, with another platform nearby to accommodate the necessary brass band, and radiating from there were a number of roped-off, tapering areas, each showing the name of the Sunday school it was reserved for. Outside the wide ring were seats for parents and spectators, although many preferred to sit on the grass.

Allowing plenty of time, each Sunday school—pupils, teachers, minister, choir, parents—started to walk in procession to the park, sometimes as much as 2 miles away. Each of the processions due at Endcliffe Woods entered by the Rustlings Road entrance and was conducted to its allotted area. The officiating minister, without the aid of any loud-speaker, opened the service, and every man and boy bared his head. The opening hymn was announced, the conductor raised his baton, the band played the opening bars, and then the singing of the first hymn written for the 'Whit-sing' began. This was Sheffield, so each singer faithfully obeyed the conductor's beat, and soprano, alto, tenor and baritone raised their voices in delightful harmony. The 'sing', with several prayers, lasted perhaps an hour, then the groups one by one left the park, homeward bound. Usually, in the afternoon all met again at their chapel and marched to a field where races were run, games played, and tea and sandwiches enjoyed.

The other religious denominations probably held their own special Whitsuntide ceremony, but the delightful 'sings' in the parks seemed to be specially organized and enjoyed by the Nonconformist Sunday schools.

Another happy ceremony for the Sunday school children was the 'anniversary' or Flower Sunday. Tiers of seats were arranged surrounding the pulpit in the chapel, facing the assembled congregation, and each child climbed to a seat holding a bouquet of flowers. These were to go to the hospitals, and as each child left at the end of the service the flowers were handed to officials. Hundreds of bouquets went to hospitals that day, almost all having been gathered from the gardens of parents or relatives.

It has been claimed that after the first quarter of the twentieth century even the long-established, traditional games were being played less and less by children, and that children today know little of such games. All the games had an origin away back in history, or had a folk-lore background, and some were seasonal. The historic singing-games come first to mind, always played by *groups* of children. Probably unrealized by the children of a later age, the symptoms of victims of the Great Plague were recorded in the game played by children holding hands and skipping in a ring, singing

"Ring o' ring o' roses   (the bright spots on the victim's chest)
A pocket full of posies   (the herbs carried as a preventitive)
*Tish*ew; *tish*ew!   (the victim's violent sneezing)
All fall down!"   (the victim's sudden collapse).

At the last line the whole group fell to the ground.

Then:

> Orange and lemons
> The bells of St. Clemens
> I owe you five farthings when I get rich;
> Here comes a candle to light you to bed,
> Here comes a chopper to chop off your head—
> Chop! chop! CHOP!

In this singing game two children with hands joined and raised faced each other whilst the others, each holding the back-stretched hand of the child ahead, formed a circle trotting between the two stationary players who moved their joined hands up and down to the rhythm, one player at a time in the moving circle being able to escape as the 'chopping' pair had their hands raised. Excitement grew towards the last line, as the child caught by the descending hands on the final "CHOP" was beheaded and therefore 'out'.

The bells of St. Clemens were those of St. Clement Dane's in London; "when I get rich", referred to the bribery towards preferment; the 'candle' and the 'chopper' tell their own story of Tower Hill.

At a certain date (how did they know when?) local boys made 'touch burners', small lidless boxes made of clay, with a round hole in the middle of each of the four sides. The burners were filled with 'touch-wood' collected from rotten tree stumps, then a lighted match was applied and the owner ran swiftly in a wide circle, the draught making the touch-wood glow as the burner was held in his raised hand. The faster the boy ran the brighter was the glow.

Other seasonal games were shuttle-cock and skipping for girls, and peg-top and whip-top for boys. Rim and hop-scotch were seasonal games also, played individually by boys and girls.

There was tiggy, a strenuous running game, in which the child who was 'on' had to try to 'tig' another child, who in turn was 'on' until another child was successfully 'tigged'.

There were the group games, blind man's buff and tug-of-war, and the two-boy game of conkers, a seasonal game using treasured horse-chestnuts each strung on a foot-long piece of string.

A singing game with historic associations was:

Mary, Mary, quite contrary,
How does your garden grow?
With silver bells and cockle shells
And four maids all in a row.

This refers to Mary Queen of Scots, the silver bells and cockle shells having religious significance, and the four maids being her four Marys.

Another 'tug' singing game was played in May by both boys and girls.

Here we come gathering nuts in May. . . .

Who will you have for your nuts in May? . . .
We will have —— for our Nuts in May . . .
Who will you have to fetch her away? . . .
We will have —— to fetch her away . . .
On a cold and frosty morning.

Two lines of children with clasped hands faced each other a few paces apart, and as alternate lines were sung, in turn each of the facing groups skipped forwards and backwards to the tune. When the "nuts in May" was chosen by one side and the one to "fetch her away" by the other side, the chosen two tugged each other, the winner recruiting the loser to his side. The game continued until one side won all the others—or until exhaustion set in.

It is a salutary experience, as the last quarter of the twentieth century is approached, to glance back at the ordinary everyday happenings in the town almost a century ago, and to realize that today much has been lost, as well as gained.

And Sheffield had so much that was denied to other towns; the hills, the woods and the moors were always present. It has been claimed that Sheffield has always been known for its large number of enthusiastic ramblers. This still is the case. The year 1900 saw the birth of a rambling club which set the pattern for many others to follow—and for the addition of superb colours to our Portrait, for they were responsible for creating and crystallizing the determination to save and preserve for all to enjoy our wonderful heritage of superb countryside.

In the *Sheffield Morning Telegraph* of 5th September 1970 an article by Ken Morgan recalls the details of the founding of the Clarion Ramblers by that remarkable son of Sheffield,

George Henry Bridges Ward, affectionately known as 'GHB'. Ken Morgan wrote:

The year 1900 was a year for dreaming dreams, the start of a new century . . . there were idealists, philanthropists, humanists, Socialists (very odd, many people thought them), who looked beyond the drab prosperity of the industrial scene towards a better, more meaningful future for all men. A penny weekly, "The Clarion" was the inspiration of some of these dreamers, including a civil servant George Henry Bridges Ward, of Sheffield, whose dreams included such modern ideas as the preservation of Britain's beautiful countryside as a leisure inspiration for the poor as well as the rich. . . .

GHB put an advert in "The Clarion" asking all like-minded people to meet him at Sheffield Midland Station on the first Sunday in September 1900, in time for the first train to Hope and thence a ramble round Kinderscout. Thirteen people answered the advert and so the Sheffield Clarion Ramblers were born. . . . That first meeting was so successful that others followed and the Clarion's name and fame grew steadily.

But consider the difficulties they faced; there were no motor-cars, virtually no public transport, they had to footslog to and from their homes to the railways. Sometimes they despised even the railways and walked all the way out of the city. And when they really started their ramble, usually in the Peak District, they often had to face battles with landowners over disputed rights of way.

The Clarion was a democratic club, love of walking and the countryside, notably the Peak, was the only requisite. "A rambler made is a man improved" is the club's motto. Early members included miners, university lecturers, clerks and steel workers. The Clarion handbook (largely written by GHB) . . . soon became an amazing booklet, a rich ragbag of club chronicles, nature and history notes and Private Eye reminiscences of some of Sheffield's early great folk.

Today, some of Clarion's veterans . . . can recall grim clashes with landowners over ancient rights of way. But there was one hilarious occasion when a small party was trekking over Kinderscout, led by GHB, of course. A keeper came pounding after them but their steady marching pace so exhausted him that when he caught them he had to sit, purple-faced, on a rock to recover. GHB looked at the man with feigned concern and said to his friend, Bill Whitney, "Doctor, I think this man needs attention." Whitney gravely took the poor keeper's pulse, then announced in Harley Street style: "You must go home quietly and have two days in bed." The keeper crept off quietly and the Clarion continued their merry 'trespass'.

Throughout the years, virtually until his death in 1957 at the age of 83, GHB remained the father figure of the club, indeed of all Sheffield ramblers, and led local work for access to the countryside which came to a triumphant conclusion with the 1949 Act. And, as Fred Heardman, of Edale, one of the great ramblers of the Peak stated, "We always respected the ground we walked on."

As a testimonial from his fellow ramblers in 1945 an area of fifty-four acres at the dramatic summit of the Peak's Lose Hill was purchased, and in April 1954, on site, 'Ward's Piece' was ceremoniously handed over to the National Trust.

In 1956, Sheffield University marked GHB's achievements with an honorary M.A. Sadly, the ceremony was held at his hospital bedside.

The battle for access is won, now they fight for the conservation of the countryside.

In his article Ken Morgan has revealed the love which so many Sheffield people have for the hills climbing from the heart of Sheffield; their determination and practical efforts to conserve the fine countryside, and their ever-present, impish sense of humour.

Perhaps another side of GHB—which will surprise none who knew him—should be mentioned, and that is his practical humanity. Just a few years before his death news came that an elderly shepherd named Tagg and his dog were missing on one of the loneliest parts of the moors; at once a rescue search-party was organized and led by GHB. It was many weeks before Mr. Tagg's body was found, still being faithfully guarded by the old sheepdog.

Having indicated above the long record of Sheffield people's interest in outdoor pursuits, it will be appropriate to make reference to the city's remarkable acreage of fine parks, woodlands and recreation facilities, an acreage greater than is possessed by any other city in the country.

The many recreation grounds and parks include facilities for boating (canoeing, rowing, speedboat, and children's paddle-boats), angling, archery, athletics of all types including training areas and grounds for athletic meetings cross-country running, bowls (forty-five greens, largely used by senior citizens), tennis (130 courts), basketball and netball, golf (9-hole and 18-hole courses), putting, walking and rambling, riding on bridleways, football and cricket, hockey and rugby, swimming (both indoor and outdoor); there are fifty equipped playgrounds for children, and nature trails. The provision of all these facilities together with the upkeep of all the parks and landscaped areas and open spaces come under the control of the city's recreation department.

Sheffield's largest park is Graves Park, which was acquired in 1925, 1932 and 1935, presented by Alderman J. G. Graves, J.P. This park, covering more than 206 acres, climbs from Woodseats up to Norton, and was formerly the estate of Norton Hall.

Ecclesall Wood, an area of natural woodland clothing the hillside from the River Sheaf to Ecclesall has some 306 acres, and in addition to pedestrian footpaths has several specially designated bridleways for riding. The Rivelin Valley has more than 128 acres and through it is laid a nature trail. Blacka Moor covers an area of nearly 450 acres and was presented to the city in 1933 by the J. G. Graves Charitable Trust. From this site there is a magnificent panorama in almost every direction from the slopes of Blacka Dike, Strawberry Lee Plantation and Linney Hill. Footpaths cross this moorland, and there are bridleways for horseriders. This fine stretch of woodland and moorland lies to the south-west of the city.

To the north of the city is Concord Park, covering 153 acres. It was presented by Alderman J. G. Graves in 1929, with extensions in 1932. In 1932 Mr. Charles Boot presented a pair of impressive, wrought-iron gates, which formerly were at the entrance to Hayes Park, Kent, the residence of William Pitt, Earl of Chatham. This is a remarkable site rising to the hill top at Shiregreen, where, alongside an ancient way, is a fine cruck building, just inside the park.

A park of an entirely different kind is the Botanical Gardens, with the main well-designed entrance on Clarkehouse Road just over a mile from the city centre. In 1833 the Sheffield Botanical and Horticultural Society was formed, and purchased the site from the Wilson family of Sharrow. The grounds were laid out tastefully, and on the north side of the Broad Walk three attractive 'Paxton' pavilions were erected to house tropical plants. This was a business venture which lasted for some sixty years, and then the gardens were vested in the town trustees in 1898, being administered by them until 1951, when they were leased to the parks committee for a nominal rent. The gardens have now been largely remodelled and contain approximately 3,000 varieties of plants, an aviary and an aquarium. In 1967 the gardens were further developed as an educational centre of great interest to the amateur gardener. They extend to about 20 acres.

Another interesting park is the 45-acre Meersbrook Park, just over 2 miles south from the city centre. To quote the City of Sheffield's handbook "Recreation in Sheffield Parks":

> An undulating, wooded parkland, with magnificent views over the city, acquired by the Corporation in 1886, 1928 and 1946 as a public park. . . . The park was formerly the estate of Meersbrook House, built in the mid-eighteenth century by Benjamin Roebuck, one of four eminent sons of the Sheffield manufacturer and cutler, John Roebuck. It was Benjamin Roebuck (1712–1796) who in 1770 in partnership with John Shore established the first Banking House in Church Street, which is now the bank of Williams Deacons, Ltd. . . . Meersbrook House was opened by the Earl of Carlisle in 1890 as the Ruskin Museum, which use continued until 1953 when due to a decline in the number of visitors the Ruskin Collection was transferred to the Sheffield City Museum. . . .

To describe the park as "undulating" could be regarded by those from less hilly regions as an understatement, for in fact the park clothes part of the steep hillside which climbs the higher part of the hill from above Heeley to Norton Lees. The substantial Georgian Meersbrook House (now used as the headquarters of the city's recreation department) stands at the bottom of the park alongside Brook Road, and high up the hill at the top of the park by Norton Lees Lane stands a fine half-timbered building known as the Bishop's House. This lovely post-and-truss building dates back to at least the fourteenth century, and fortunately has been well preserved; but regrettably about a century ago the first building, a very sturdy cruck building of Anglian date, was demolished. The half-timbered house at the top of Meersbrook Park was built as the house for the family of that period to replace the living accommodation in the original aula, the great cruck building, which from that time functioned as a barn. From the days of the original settlement the farm must have been very desirable, and it is not surprising that it remained so throughout the centuries. At a later date the house and its extensive farmlands and buildings was acquired by the Blythe family, which provided two bishops—Geoffrey Blythe, Bishop of Lichfield, and John Blythe, Bishop of Salisbury.

Being aware of the love of walking shared by most Sheffield people, the recreation department laid out a round walk—not around the whole of Sheffield, but through a number of the amazingly beautiful parks and woodlands owned by the corporation in the city's south-west area. The round walk gives ready access over a 10-mile route to some 1,100 acres of lovely scenery which has much of historic interest also.

The walk begins at Hunter's Bar. The toll bar has been re-erected on its original site, now laid out as a roundabout. This last-remaining Trust-owned toll bar in Sheffield was torn down on Friday 31st October 1884 when a boisterous crowd threw the gate into a field nearby. They were tired of having to pay tolls in order that their sheep, pigs, cattle and horses could pass along Ecclesall Road. Here the walk enters Endcliffe Park, and continues up the valley of the busy little Porter Brook (or perhaps one should say the *once* busy Porter Brook, for the stream once powered twenty wheels), through Whiteley Woods to pass the Forge Dam and on through the lovely Mayfield Valley to Porter Clough near the head of the brook.

The walk turns to the left along Fulwood Lane to the charming hamlet of Ringinglow at a height of 1,000 feet above sea level, past the octagonal Round House, which was a toll-bar house built between 1758 and 1760. A few yards along the Houndkirk Road brings the walker to a footpath turning to the left leading down the valley of the Limb Brook to Whirlow Bridge and the entrance to Whirlow Brook Park, which has notable rock-gardens. The residence in Whirlow Brook Park was the home of the Sheffield industrialist Sir Walter Benton Jones, and is now a popular restaurant. Adjacent to this park are the Whinfell Quarry Gardens, presented to the city in 1968 by James Neill Holdings Ltd. as a memorial to Sir Frederick Neill who lived many years at Whinfell, and had the old quarry converted to a lovely, sheltered garden.

Across the main road the walk enters Ryecroft Glen parallel to the Whirlow Playing Fields and continues through the western part of the extensive Ecclesall Wood. In the woods near to Abbey Lane, among the undergrowth stands a slab of stone, now protected by iron railings, bearing the legend: "In memory of George Yardley, wood collier, he was burnt to death in his Cabbin on this place, 11th. October, 1786." Four names follow the inscription: William Brooke, salesman; David Glossop, game-keeper; Thomas Smith, besome-maker; Samuel Brookshaw, innkeeper. The corporation's little handbook, *Sheffield Round Walk* has the informatory paragraph:

Yardley, apparently, was a wood collier, a charcoal maker. He was one of the men, usually from the east end of Sheffield who bought wood, made charcoal from it and sold it to the steelworks. The sticks were built into a long stack, circular in form and narrowing at the top. They were covered with grass sods and slowly burned. One of the most important factors was the timing. The fires were lit on Sunday to enable the wood to be converted into charcoal by the following Friday or Saturday when the men could be sure of pay-ment from the steelworks. Charcoal burners could be found in Ecclesall Woods in the early years of this century and their cabins remained intact until comparatively recently. The four men who caused the stone to be raised have been identified—Brookshaw, the innkeeper kept the Rising Sun; Brooke, the salesman, it is believed, sold the wood to the burners; Glossop the gamekeeper would know Yardley from his patrols in the area; and Smith the besome-maker made his long brooms near the cabin.

Of the 305 acres of Ecclesall Wood an area of 42 acres is reserved as a bird sanctuary. The wood is known to have more than fifty-six varieties of wild flowers and some remarkably fine timber specimens.

Crossing the main road to the east of the Woods the walker sees the small Beauchief Garden by the Dam on the other side of the road. The dam serves to power the wheels of the Abbeydale Industrial Hamlet, formerly a scythe works. This interesting site has been restored and is being preserved as an industrial museum. Those who speak of the ugliness of Sheffield's early industries would do well to visit this remarkable site, in its lovely setting alongside the River Sheaf.

By continuing along Abbeydale Road to the south the walker soon reaches Twentywell Lane which climbs the hill beyond the Sheaf to the left, and just over the railway bridge a footpath to the left leads into Ladies Spring Wood. In 1954 the Nature Con-servancy declared this 34-acre wood (acquired by the Corpora-tion in 1931) to be an area of special scientific interest for natural history.

A left turn down Beauchief Abbey Drive leads to the historic

Paradise Square
The City Museum and Mappin Art Gallery in Weston Park

Beauchief Abbey, founded by Robert Fitzranulph in 1183 as a house of the Premonstratensian Order, and closed at the Dissolution in 1536. It was acquired by Sir Nicholas Strelley and in 1648 passed to the Pegges. In 1931 the abbey and grounds were presented to the city by Messrs. F. and F. M. Crawshaw.

The walk now leads through Parkbank Wood, and across Bocking Lane to Chancet Wood, and by continuing through this wood the Meadowhead entrance to Graves Park is reached—Sheffield's largest park and the end of the Round Walk.

The round walk is well signposted, and is both beautiful and interesting.

Before closing this chapter mention must be made of the city's long story of cricket and football. Up on the hill overlooking the city centre, near the new Hyde Park Flats, is what is known as Hyde Park Stadium. Originally this was a cricket ground—even before 1826—and it was here in 1833 that the first county match was played by Yorkshire against Norfolk. There was no official Yorkshire club at that date, and matches were organized by interested private individuals.

At an inn with a dignified façade, the Adelphi Hotel at the corner of Sycamore Street and Tudor Way, the present Yorkshire County Cricket Club was founded on 8th January 1863. In 1867 the Sheffield Wednesday Club was formed at a meeting here. Alas, this well-known hotel with its pleasing exterior was closed in 1969, to be demolished to provide a site for the new Sheffield Theatre.

To the south along Abbeydale Road stands Abbeydale Park, which is claimed as the home of one of the biggest and most comprehensive sports clubs in the country. It is the home ground of the Sheffield Club, formed in 1857, the first Association Football Club in the world.

At Bramall Lane, not far from the city centre, is the home ground of Sheffield United Cricket and Football Club, where Yorkshire County Cricket Club play. The first important cricket match to be played here took place in 1855, when Yorkshire played Sussex.

Within the last century Sheffield has produced harriers (cross-country runners), swimmers and sprinters who took their places in national championships.

11

The Cholera Monument in Clay Wood

XIII

THE QUEEN COMES

BY THE beginning of the year 1893 it was realized that fifty years had elapsed since the date of incorporation—fifty years of hard work and steady progress—and in February 1893 the council petitioned the Queen asking that the title of City be conferred upon the borough to commemorate the Jubilee of Incorporation. In due course a reply was received from the Home Office informing the council that the Queen had granted this petition. A request was made that a cheque for 100 guineas be forwarded to cover the expenses involved in issuing the necessary letters patent. Steps were then taken by the council to obtain a grant of supporters to the arms of the corporation to which it was entitled on attaining the dignity of a city.

In 1893 it was agreed in council that the Municipal Buildings should be called the town hall, and the former town hall in Castle Street should be the court house. The site for the new Municipal Buildings had been purchased in 1886, costing £49,000, although at the time of purchase it was not envisaged that this would be the site of a new town hall. A good deal of slum property had to be cleared to make the site available, and in 1889 it was decided to proceed with the erection of the new building. In October 1891 the foundation stone was laid by the mayor, Alderman G. W. Clegg.

In 1893 it was agreed to have the main staircase and corridor lined with marble, and in 1894 it was decided that the whole building should be wired for electric lighting. As time passed new extras were decided upon.

Her Majesty Queen Victoria came to open the completed new town hall on 21st May 1897, and it was at once both a royal and a festive occasion. The building itself certainly was worthy of the honour of being opened by the Queen. The city was decorated with garlands and triumphal arches; a detachment of Lancers and other troops were in the procession and the Queen had a Sovereign's Escort of Life Guards. Shortly after this colourful opening ceremony there came word from the Queen graciously conferring the title of lord mayor on the city's chief citizen, by letters patent. A baronetcy was conferred on the master cutler, Mr. A. Wilson, and a knighthood on the deputy mayor, Alderman C. T. Skelton.

The first lord mayor was the Duke of Norfolk, who was serving for a second year as mayor. The town hall was constructed of local material, the lovely Stoke Hall stone. Mr. F. W. Pomeroy, R.A., was responsible for the interesting frieze, 70 feet by 36 feet on the front elevation, representing various Sheffield trades, the figure of Justice in the large gable facing Cheney Row and the figures of War and Peace in the niches on the Surrey Street elevation. Mr. E. W. Mountford was the architect.

In 1899 the duke presented to the city the ceremonial mace which is carried before the lord mayor on all official occasions. Over twenty years previously in 1874 the council had authorized the mayor to wear "an official robe of scarlet trimmed with sable fur at all General Meetings of the Council" and on other official or ceremonial occasions. In the same year the custom was instituted that he should attend Divine Service with the other members of the council on the Sunday morning following his election, "as a good example to the people".

It will be appreciated that discussion concerning the building of a dignified, worthy town hall occupied a good deal of the council's time, and even small economies were considered. For example, electric lighting having been agreed upon, the committee passed a resolution that, as such lighting would be used for only six months in the year and the boilers for six to eight months, it was not necessary to have a skilled man as engineer and electrician and that a competent stoker was all that was needed together with two window cleaners and an attendant at each entrance. The total cost of the building in 1893 was £182,128.

Only a few years later the question of much-needed extensions came up for consideration, and in 1901 the city expansion made it essential that the town hall be enlarged. By the Sheffield Corporation Act of 1903 powers were granted to acquire part of St. Paul's Churchyard and to stop up part of Cheney Row, a new footpath being made in its place. The estimated cost of the proposed additions amounted to £36,000 and this evidently alarmed the council, but in 1908 it was decided that enlargements were now a matter of urgency. Eventually new plans were agreed and in May 1914 tenders were accepted for the town hall extensions. And then came war, which necessitated the deferment of the work. In February 1919 it was considered expedient to proceed with the building and by 1923 this work was completed. The extensions were officially opened in 1923 by the Prince of Wales (now the Duke of Windsor).

Sheffield's town hall, with its well-designed high tower supporting the figure of Vulcan (the Roman god of fire and the working of metals) at the summit, is a Municipal Building of which citizens may well be proud.

H. Keeble Hawson's interesting book, *Sheffield. The Growth of a City 1893–1926*, has an interesting paragraph about the Town Hall Square, the area outside the town hall's main entrance:

The Monolith which had been erected in the centre of what is now called Town Hall Square to commemorate Queen Victoria's Golden Jubilee in 1887 was removed in May 1904 to make room for Queen Victoria's statue and was stored for a time pending a decision for its re-erection. The Parks Committee wanted to re-erect it in Wincobank Wood but the council decided that it should be re-erected in Endcliffe Woods on the site near Rustlings Road where it now stands. Queen Victoria's statue followed it in due course in 1931 to make room for a novel system of traffic control, which involved a police officer sitting in what was irreverently referred to as an ice-cream kiosk, to control railway-type signals on the various roads leading into the Square.

In their busy programme of work the council managed to include in 1895 the presentation of a petition in favour of legislation to allow autocars "or other horseless carriages on the highways".

In August 1894 the council confirmed a resolution of the Parliamentary Committee in favour of a Bill, which was then before Parliament, which would have given votes to women.

In October 1899 the council agreed to exercise its powers to create Hon. Freemen of the City. This was proposed by Alderman W. E. Clegg, and the distinction was conferred on the Duke of Norfolk, Sir Frederick Thorp Mappin and Sir Henry Stephenson, the formal presentation taking place in March 1900.

In 1902 the city's General Purpose and Parks Committee passed a resolution in favour of the use of the metric system in the British Empire being made compulsory. This was accepted by the council. (What a lot of trouble this would have saved the citizens of 1971 who in February of that year had to struggle with the official change-over to the decimal currency system!)

In 1902 also was passed a resolution to establish a gold assay in Sheffield. This was carried out.

In June 1912 the council sent a deputation to wait on Mr. Winston Churchill, then the First Lord of the Admiralty, asking for a battleship to be named *Sheffield*, in view of the fact that Sheffield for many years had made armour plate and guns for the navy. The First Lord replied that cruisers, not battleships, were named after towns, and this would be considered. Disappointed, the council decided to leave the matter over for a time. It was not until July 1936 that a cruiser was named *Sheffield*, and she had so much stainless steel in her fittings that she was known throughout the navy as the 'Shiny Sheff'. The city was very proud of H.M.S. *Sheffield*, and especially of her excellent record in the Second World War. From time to time visits were exchanged between representatives of ship and city, and in 1951 the council presented to the ship the drum major's mace.

In 1962 the 'Shiny Sheff' went into reserve prior to being broken up, and her silver plate was given to the city for safe keeping. Her ship's bell is today hanging in the cathedral.

One of the urgent problems awaiting the council's attention was that of improving the major roads, some of which could still take only single-line traffic. Road widening was needed as well as the construction of several new roads. This undertaking posed the problem of buying up properties to permit road widening, and each and every plan seemed to meet with considerable opposition. In 1894 and over the next few years many arguments occurred about methods of road surfacing, and the use of granite setts featured prominently in these arguments. The surveyor reported that the use of granite setts was desirable because they were less costly and very hardwearing; others objected because of their slippery surface when wet. One alderman stated that he had had the shafts of four dogcarts broken under him because his horse had fallen on slippery setts, and these mishaps had occurred on level roads, not on gradients. The controversy continued.

Feelings ran higher than ever when the tramways extensions were planned, and the old tramways were re-laid for electrification; for this work wood-block paving was advised, and was largely carried out for the main streets. But still certain experts stuck to their preference for granite-sett paving.

It was during one of these arguments that Councillor Herbert Hughes, a solicitor, evidently found himself getting a little tired of expert advice in favour of granite, for he remarked, "I have been dealing with expert advice all my life. It is very useful if you don't know the facts."

At that time every street-widening plan needed to be authorized by either an Act of Parliament or a Provisional Order. The Corporation Act of 1897 listed thirty-three required widenings and the 1900 Act listed thirty-two. In 1893 the improvements committee seriously faced this problem, and in the Provisional Order of 1875 had already succeeded in getting powers for:

(1) The widening of Moorhead between Backfields (now dis-appeared as the result of later Moorhead redevelopment) and Coal Pit Lane (now Cambridge Street), a new street from Moorhead to the junction of Pinstone Street with Cross Burgess Street and the widening of Pinstone Street from Cross Burgess Street along the whole of its length. This produced the Pinstone Street we know today.

(2) The widening and improving of Fargate from Pinstone Street to High Street.

(3) A new street from Norfolk Street to Fargate, thus giving the length of Surrey Street along the east of the Town Hall, originally known as New Surrey Street.

(4) A new street from Fargate to the junction of Church Street and Bow Street. This is now Leopold Street.

(5) The widening and improving of Pinfold Street, Trippett Lane and Townhead Street.

(6) The widening of Church Street from St. James's Row (now St. James's Street) to Townhead Street.

(7) The widening and improving of Attercliffe High Street (now Attercliffe Road) and Attercliffe Bridge and its ap-proaches.

The original 1875 proposals had included plans for the widening and improving of High Street and Market Place on the south side, but this incurred so much opposition that in order to get the other plans approved it was agreed to drop these two. High Street was very narrow, but the plans for its widening were actually postponed for almost twenty years.

In 1893 the improvements committee was carrying out the continuation of Lady's Bridge to West Bar with the widening of Bridge Street and Snig Hill, and the part widening of West Bar, Gibraltar Street, Shalesmoor and Infirmary Road—and the proposed widening of High Street.

In May 1892 a special committee, known as the High Street Committee, was appointed. After considerable opposition their recommendation was eventually accepted by the council in October, and it was agreed to promote a Bill for the improvement of High Street, Market Place and Fruit Market, this latter being the name given to the lower part of High Street below its junction with Angel Street. There was still opposition to the High Street widening plan. H. Keeble Hawson states that in 1893, during a debate on this question, one member of the council said that High Street was wide enough for all time and all eternity, but: "In this instance eternity lasted until the 1950s, when the Sheffield Development Plan approved by the Minister for Housing and Local Government provided for a further widening."

In 1910 a scheme was carried through by the council, and was considered to be a great improvement, when Fitzalan Square was re-designed and was formally opened by the lord mayor. The old cabmen's shelter was removed, the oval space in the centre was reconstructed with modern facilities and would receive the Statue of King Edward VII a few years later, and the new head post office just completed on the west side of the square was considered very suitable. In 1910 it was also agreed that Scotland Street should be widened.

Another topic which the city council knew needed strong action was public health, with the closely connected problem, sanitation. The city's industrial preoccupation together with the poor sanitary arrangements made inevitable a high death-rate due to disease. It was only the health-giving breezes from the surrounding hills together with the fact that Sheffield people have always been fond of getting out to the country, which prevented a far worse health situation. There were several serious factors contributing to the poor health record, and each of these had to be tackled by the council.

In 1893 the health committee consisted of fifteen members, and had in its hands the management of public baths, the investigation of nuisances, the cleansing of closets and ash-pits, the restriction of offensive trades, the scavenging, cleansing and watering of the streets, plus a number of other duties imposed by Act of Parliament.

In 1893—the year which saw the last threat of an outbreak of cholera, which fortunately was averted—the Medical Officer of Health presented a detailed report covering the whole question of public health. It makes grim reading.

The report presented by the medical officer in 1914 shows considerable improvement in the health situation, and the death-rate had fallen significantly. But there was still much work to be done. In his 1913 report he stated: "The wages for women are very low. Fifteen per cent of the houses in the City are back-to-backs. The common yard system which prevails is likely to spread infectious diseases. More than 20% of the houses still have middens. Another 20% have large fixed ash pits for house refuse. There is the bad effect of the grinders' trade causing consumption and the less marked effect of other dirty trades in causing diseases of the respiratory system. Twenty-five per cent of the natural sunshine is cut off by smoke in certain areas of the City." He added that as late as 1888 rubble sewers were still being constructed in Sheffield.

Obviously the situation was overdue for attention.

It was in 1878 that Winter Street Hospital was built, with sixty-four beds, to deal with infectious diseases. In 1887 there was a serious smallpox epidemic, and right out at Lodge Moor 42 acres were purchased on which temporary wooden huts to contain 120 beds were erected at once. In 1896 it was decided to purchase a site on Crimicar Lane on which to build a smallpox hospital, following a ruling that smallpox patients should be isolated from those suffering from other infectious diseases, but it was not until 1902 that this building was completed for twenty-six beds and an isolation block of four beds. By 1904 the wooden structures at the Lodge Moor Hospital had been replaced by blocks of modern stone buildings, and the accommodation considerably extended.

In February 1901 a joint meeting between representatives from the two boards of guardians and the sanitary sub-committee agreed that a sanatorium should be established for the treatment of consumptives. In December 1905 it was decided to convert Winter Street Hospital from a fever hospital to a sanatorium for tuberculosis patients, at first for twenty men and later for 110. And at the same time it was agreed to use Crimicar Lane Hospital for infectious cases other than smallpox, provided that should there be an outbreak of smallpox these patients should be removed at once to other accommodation.

It was pointed out that in Sheffield 5 per cent of the deaths were due to tuberculosis, and the hospital facilities were totally inadequate. In 1908 a tuberculosis hospital with twenty beds for female patients was established at Moor End, Commonside, Walkley.

An important step was taken in 1908 when the Medical Officer of Health visited the German cutlery centre of Solingen, and as the result of this visit it was decided to press the Home Office to make more stringent regulations in the cutlery industry to secure better protection for the workers in the problem of dangerous dust-inhalation, and for more cleanliness.

It has been noted above that a statue of King Edward VII was erected in Fitzalan Square; this was the result of public subscription, and it was decided that the bulk of the money subscribed should be used to provide a hospital for the treatment of children who had tuberculosis other than tuberculosis of the lung. The site was donated by the Duke of Norfolk in Rivelin Valley, and by 1916 all arguments had been settled and the building completed. It was opened by the Duchess on 26th July 1916, as the King Edward VII Hospital. As time passed further hospital and dispensary arrangements were made, with the satisfactory result that tuberculosis claims many fewer victims.

Getting off to a slow start, owing to the enormous amount of work entailed, the council with increasing success tackled the problem of converting hundreds of privy-middens to water-closets, having open drains replaced by earthenware pipes, and asphalting backyards and courts. Further, it was decided to replace the rubbish-tipping system by incinerators. The cleansing department's report for 1913 stated that "the whole of the offensive refuse of the City was sent to destructors except a small quantity which was sent to farmers".

The cleanliness of the milk supply also concerned the council. Adequate provision was made for the supply of dried milk for infants, maternity and child welfare clinics were established, and the famous Jessop's Hospital for Women extended its facilities. A slow, steady decrease in infant mortality resulted.

The care of the blind was another urgent problem. Some years previously a blind school had been established in Manchester Road and was controlled by the Royal Sheffield Institution for the Blind. It was not until almost 1921 that adequate arrangements were made to help blind persons of all ages.

The care of mentally defectives was seriously tackled in 1913 following the passing of the Mental Deficiency Act. One problem was the provision of suitable accommodation. Wales Court at Kiveton Park, which can accommodate sixty patients, was opened in July 1919, and in 1923 it was arranged that the Industrial School at Hollow Meadows (known as the Truant School) should be taken over to accommodate forty-eight male patients. The city council's efforts included much hard, uphill work, but definite headway was being made.

In the 1890s there were a number of claims against the owners of steam traction engines for the damage being done to the surface of highways. One council member wanted these giants to be barred altogether from using the streets. In 1898 bye-laws were proposed limiting traction engine traffic to certain streets and during certain hours only, but it was not until 1901 that this bye-law was approved.

In 1906, by arrangement with the Vicar of Sheffield, the very narrow Church Street was widened by adding the footpath to the street width and making a new footpath behind the railings which then existed along the churchyard. Later, in 1960, the footpath was extended further into the churchyard, much of which was paved and made available as an open space with seats, and a garden was made over part of the area.

Arrangements were made in 1906 for the removal of the last toll bar on a main road in the city, which was still collecting tolls. This private toll bar belonged to the Shrewsbury Hospital Trustees and was on the Meadowhall Road; it was purchased by the council for £1,200 in settlement for several years' tolls. The posts and gate were removed. Each toll bar had erected alongside a large board showing the tolls to be paid. Fortunately, one of these enormous notices was saved. There must have been quite a hold-up of traffic whilst road-users searched the board to ascertain the amount of toll payable in their particular case. We quote some of the conditions:

> Turnpike Road from Worksop in the County of Nottingham, to the North-East end of Attercliffe in the County of York.
> A TABLE of TOLLS to be taken at this BAR pursuent to the Directions of an act passed in the sixth Year of the Reign of his Majesty King George the fourth   Viz.
> For every Horse or other Beast drawing any Coach Barouche Sociable Berlin Charriot Landau Chaise Calash Gig Chair Phaeton Caravan Whiskey Hearse Litter Curricle or any Carriage on Springs
>
> s. d.
>
> drawn by more than one Horse or for any taxed cart the sum of $4\frac{1}{2}$
> For every drove of Calves Swine Hogs Sheep or Lambs the sum of sevenpence halfpenny per score and so on in proportion of any less
>
> s. d.
>
> number - - - - - - - - - - - $7\frac{1}{2}$

In 1905 the council made several interesting decisions, one being to experiment with the use of tarmacadam for road surfacing. Another was to propose the further taxation of motor vehicles to provide funds from which local authorities could obtain a grant towards the additional expense incurred by the extra watering of highways to reduce the dust. The increasing number of motor vehicles was causing a serious dust problem, and the highway engineers were considering new surfacing materials to try to deal with the nuisance.

The 1909 report from Mr. Hadfield, Surveyor of Highways and Deputy City Surveyor, contains the information that the total length of adopted highways (there was a considerable length of unadopted roads) in the city was 302 miles, of which approximately 54 miles were paved with granite, 52 miles with freestone, 26 miles with boulders, nearly 10 miles with wood and 2 miles with whinstone, while of the remainder, 135 miles were surfaced with dry macadam and $12\frac{1}{2}$ miles with tarmacadam. It was found that the macadam-surfaced roads in the city which had been treated with either tar or calcium were relatively dust-free and remained in better condition. Tar was not used on roads with a gradient of more than one in twenty.

It is worthy of note that Sheffield's Surveyor of Highways did much pioneer work on asphalt paving and surface dressing, which was recognized at national level.

The 1914–18 War interrupted the city's road-improvement

plans, and by the end of the war there was the problem of catching up with repair of road-damage due to unavoidable neglect and heavy use. Plans were afoot to deal with this when the dreadful period of unemployment began to effect the city seriously in 1920. It was decided to give work to the many unemployed by carrying out new road schemes. This work began with the construction of a new arterial road between Intake and Darnall (Prince of Wales Road), the widening of Abbey Lane, the widening of Abbeydale Road South, and a new road from Millhouses to Whirlow (Whirlowdale Road). As the unemployment situation continued men were found work in the construction of several other new roads, and in much road improvement.

H. Keeble Hawson has described this post-war achievement of the highways department in the following words: "The Department's main achievements in the post-war period to the end of 1926 can be summed up as, first, the pioneering and use of modern materials and methods of road surfacing to meet the needs of the motor age and the substantial reduction in costs achieved by the use of such materials and methods; and secondly, the construction, largely as unemployed relief works, of new traffic roads, the benefit of which we are feeling increasingly today."

The new city's council lost no time in getting to grips with plans to extend the tramways. As we have seen above all legal requirements were eventually satisfied and the council acquired the system from the tramways company on payment of an agreed sum, in July 1896. Promptly the newly appointed tramways committee agreed to continue the former company's standing contracts for advertising, the conveyance of post office officials, the removal of manure, the providing of stable requisites, and the issue of tickets for pupil teachers. They continued the forage contract, bought another twenty-four horses and appointed a veterinary surgeon. Investigation was being made into the various existing systems of traction, a deputation being appointed to visit places in the United Kingdom and in Europe to recommend which system should be used in Sheffield. In February 1897 the deputation reported that traction by overhead electric wires was recommended, and this was accepted by the council. At once work was started to electrify the Nether Edge–Attercliffe route, and this was extended from Attercliffe to Tinsley. Rails were purchased and a contract for the supply of cars, trolleys, wires, poles and electrical equipment at a total cost of £41,185 13s. was agreed with British Thompson Houston Limited.

The first electric cars ran on the Tinsley and Nether Edge routes on 5th September 1899. It was required that tram bells should be sounded as little as possible when passing churches and chapels on Sundays. From the first the system was successful, and as early as December 1898, resulting from the profits of the first year's working, the tramways committee transferred out of their profits the sum of £7,000 towards the relief of the rates. At various times substantial grants were made from their profits to Sheffield University, for the provision of music in the parks, towards municipal winter concerts, and a payment of £500 spread over five years to the Cutlers' Company as a contribution towards their fund for protecting the name of Sheffield against infringements by firms not carrying on business in Sheffield.

It is recorded that tram traffic was dislocated in February 1900 by heavy snow, but most of the horse-cars managed to get through. In February 1900 a horse and trap was provided for the use of the traffic superintendent!

In 1910 there was considerable discussion in the council concerning a proposal to erect tram shelters. In the same year an arrangement was made with postal authorities that posting boxes should be carried from every suburban terminus each night on the tram leaving the suburb at about 9.0 p.m. This proved to be very popular. In 1910 also tram conductors were instructed by the committee that miners in their pit clothes must not be allowed to ride inside the trams!

During the 1914–18 War there was a great increase in the number of passengers carried, because of the influx of munitions workers, and it is said that queues originated at this time—for which the council wisely erected barriers to prevent queue-jumping.

The first electric cars were double-deckers, with the upper deck unenclosed. With the years there were many improvements, and the last cars made—still carrying the famous dark blue and cream colours—were the fine, comfortable cars, ordered after the 1939–1945 War, and which were taken off the road in 1960 when they were replaced by the less reliable, much more costly motor bus. The tram fare throughout much of the tramcar era had been one penny from suburb terminal to city centre. Today, the fare on many of these routes is measured in shillings. Appropriately, the last route to carry electric cars was the Tinsley route, which had, with Nether Edge, been the first in September 1899.

As early as 1905 the council passed a resolution that application should be made to Parliament for powers to run "omnibuses and other vehicles powered by mechanical means in connection with or in extension of the tramways system". In the mid-twentieth century as motor buses replaced electric trams the routes were extended to link up with certain other towns, and to offer more routes in the city.

XIV

THE SCHOOL BOARD

It is appropriate at this point to take a further look at our city's not inconsiderable educational attainments.

We have noted above that since before the turn of the sixteenth century a number of enlightened citizens were striving to introduce educational facilities to the then small, isolated little township, and that their efforts in several instances were outstanding, setting an example which was adopted elsewhere. By the last quarter of the nineteenth century it was clear in Sheffield, as indeed in a number of other growing towns, that efforts must be made to unify and extend educational facilities.

The first public local authorities to control education were the school boards, created under the education Act of 1870. The Act required that a school board was to have "not less than five nor more than fifteen" members. Sheffield was entitled to have fifteen members. A public meeting was called on 11th November 1870 by the mayor (Mr. T. Moore), who chaired the meeting which was held in the Temperance Hall, Townhead Street, and it was hoped that the meeting would adopt fifteen gentlemen. There were the usual arguments and differences of opinion, and the town clerk, who was present, expressed the opinion that "the Act of Parliament undoubtedly vests the election in the burgesses of Sheffield". Fifty-one names were suggested.

The election took place on 28th November 1870, the following fifteen citizens being elected:

Name and place of Abode	Description	No. of Votes	Religion
(1) Michael Joseph Ellison, Norfolk Cottage	Conveyancer and estate agent	17,057	Roman Catholic

Name and place of Abode	Description	No. of Votes	Religion
(2) Henry Wilson, Westbrook	Gentleman	12,489	Church-man
(3) Charles Wardlow, 268 Glossop Road	Steel manufacturer	11,464	Free Church-man
(4) William Cobby, Beech View, Burngreave Road	Goods Agent for Midland Railway Company	11,372	Wesleyan
(5) Thomas Moore, Ashdell, Broomhill	Common brewer	10,823	Church-man
(6) Mark Firth, Oakbrook	Manufacturer	10,316	New Connection
(7) Skelton Cole, 343 Glossop Road	Draper	10,315	Wesleyan
(8) Charles Doncaster, Crookesmoor Road	Steel merchant	9,762	Society of Friends
(9) William Fisher, Norton Grange	Merchant and manufacturer	9,756	Unitarian
(10) Sir John Brown, Endcliffe Hall	Merchant and manufacturer	9,344	Church-man
(11) Richard Wainman Holden, 100 Nottingham Street	Cattle dealer	9,303	Primitive Methodist
(12) John Fairburn, Broomhall Park	Lead merchant	8,310	Wesleyan
(13) James Crossland, Norfolk Road	Soap manufacturer	7,215	Church-man
(14) Alfred Allot, Brincliffe Crescent	Accountant	6,947	Independent
(15) Robert Thomas Eadon, Lord Street, Attercliffe	Saw manufacturer	6,624	Unitarian

"As witness my hand this twenty-ninth day of November 1870
JOHN YEOMANS,
Town Clerk and Deputy Returning Officer."

The War Memorial in Barker's Pool

The first meeting of the newly elected body was in December 1870 in the mayor's parlour, council chamber, then in the old Central Library, Surrey Street, on which site the Central Library has now been built. Sir John Brown was elected chairman and Mark Firth vice-chairman. The members of the Board served for three years, or longer when re-elected.

The education department of the Privy Council seemed anxious to have no time lost in providing the required educational facilities for all children between the ages of five and thirteen, and reports were asked for from the board with a view to obtaining reliable information on a number of points.

All these details received prompt attention, with the result that very soon it was possible to have a building programme under way. Newhall School was the first to be built, "designed to accommodate about 750 children in three departments". The board's first report proudly states that Newhall School was "... the first new Board School building commenced under the Elementary Education Act of 1870". It was opened by Sir John Brown, chairman of the board in January 1873, after several unavoidable delays. The report of the board to March 1873 gives a list of

. . . new school buildings either completed or in progress:

Name of School		Children to be accommodated	Cost of Buildings Fittings and Furniture		
			£.	s.	d.
Newhall	Completed	750	3,419	0	0*
Broomhill	Completed	350	2,377	0	0*
Netherthorpe	To be completed July 1873	950	6,305	0	0
Philadelphia	To be completed Apl. 1873	950	5,090	0	0
Walkley	To be completed Oct. 1873	720	5,600	10	0
Attercliffe	To be completed Sept. 1873	800	5,424	0	0
Grimesthorpe	To be completed Oct. 1873	756	5,507	0	0
Crookesmoor	To be completed Sept. 1873	750	6,390	0	0
Darnall Road	To be completed Oct. 1873	700	5,735	0	0
Carbrook	To be completed Oct. 1873	750	5,994	0	0
Lowfield	To be completed Oct. 1873	706	5,715	15	0
Pyebank	To be completed Nov. 1873	800	6,712	0	0

* Exclusive of fittings.

12

The Castle Square pedestrian underpass or 'the hole in the road'

The first mention of 'free' education appears to have been in September 1885, when a resolution was submitted: "That, in the opinion of this Board, the time has arrived when, in the interests of education and the country generally, it has become desirable to abolish the present system of charging fees in schools which are managed by persons who have been elected by, or are directly responsible to, the ratepayers." As was customary, this was argued back and forth without decision, and parents still had to pay a few pence every week for each child at school.

Naturally, there was strong feeling on this question, but it was not until January 1890 that the board, by eight votes to five, passed the resolution: "This Board respectfully calls upon Her Majesty's Government to take immediate measures for giving free education in all schools under popular representative control, to promote a continuous and progressive course of Kindergarten teaching, to establish in all school districts Continuation Schools, and to increase the facilities for Technical and Intermediate Education."

It is of interest that many of the town's enlightened citizens, as well as a proportion of members of the school board, were very concerned that a *free* system of education should be made available to all children from the age of 5, but this was very forward thinking, and could only 'make haste slowly'.

The board's schools were very well built, of stone, and unless they have been demolished deliberately are standing today, proudly conscious of their style and quality compared with the flat, land-consuming, concrete erections for modern school buildings.

The work contributed by the board's members seems to have been carefully noted by numbers of people genuinely interested in educational facilities, and at each triennial election efforts were made to return members whose work was deemed to have been good, and to have replaced those who were considered to have been unsatisfactory. At the 1876 election one of the three members not returned was Mr. Cobby concerning whom a letter had appeared in the *Sheffield and Rotherham Independent* of 16th November 1876:

Mester Edditor,
    Can yo inform me, thro t'medium o' yor valable paper, how meney times Mester Cobby has attended t'Appeal Committee during

t'last six year, as Oive heerd it on good authority that he's neare
been near a single meeting. As a reason, he says he's t'Midland
Company's interests to attend to. Na, Mester Edditor, what I want
to know is, supposin' Mester Cobby gets in again, will he attend to
t'Appeal Committee Meetings as well it futur as he has it past. If so,
I think he'd be better aat, and let somedy go in 'at would attend to
aar interests.

Jack Weelswarf, from aar hull hartstone.

'Jack Weelswarf's' letter evidently was effective; and equally
evidently it was written by one who knew how to express himself,
albeit in simulated dialect.

The Sheffield School Board operated from 1870 to 1903, and
their work played a notable part in establishing Sheffield's proud
educational standards. The first chairman of the board, Sir John
Brown, steered the board through its difficult years, and to him
Sheffield owes much. On his retirement from the board after
serving for nine years the board placed on record "its deep sense
of the value of those services—of the ability, discretion and cour-
tesy with which he has discharged the duties of the office, and also
its sincere regret that the state of his health compels him to withdraw from the position which he has so honourably filled for the
past nine years". A bust of Sir John Brown, paid for by voluntary
subscriptions, is now in the boardroom of the education committee.

"Sir John was born in Favell's Yard, Fargate, in 1816, the
second son of Samuel Brown, slater. He was educated at a small
school held in an attic and in his fourteenth year was apprenticed
to a small firm of cutlery and file manufacturers, in Orchard
Place. He was later taken into partnership, and in the great days of
the steel trade built up the Atlas Works. He died in 1896, and is
buried at Ecclesall." This is quoted from Alderman J. H. Bingham's *The Period of the Sheffield School Board, 1870–1903* (1949).
Of Mark Firth who left the Board at the same time, Alderman
Bingham says: "Mark Firth was born in 1819, and educated at
Eadon's Academy, Red Hill. His father was a working man, a
steel melter, and with his two sons, Mark and Thomas, went in
business on their own account and built up the great steel works
of Thomas Firth & Sons. He died in 1880 and is buried in the
General Cemetery. . . . Both were really fine types of 'self-made
men' with a large sense of social responsibility. They did a great

service to local education, laying the foundations with courage, decision and wisdom."

From its inception the Sheffield School Board had in mind plans for higher education, and their report for the period November 1870 to November 1876 shows their intentions. It stated that the plan for the Central School was intended:

> To furnish (in addition to some accommodation similar to that in other elementary schools) a distinct higher department to which may be drafted deserving and clever pupils from other schools of the town . . . irrespective of class . . . and that in addition to the ordinary subjects for higher standards, subjects set forth in the Fourth Schedule of the New Code of the Education Department, viz., Literature, Mathematics, Latin, French, German, Mechanics, Animal Physiology, Physical Geography, Botany and Domestic Economy (for girls) should be taught. There should also be taught other subjects specially bearing upon the industries of this district, which may be taken under the regulations of the Science and Art Department . . . such as Drawing, Chemistry, Geology, Minerology, Principles of Mining, Metallurgy, Machine Construction, Steam, Building Construction, etc. In both senior departments special attention should be given to the training of boys and girls intending to become pupil teachers. . . . To scholars of special ability passing the competitive examinations . . . it is intended that aid should be given of a financial character where necessary. Such an arrangement will . . . enable scholars to better fit themselves for most useful positions, either connected with the industries of the district or with educational work. It is also important that facilities should be given for evening classes. . . . In connection with this subject . . . the Board have encouraged the establishment of a system of scholarships with very gratifying results, as the pupils who have been received into the Collegiate and Grammar Schools are fully justifying the hopes which were entertained by the promoters.

The report also states: "The scheme for Central Schools is looked upon with great interest, far beyond the confines of this district, and is a decided step in advance, which is not unlikely to be followed throughout the country. . . . The plans of the building have been prepared specially with the object of providing for such a scheme of education."

Throughout all these new educational advances considerable support was accorded by Mr. A. J. Mundella, one of Sheffield's Members of Parliament.

The formal opening of the Central School took place on 15th July 1880. In March 1876 a minute of the board fixed the site of the Central School and of the school board office, agreeing to "the purchase of property in Bow Street, Church Street, Smith Street, Orchard Lane and Orchard Street ... at a cost of £17,000". In April 1877 an area of land fronting Bow Street and Smith Street was to be sold to Mr. Mark Firth for £2,750 "as a site for his proposed University College Buildings".

When opened in 1880 the Central School had 976 scholars and many evening-class scholars. In October 1898 work began on the building of the new Pupil Teachers' Centre, in Holly Street. This whole group of new educational buildings made a very substantial contribution to the increasing dignity of the buildings in the town centre, and the new, wide Leopold Street made suitable access from what is now Town Hall Square.

Firth College (the forerunner of the university) was founded in May, 1879 by Mark Firth, entirely at his own expense. Later, this building became the Central Secondary School for Girls, and later still, the Junior Technical College.

Many outstanding names have been associated with the educational organizations represented in this historic block of buildings. In 1880 William Ripper was appointed as science teacher for the Central Schools (four years previously he had been appointed headmaster of the Walkley Temporary School). In November 1884 he took up the post of assistant professor of mechanical engineering at the Sheffield Technical School; he later became professor of engineering and Dean of the Faculty of Applied Science, and eventually became Vice-Chancellor of the University of Sheffield.

In July 1876 Mr. Henry Coward was appointed headmaster of the Park School. His ability was outstanding, in music as well as academically. The National Union of Teachers asked Mr. Coward to train and conduct a choir of 500 scholars and teachers. He left the service of the school board in January 1879 to accept the headship of the Free Writing School, thus, as he said, "escaping the trouble, turmoil, red-tape and anxiety of the yearly uncertainty of grant based upon H.M. Inspector's examination". Sir Henry Coward became a national—and international—figure in music.

Miss Isabel Cleghorn in November 1879 was appointed to be

headmistress of a girls' school. She became the first woman President of the National Union of Teachers.

Mr. W. B. Marshman, affectionately known as 'Benny' by his pupils, was appointed to the Central Higher School as assistant in 1896. He proved to be a quite brilliant producer of drama, specializing in Shakespeare's plays. W. B. Marshman was in the boys' school, and his plays, with casts drawn entirely from among his pupils, were enjoyed by boys and audience alike.

There were many outstanding pupils of whom Sheffield must be proud; but one case worthy of mention was W. W. S. Legge, who was a former scholar and then a pupil teacher at Crookesmoor Boys' School. In the Queen's Scholarship Examination in 1901 Legge came out first in the whole country.

Alderman Bingham's interesting book mentions:

In June, 1897, an understanding had been arrived at between the Board and the Sheffield Technical School Committee whereby "one scholarship of the value of £15 for the first year, £20 for the second year and £25 for the third year, tenable at the Technical School, be offered to scholars of 15 years of age and upwards attending the Central Higher School. The Scholarship to be awarded on the result of an examination in all subjects taken by the boys in the Mechanical Section of the Central School, to be only given providing that candidates of sufficient merit present themselves: the examination to be conducted by the Head Master of the Central School in conjunction with the Principal of the Technical School". . . .

The scholarship tenable at the "Technical Department of the University College in 1902 was won by Thomas Swinden of 28, Holland Road, aged 15 years and 10 months, who became D.Met. of Sheffield University in 1913, and at his death in 1944 was Director of Research for United Steel Companies, Ltd., and a Director of Samuel Fox & Company, Ltd. and other Companies".

Alderman Bingham also describes a royal occasion—the celebration of Queen Victoria's Diamond Jubilee, in 1897:

A "dutiful address" was presented to Her Majesty by the Board under its Common Seal, which noted the fact that 40,000 to 50,000 elementary school children "through the kindness of our Mayor, His Grace the Duke of Norfolk", will have the "inexpressible delight of giving their Queen a loyal and loving welcome in Norfolk Park".

50,561 scholars and about 2,000 teachers were present, and formed a choir conducted by Mr. Henry Coward—as he was then. There were nine military brass bands, and the conductor, on a stand thirty feet high, had a baton "about six feet long with a little flag at the end". High tribute was paid to "the organization of the children by Mr. Quine, and their "clockwork precision of movements".

The Sheffield School of Art was founded in Arundel Street in 1857; in 1901 this school was taken over by the city council.

At national level the Education Act of 1902 provided for the transfer of primary education from the school boards to local authorities, and the provision of greatly extended powers to provide secondary education. Several of the conditions imposed caused the usual fierce arguments. In addition to all the city's board schools, the new committee took over the Pupil Teachers' Centre in Leopold Street and the College of Cookery and Domestic Science in York Street.

In 1904 following upon a comprehensive report made by Mr. Michael E. Sadler it was arranged to amalgamate the Royal Grammar School and the Wesley College to form the King Edward VII School. The head of the new school was Mr. J. H. Hitchens, M.A.: in the period until his retirement in 1926 he built up a school with a very fine academic record.

When the King Edward VII School opened in October 1905 on Clarkehouse Road its former building in Ecclesall Road was used to establish a training college for teachers, and the former headmaster of Wesley College became principal of the new training college.

Up to the outbreak of war in 1914 educational standards in Sheffield, at all levels, were quite remarkable. In June 1914, when presenting prizes at the nine-year-old King Edward VII School, Dr. H. A. L. Fisher, Vice-Chancellor of Sheffield University said: "I do not believe that there is a school in England with a history at once so short and so distinguished."

In 1924 'intermediate schools' were founded at Greystones and Marlcliffe, at Carfield in 1925 and Owler Lane in 1926.

Back in 1879 Firth College was opened, and it was then that Bayley's highly successful People's College founded in 1842, closed. The Mechanic's Institute, founded in 1832, continued until 1890, when its resources were handed over to found twelve exhibitions at Firth College. In 1897 all the balance of cash of the institute was disposed of when Firth College became the Sheffield University College. As the city's educational facilities expanded, the older charity institutions tended to merge and amalgamate, but their former undoubted value had laid the foundation upon which the new institutions were built.

The old Pupil Teachers' Centre became the City Grammar School for Boys and Girls, and the Central School was transferred to High Storrs as two grammar schools, one for boys and one for girls. After the Second World War a new College of Housecraft was opened at Totley Hall, and a further training college at Thornbridge Hall, near Bakewell.

Technical education came decidedly to the fore after 1945; a huge new college, the Sheffield Polytechnic, was formed in January 1969 when the Sheffield Colleges of Technology and Art were merged. In recent years the Granville College of Further Education, the Richmond College of Further Education, the Shirecliffe College of Further Education and the Stannington College of Further Education have been established. And within the last few years the comprehensive schools have been, and are still being established.

At the apex of this truly substantial pyramid of educational facilities of all types—a structure second to none in the country—is the University of Sheffield.

Very fittingly, the university grew from three earlier educational institutions, the Sheffield Medical School founded about 1830, Firth College founded at his own expense in 1879 by Mark Firth (at that date he was mayor of Sheffield), and the Sheffield Technical School founded in 1884 largely with the help of Sir Frederick Mappin. In 1897 by royal charter the three educational institutions were united as University College, Sheffield. This was helped considerably by public subscription, the public fund collected to celebrate Queen Victoria's Diamond Jubilee being donated towards the endowment of the new University College.

The years immediately preceding the founding of the University College were by no means free from financial worry, and in fact it was largely through the determination and generosity of Sir Henry Stephenson, and the devotion of W. M. Hicks that these storms were weathered. W. M. Hicks was Principal of Firth College from 1883 and then of the University College; later he became the first Vice-Chancellor of the university.

New buildings were started on a fine site at Western Bank for the Departments of Arts, Science and Medicine; public subscriptions were made on a generous scale. Efforts were next made to secure a university charter, and this was granted on 31st May 1905. King Edward VII came, with Queen Alexandra, to open the new building in July 1905.

The university was very small at first, but the number of students, from an increasingly wide area, rose rapidly. The original buildings have been enlarged several times and today, in addition to the original buildings at Western Bank and St. George's Square there are extensive buildings dominating a wide area, housing the tremendously expanded Faculties of Art, Law, Pure Science, Medicine, Engineering and Metallurgy.

The Firth Chair of Chemistry was endowed by Mark Firth when he founded Firth College. The Faculty of Medicine is a direct continuation of the early medical school of 1828, and with it are associated some famous names, including Sir Howard Florey, famous for his work on penicillin; H. A. Krebs who was a Nobel Prize-winner in 1953; Sir Edward Mellanby whose work on diet and disease was largely instrumental in overcoming rickets, once so terribly prevalent; and several others.

The department of Glass Technology, started during the First World War, became outstanding in this country and indeed in the world. It is now housed in separate premises. The Faculties of Engineering and Metallurgy, also world-renowned, remained faithful to the aims of the old technical school, in that in addition to the day-time graduate courses, evening students were very well catered for, and advanced courses offered. Today, the Sheffield Polytechnic is able to accept these numerous evening-class students, in modern, up-to-date premises.

The university has always been conscious that an important part of its role involves spreading its learning to all types and classes far beyond the university itself. It was to further this important aspect of its work that in 1947 a Department of Extramural Studies was instituted under a full-time director. Today the university's Extramural Department caters to more than 5,000 people over a very wide area, providing popular courses at a number of centres throughout the area as well as in the university building itself.

In *Sheffield and its Region* Dr. A. W. Chapman says of the

university: "the foresight and generosity of the early supporters have borne fruit; the scale of its work has now grown far beyond the dreams of its founders; the horizon of its influence has extended from the locality to the nation and beyond; yet it remains ever more effectively a focus of enlightenment for its immediate region and a source of legitimate pride to its city".

XV

MURDERS AT THE THEATRE

In an earlier chapter the average Sheffielder's love of music has
been mentioned. The love of drama was almost equally marked.
This interest in music and drama is still very evident today, though
its pattern has changed somewhat. The part played by theatre and
music hall in Sheffield in the late Victorian period is excellently
described in an article written by John Barry in the *Sheffield
Telegraph* of 17th November 1962, entitled "When West Bar
was the Piccadilly Circus of Sheffield:

> "Hey up, Bill, will ter goa wi' me t'Tommy's toneet?"
> "Why? Is't owt speshul?"
> "I shud say it wus—theer's three murders i't fust act."
> And that [writes John Barry] in one classic Victorian conversation,
> was Sheffield's night life a century ago. . . .
> Tommy's was the Surrey Music Hall in West Bar, not on any
> account to be confused with the Music Hall, Surrey Street, where
> more dignified pursuits were the rule. For, in the days when
> Sheffield had more music halls than there are cinemas today, when
> West Bar was called 'The Piccadilly Circus of Sheffield', Tommy
> Youdan was king. His Surrey Theatre specialized in lurid melodrama
> until, in March 1865 he over-reached himself and, during a particu-
> larly realistic staging of 'The Streets of London', the theatre, with
> menagerie attached, was burnt to the ground.
> Undismayed by a £30,000 loss, Tommy Youdan bought 'The
> Royal Alexandra Theatre and Opera House' in Blonk Street. Because
> it had one of the largest stages in England—it projected over the
> river, and chorus girls had to change under that stage—all the operas
> used to come. But to placate the Sheffield audiences, singers used to
> put popular song-hits between the arias. For three months every
> year, the Alexandra put on fabulous pantomimes. . . .
> Sheffield's idols included men like George Leybourne, who sang
> 'Champagne Charlie is my Name' and drove to the theatre in a

carriage and four; or J. W. Rowley, the Yorkshire dialect comedian; or J. W. Ashcroft, 'the solid man'. Then there was adorable Jenny Hill, 'the vital spark', who started in Bradford and for 15s. a week scubbed floors all day, and sang twenty to thirty songs each night. Finally, she came to Sheffield at the biggest wage ever paid to a panto artist at that time. . . .

Opposite the Britannia stood the old Gaiety, at the corner of Corporation Street. . . . At the edge of the stage, above the orchestra —never more than six-piece, and usually only piano, violin and cornet—was the chairman's table. One of the best in Sheffield was W. B. Field, who sang 'Tommy, Make Room for Me'. . . . Chairmen had to be ready to perform, because artists were wildly unpunctual. Even the managers could lend a hand. Arthur Holmes, manager of the Empire from 1896, had been Prof. Holmes, the conjurer, then Olmos, the trapeze artist, and was a champion plate-spinner. . . .

At the bottom of Snig Hill was the West Bar Hall, later called The Grand. That was owned by a man with a bad squint and a marvellous collection of oil-paintings. . . . There was the Alhambra in Union Street, burnt down in 1882. The Pavilion in Surrey Street gave away legs of mutton on Friday nights, and once advertised, in the same bill, 'Hamlet', followed by a side-cracking farce, 'My Wife's Second Floor'.

The Fleur de Lys, 'a very select house', stood where Cochayne's are today, and the Union in Barker's Pool was small but good. The London Music Hall, more properly called 'The London Apprentice', on the corner of West Bar and West Bar Green, was particular. The manager admitted no man in cap and muffler, no unescorted woman, and no woman in a headscarf.

But whatever the hall, the artists were fabulous. Regular Sheffield stars in those days read like an A.B.C. of the music hall. Even today, they are remembered. Dan Leno, whose parents kept a hall, 'Leno's Varieties', where the Lyceum is now. Dan was the world champion clog dancer, and his 'double shuffle' is still the basis of tap routines. Vesta Tilley, 'the idol of the halls'; Coram, the Sheffield ventriloquist who made a fortune in London; the great Lottie Collins, followed on the boards by her daughter Josie; Gertie Gitana; Fred Earle; G. H. Elliot.

And the songs . . . Charles Coburn's 'The Man Who Broke the Bank at Monte Carlo' and 'Two Lovely Black Eyes'; Eugene Stratton's 'The Lily of Laguna'; 'My Old Dutch' by the incomparable Albert Chevalier, and Gus Elen's richly sardonic 'If It wasn't for the Houses in Between'. . . . But perhaps the most moving of all was Ella Shields, with 'I'm Burlington Bertie from Bow'. One verse ended: '. . . I had a banana with Lady Diana, I'm Burlington . . .'

Lady Diana was Lady Diana Manners, later married to Douglas Duff-Cooper, and she was the darling of England. To be immortalized in the words of one of the most famous songs ever sung, is there any greater honour than that?

After the turn of the nineteenth century movies were coming, and there remained only two main music halls, the 'Empire' and the 'Hippodrome', and two theatres, the Theatre Royal and the 'Lyceum'. Outstanding plays and operas with famous artists were the order of the day. By the mid-twentieth century only the 'Lyceum' remained. Fine concerts were given at the Victoria Hall in Norfolk Street, and each season, in the first half of the twentieth century, internationally famous singers, pianists, violinists and elocutionists appeared there. The Second World War changed this pattern.

But Sheffield's love of singing and music was not diminished, and today there are no less than twenty musical societies and orchestras, ten operatic societies and a dozen dramatic societies. The number of cinemas has dwindled to half a dozen, as a result, perhaps, of the popularity of television.

In addition to the Lyceum Theatre there is the Sheffield Playhouse, controlled by what is claimed to be one of the country's leading repertory companies. This is shortly to be greatly expanded in scope and will move to larger, specially built premises soon to be completed, and described as: "unique in this country with unrivalled audience facilities. It will be the first full-scale theatre in this country committed to the concept of a deep thrust or promontory stage with the audience seated on three sides; the main auditorium of the theatre will seat 1,000 people and a small octagonal experimental theatre will house up to 250 more". This is to be called the Crucible Theatre.

The corporation's present plan is to constitute the vicinity of Arundel Gate and Angel Street as the main entertainment area.

Happily, the City Hall in Barker's Pool is available for concerts of all types, including orchestral concerts. Here also are facilities for lectures and conferences.

It was in the middle of 1916 that an idea was mooted for building a public hall for the use of Sheffield's citizens; this was adopted eventually by the council as a recommendation. Immediately after the war the lord mayor's advisory committee considered a suggestion that, as a war memorial, a memorial hall should be built. In February 1919 it was decided that a Roll of Honour of Sheffield men who had fallen in the war should be erected, with a piece of statuary as a memorial. Designs for the proposed war memorial hall were invited, and that of Mr. E. Vincent Harris was chosen. The scheme was then postponed for a time, owing to the general financial situation then obtaining. In 1922 the advisory committee recommended that the Memorial should be erected in Barker's Pool, and of the designs submitted that by Mr. Carus Wilson was accepted. His design featured a very tall, tapering flagstaff of stainless steel, rising from an interesting, finely sculptured base. This work has been criticized, but there is no doubt that it is a striking, well-designed memorial, and could be claimed to be unique. The site, also in Barker's Pool, for the erection of the war memorial hall required that thirty-one houses be demolished, and work could not proceed until suitable alternative accommodation was provided for the evicted households. The architect's plans included a hall to accommodate 3,500 persons, a small hall to accommodate 500, and three halls in the basement, two of which accommodated 340 each, and the third, 780. In addition there were three conference rooms, cloakrooms, retiring rooms and caretaker's quarters. The building was not actually started until 1928, the foundation stone being laid by the lord mayor (Alderman Harry Bolton) in June 1929. The hall was opened in 1933 by the lord mayor (Alderman T. H. Watkins), when the council had decided that the building should be called the City Hall, and that the smaller hall should be the Memorial Hall.

And so, near the site of the early important Barker's Pool there arose, in the twentieth century, a finely designed public hall facing the city's memorial to the men who fell in the 1914–18 War.

The effects of the 1914–18 War on Sheffield were diverse and lasting, although it was probably some years after the cessation of hostilities before the full story could be told. Because of Sheffield's importance as a centre of the manufacture of armaments and war materials, many extra workers were needed, and when all available accommodation was exhausted, wooden buildings were erected to house them as near to the east end works as possible. All the city's facilities were stretched to the utmost. And then, on a bright, moonlight night, 26th September 1915 there came an enemy air attack. It was known that Sheffield was beyond the range of the German aeroplanes of that date, but it was another matter for the huge Zeppelins. Just before 10 p.m. people living beyond the city's southern boundaries heard a loud, droning sound approaching, and on looking out saw an enormous cigar-shape in the sky, white in the moonlight, cruising majestically towards Sheffield. It seemed that the great air-ship had followed the brightly shining railway lines from the south. It passed on to the north, and some time later people heard the muffled roar of dropped explosives over Sheffield, followed by the glare of fires. Houses were destroyed and twenty-eight people were killed, but the east end works and the railways were unharmed.

A story is told of how what could have been serious panic was averted at the music hall, the Sheffield 'Empire'. This hall had considerable capacity, and that night a crowded audience enjoyed listening to George Robey. Shortly before the end of the perfor-mance he was singing, in his inimitable style, a song in which each verse ended with, "Aw, shurrup!" During his song the drone of Zeppelin engines was heard approaching, and it seemed likely to pass over or very near the crowded 'Empire'. There was, understandably, a gasp of fear throughout the audience, and there could have been panic, with serious results. George Robey stopped singing, listened quizzically to the rapidly increasing overhead noise, then waved a derisive arm towards the roof, shouting in a tone of disgust, "AW, SHURRUP!"

The burst of laughter shared by the whole audience dispelled any inclination to panic, and the still giggling crowd made a leisurely, unperturbed exit.

It was after the war that Sheffield experienced a period of serious depression. A wise scheme to overcome unemployment by im-proving existing roads and constructing excellent new roads was adopted by the corporation between about 1921 and 1926.

By the year 1893 the efforts of those early stalwarts who worked so well, as we have seen, to try to establish library facilities for the public, were coming to fruition. The Central Library was opened in 1856, Sheffield being one of the first towns to adopt the Public Libraries Act of 1850. Branch libraries were opened—Upperthorpe in 1869, Brightside (now Burngreave) in 1872, Highfield in 1876 and Attercliffe in 1887. Later, the opening of the Walkley Library

in 1905 and the Tinsley Library in 1911 were greatly assisted by
grants generously made by the Scots-born philanthropist Andrew
Carnegie.

The Central Library had to struggle along for many years in
unsuitable premises, although in 1893 three separate committees
were set up to deal with the important matters involved in the
control and expansion of a public library and museum service. A
museum had already been established in Weston Park, with the
Mappin Art Gallery nearby, and by 1892 both were attracting a
large number of visitors.

The Central Library, in a fine new building which was opened
in July 1934 by Queen Elizabeth the Queen Mother (then Duchess
of York), today offers one of the finest public library services in
the country. Its department of local history and archives has a
notable collection of manuscripts; it is recognized by the Master
of the Rolls as a repository for manorial and local public records;
there are special collections, and important loan deposits including
the Wentworth Woodhouse Muniments, the Arundel Castle
Muniments and the Wharncliffe and Crewe Muniments. Another
of the Central Library's important departments is the Library of
Commerce and Law, Science and Technology, the latter section
having a nationally important steel specifications index and being
the headquarters of the Sheffield Interchange Organization. In
addition to the lending library section, there is a music lending
library, and a general reference library. There is a school libraries
department which controls 278 libraries in schools; there are
twenty-five branch libraries and three mobile libraries serving a
wide area on the city's outskirts. This remarkable library service
can only be regarded as a very real tribute to the efforts of the
early pioneers. The Central Library has a newsroom and a lecture
theatre, and also houses the busy Civic Information Service.

The museum in Weston Park was founded in 1875, and has a
very proud record. Originally known as Weston Park Museum,
it was formerly the home of a family who were generous bene-
factors to the town. It has been noted that Sheffield is in an area
of outstanding archaeological interest, so it can occasion no surprise to find that from its inception the museum acquired an
enviable collection of local archaeological 'finds'. In January 1893
the museums committee purchased for £1,610 the valuable collection of local material made by Mr. Bateman of Youlgreave, a

A carved post in 'The Old Queen's Head', Pond Hill

local antiquarian. Several attempts were made to have the Weston Park Museum enlarged, but without success until the end of the first quarter of the twentieth century. Extensive rebuilding was then started, and the present fine building—now known as the City Museum—was opened in 1937. To this new building in 1953 was transferred the collection—including a fine display of geological specimens—which had been founded by John Ruskin, housed at Meersbrook House in Meersbrook Park, and opened by the Earl of Carlisle in 1890 as the Ruskin Museum.

The City Museum today houses, in addition to a notable collection of local archaeological material from early prehistoric times, a world-famous collection of cutlery and of old Sheffield Plate, considerable material relating to birds and animals, and an interesting Collection dealing with the life and work of the famous Sheffield scientist Henry Clifton Sorby.

Under the control of the museum's committee are the unique Shepherd's Wheel in Whiteley Woods—a water-driven cutlery grinding wheel dating from the early sixteenth century, and long before that date probably a corn-grinding wheel—and the remarkable Abbeydale Industrial Hamlet on the River Sheaf. The Shepherd's Wheel is on the Porter Brook. Both these interesting industrial wheels have been acquired and restored to working condition, an undertaking calling for skill and knowledge, by the Council for the Conservation of Sheffield Antiquities, and developed by the corporation as a museum. They both stand in quite delightful surroundings.

The Abbeydale works seems to have been founded in the eighteenth century as a scythe works, a use which it always retained. At Abbeydale it is possible to trace the manufacture of a steel edge-tool through every process from the raw materials to the finished product. We quote from the pamphlet available to visitors:

Also preserved on the site is an early furnace for producing steel in crucibles of the type developed by Benjamin Huntsman about 1742; the invention of such a furnace laid the foundations for the production of high quality steel for which Sheffield is world-famous. The Works are situated about three and a half miles to the south-west of the City centre between Abbeydale Road South and the River Sheaf.

The crucibles in which the steel was made were produced here and

13

Bishops House, Meersbrook
Detail of the plaster-work over a chimney breast in Bishops House

the workshop where the clay was kneaded with bare feet prior to being made into 'pots', as they were called, is still extant. The high quality steel was made from a charge of iron and scrap which was heated in the pot for about four hours, the requisite carbon being added. The pot was then lifted from the furnace and after skimming off any slag, the fluid metal was teemed into moulds and allowed to cool to a red heat before removal. When cold the quality of the ingot was tested.

The ingot was then ready to be forged roughly into shape. It was re-heated in a hearth in the tilt-forge where the temperature required was achieved by means of an ingenious water-driven air blowing machine for the fires. The forging then took place under tilt-hammers which were also water-driven. The hammers were lifted by cogs on the wooden main shaft which tilted them to give the correct rapid forging action which was needed to sandwich a piece of carbon steel between an outside composed of wrought iron. Thus great strength and reliability was given to the central cutting edge. The various hand-forges were used by craftsmen who tempered and straightened the blades and also forged other articles from bar steel made under the tilt-hammers.

The grinding machinery, currently being restored, was driven by an eighteen-foot water-wheel and during the nineteenth century a horizontal steam engine was added to provide the motive force in times of water shortage. Adjacent to the grinding shop is the hafting and boring shop which has a further water-wheel used to drive the machinery for these processes. In addition to the main workshops there is a large warehouse, offices, a row of workmen's cottages and a manager's house.

The restoration was carried out by the Council for the Conservation of Sheffield Antiquities with funds resulting from a public appeal. The hamlet was opened to the public on April 30th, 1970, and is now maintained by the Sheffield City Council as a museum of the City's industrial history.

Part of the former warehouse has been fitted up as a most interesting museum displaying a variety of Sheffield's industrial products, including a 'Sheffield thwittle'. One exhibit which deserves mention is a Memorial Stone "In Memory of JOSEPH WHITTINGTON, GRINDER, who by correct taste united by Rare skill as a workman enhanced the fame of Sheffield in its Staple Manufactures. Numerous specimens of his workmanship are in the show-rooms of Joseph Rodgers & Sons. His private worth equalled his skill, as a citizen. And this tablet has been erected to his Memory, By his fellow workmen, in token of their estimation of his character and ability. 1854."

In its two art galleries Sheffield has a number of very valuable works. John Newton Mappin's generosity was instrumental in founding an art gallery in Weston Park, alongside the Weston Park Museum, in the last quarter of the nineteenth century. After being seriously damaged by enemy action, the restored building was reopened in 1966. In addition to works by British painters and sculptors of the last three centuries, there are many by Sheffield artists.

The Graves Art Gallery, over the Central Library in Surrey Street, was opened in 1934, a gift from Alderman J. G. Graves. One of the most valuable collections in this gallery is the Grice Collection of carved ivories, from A.D. 1600–1900 It is claimed that this is perhaps one of the most famous collections of Chinese ivories in the world. Among other notable works this gallery has paintings by Leonardo da Vinci, Andrea Del Verrocchio, Murillo, Cezanne and Corot. There are also collections of modern art.

The establishment in 1797 of the remarkable Sheffield Royal Infirmary indicated the merit and vision of Sheffield's medical services of that date, and that splendid vision has been logically and faithfully developed through the years by both a notable medical service and the loyalty of many citizens. The city today has a fine system of medical institutions of every type, and in addition is the centre controlling hospitals over a very wide area. The Sheffield Regional Hospital Board, one of the fourteen for England, has its headquarters at Fulwood and controls an area extending to Boston and Grimsby. The board has twenty-five hospital management committees, responsible for a total of 190 hospitals, thirty-four annexes and forty clinics.

The United Sheffield Hospitals was set up under the National Health Service Act, 1946, and embraces Sheffield's teaching hospitals, including the Royal Infirmary (1797) and the Whiteley Wood Clinic (May 1958); the Royal Hospital (1832) and the Fulwood Annexe (1908); the Jessop Hospital for Women, established in Figtree Lane in 1864, transferred to Leavygreave Road in 1878, with the later established (though recently closed) Jessop Hospital (Firth) Auxiliary at Norton Hall; the Children's Hospital (1876) at Western Bank; the Edgar Allen Physical

Treatment Centre in Gell Street; the School of Physiotherapy, also in Gell Street; and the Charles Clifford Dental Hospital, at Wellesley Road. The large new Hallamshire Hospital in Glossop Road is at present under construction; when completed in 1974 there will be 750 beds available, as well as an outpatients department.

Most of these teaching hospitals lie within the area of the greatly extended university buildings, on the magnificent slope climbing from Escafeld to the Hallam Moors.

XVI

THE THREATENED CANAL

AN EARLIER chapter has outlined the steps taken to make the town of Sheffield an inland port, with a fine water-highway from the heart of the town, through the busy industrial area, and on to the port of Hull. It was in 1819 that the first Humber keel, the steam-packet *Industry*, headed a procession of barges into the new Port of Sheffield.

Thomas Asline Ward (1781–1871) wrote to a friend: "You would have enjoyed the Canal opening. It was a glorious scene. I subscribed for a share in the adventure at its commencement, rather because I thought it proper than from any expectation of profit; but there is a fair prospect even of pecuniary advantage."

Regarding the opening of the canal, which took place on 22nd February 1819, Mr. Ward notes in his pocket diary: "The first vessels entered into the basin of the Canal at Sheffield. The public bodies went in procession. I accompanied the Cutlers' Company. Never was a greater concourse seen in Sheffield." Four days previously (February 18th) Mr. Ward records that he had walked with his brother John "along the banks of the New Canal from Sheffield to Tinsley".

Thomas Asline Ward's prophecy of "a fair prospect even of pecuniary advantage" certainly was justified. In 1815 the books of the Cutlers' Company showed the shares to be valued at £1,400 each. In 1826 one share was sold for £2,300; and in 1829 shares were worth £2,500 each.

There is no wonder that the new railway companies feared the canal as a competitor; the only way to control the tremendous amount of water transport was to get financial control of the waterway, and in 1864 the Manchester, Sheffield and Lincolnshire Railway succeeded in buying up more than half the canal company's shares, with a view to getting the traffic on to the railway.

From that date the canal was poorly maintained. This danger to the canal's efficiency was recognized by both the Sheffield Corporation and manufacturers, and in 1889 a Bill was introduced for the compulsory purchase from the Great Central Railway Company of the 57 miles of navigation so vital to Sheffield, by the newly incorporated Sheffield and South Yorkshire Navigation Company—but the railway company still managed to keep control.

The enlightened corporation of the time was still concerned about the misuse of this fine local and national asset. In 1912 a special committee was appointed to draw up plans for the improvement of the River Don, so that in addition to its commercial use, from the port of Sheffield facilities should be made available for pleasure boating and other forms of recreation. For various reasons this forward-looking plan was dropped from the Corporation Bill when it went before Parliament.

In spite of the restrictive action used against the canal, such was its value that in February 1913 the general manager, Mr. George Welch, referring to the 1 million tons carried on the canal annually said, "The Canal is capable of handling 3,000,000 tons of traffic a year without in any way needing to extend the accommodation, and the carriers—who have already at least 600 barges on the Canal—would be only too willing to undertake it."

Still greater trouble was in store, for with the coming of war in 1914 the Government took over the control of the navigation, seized large numbers of barges and sent them to Belgium and France, taking boatmen into H.M. Forces. No effort was made to maintain the canal, and the coal control and food control departments removed traffic to the railways. Throughout all these crippling actions the Sheffield City Council and leading citizens were determined that this vital water-highway must be restored to good working condition as soon as possible. By October 1918 the council had considered and approved a plan suggested by its development committee for the canal's improvement; it was urged that the present canals be modernized to provide up-to-date water connection between Sheffield and the Humber ports, and a regular boat-service be maintained. The canals in question were the Sheffield and South Yorkshire Navigation Company's waterways, namely the Stainforth and Keadby New Junction, the

Dearne and Dove, the Sheffield–Tinsley Canal and the River Don Navigation. Articles in the Press urged the removal of "the dead hand" of railway control.

A conference of manufacturers and others had been held in Sheffield and declared that the canal was inadequate to meet the needs of the district and ought to be brought up to the standard of modern requirements as soon as possible. This was followed by a conference of representatives of the councils of Sheffield, Rotherham, Doncaster and Mexborough, which passed resolutions to the same effect. Arising from these resolutions the development committee recommended the city council (1) to adopt the resolutions passed by the two conferences; (2) to declare that the council would use its influence "to secure, wherever practical and convenient, the use of the Canal, when modernized and equipped with an up-to-date service of boats"; (3) to urge upon the Government the importance of bringing the canal up to modern requirements so as to enable the introduction of mechanical haulage; and (4) (while the Committee was of the opinion that the cost of such modernization should be wholly provided by the Government and "that the navigation should be nationalized") to consider favourably the question of making some financial contribution, provided the execution of the work was not delayed, that the canal was brought under public control and "freed from all control or interference by any railway company".

In an article in the *Sheffield Telegraph Year Book* for 1919 Councillor Warlow said that the Corporation intended to purchase the canal. He pointed out that water carriage was of great importance and that it had never been developed in Sheffield as it ought to have been. He said: "We want to take the canal to the works."

But in 1919 the Government still controlled the canal. On 21st February 1919 the Press carried articles on "The Centenary of the Sheffield Canal", ending on the popular note; "The need for an efficient waterway is more urgent today than it was a hundred years ago."

The following year saw further progressive demands that the navigation be improved to take larger, motorized barges. It is heartening to recall that despite determined efforts to 'run down' the canal, the city council was a redoubtable champion of the canal's modernization, and was strongly supported by the

Chamber of Commerce. But in September 1920 came the serious news that the Government was about to hand back to the company the badly neglected, run-down waterway, and the restoration to good condition was now financially beyond the company's means. It was feared that this dreadful legacy of neglect would compel the canal's closure.

Representatives from along the length of the canal met in Sheffield, expressing determination to save it, for closure would be a calamity. Views were stated that its maintenance was essential to industry, and that if it was closed, Sheffield would find out that a very big mistake had been made. By the following year it was known that common sense had prevailed and the canal would not be closed. The company was still hoping to get some compensation for wartime neglect, loss of boats and business.

An important development in 1925 was the erection of a 2,000-ton-capacity grain silo at the Sheffield Basin, by a group of Sheffield millers.

The year 1948 was a further landmark in the story of the waterway, for in that year the nationalization of the railways included the canal, since the railway company still held a controlling interest. After several years it became obvious that determined efforts were to be made to rob Sheffield of its great water-highway, for in 1958 the rumour was heard that the British Transport Waterways were planning to close the whole of the navigation above Doncaster. Such a rumour seemed difficult to accept—but was appreciated when in 1960 the same authority informed the Sheffield City Council that it was proposed to make Thrybergh the "waterhead"! Thrybergh is a village downstream of Rotherham, so the plan, obviously the first step towards securing the proposed closure of the waterway above Doncaster, would leave both Sheffield and Rotherham with no water-highway to the sea—and that despite the fact, acknowledged throughout the world, that Sheffield and its area has the largest concentration of heavy industry in the world.

Again the city council loyally took up the cudgels on behalf of Sheffield's fine waterway, compelling the Transport Commission to withdraw their unworthy plan.

As the reason for wishing to make Thrybergh the "waterhead", British Transport Waterways stated that "there was no traffic". And at that same time a well-known, successful, long-established firm of canal-carriers based at Swinton was building extensive new warehouse facilities and wharves at Eastwood, Rotherham—a plan difficult to understand if "there was no traffic". Obviously this forward-looking, long-established firm of canal-carriers knew better than to accept the ridiculous story that on a fine, direct waterway between the country's fifth largest city and the ports there is "no traffic"!

Ever since it was opened in 1819 the Sheffield Basin had been the efficient headquarters; but as part of the amazing "there is no traffic" policy the headquarters' offices were closed, the staff removed down to Rotherham, one man only being left at Sheffield Basin. There was a substantial grain traffic to the grain silo; the lease of the great silo to the firm which had held it for many years was terminated in 1970.

An up-to-date survey reveals that at least 9,000,000 tons of cargo would be available annually were the navigation modernized right into the Port of Sheffield.

An article by Max Williams in the *Sheffield Morning Telegraph* of 25th February 1971 has the heading: "Noise: a modern torture that's getting worse." He writes:

"BOOMWATCH" has informed us that "noise is rapidly becoming one of the most disturbing features of modern society". The first report of the Royal Commission on Environmental Pollution puts the least understood aspect of pollution on the map: the row in which we have to live and work.

Noise is certainly a pollutant. Not only does it make our cities miserable places in which to exist, it has observable physical and psychological effects. . . . The Royal Commission says that the main noise culprit is traffic. It is the most general cause of noise pollution and affects the largest number of people. . . . It is worth mentioning that we already have more vehicles per mile of road than any other country. . . .

And Sheffield, the fifth largest city, with the greatest concentration of heavy industry in the world, may lose its fine water-highway to the sea! Sheffield, with a remarkably convenient large basin, with a known potential of 9,000,000 tons of water-borne cargo annually—carried economically, safely, efficiently, without poisonous fumes, and *quietly*—may be deprived of its water-route. If this incredibly retrograde plan is allowed to succeed (a plan determinedly opposed by citizens aware of the canal's economic importance), no longer from the Humber's busy tidal waters will the majestic barges move along the Sheffield and South Yorkshire Navigation to Sheffield—through placid pastoral scenes, through villages and towns, under bridges carrying thundering road traffic, rising through fascinating locks (awaiting modernization) to higher levels, rounding wooded river bluffs and limestone crags on stretches of the River Don sections of the waterway, past impressive Conisborough Castle high on its prehistoric site seen here from a good viewpoint; moving steadily and quietly through industrial scenes, through the ancient town of Rotherham, and then past the busiest scenes of all rising through Tinsley to the wide haven in the busy heart of Sheffield. Truly a noble heritage, and an invaluable asset.

As incorporated by the charter of 1843 the borough had comprised the old Parish of Sheffield with its six townships—Sheffield, Ecclesall, Upper Hallam, Nether Hallam, Brightside and Attercliffe. In 1881 Heeley was separated from Nether Hallam and established as another parish and township. At that date the area of the borough was 19,651 acres, the boundary going as far west as the ancient Stanage Pole on the western moors, and including the Redmires Reservoirs. Concerning Stanage Pole, H. Keeble Hawson has an interesting note in his *Sheffield. The Growth of a City 1893–1926*. He writes: "In the midst of the War the Council could still consider less important matters. In 1915 the old Stanage Pole was destroyed by vandals and the Council seriously debated whether it should be replaced by another wooden pole or by a stainless steel pole, stainless steel being then a recent invention of which Sheffield was very proud. After due consideration the Council decided in favour of wood and the weather beaten pole which one can see today was actually erected in 1915."

In August 1893 it was recommended by the Parliamentary Committee that the council should apply for boundary extensions to include Meersbrook, Norton Woodseats, Norton Lees and Norton Park, part of Beauchief, Wincobank, part of Shiregreen, Firth Park, part of Southey, Moonshine, Birley Carr, Wadsley Bridge, Wadsley, Wisewood, Loxley Common and Hillsborough. Until this date the borough's original boundaries had been wide enough to accommodate the rapidly expanding population. By the Sheffield Corporation Act, 1900, Sheffield acquired all the extensions named above.

Following these extensions, the city engineer's annual report for 1902 stated that with its total of 23,654 acres Sheffield was the largest city in actual area in the country, and that its 382 miles of roads approached the road mileage of some of the counties.

There were further boundary extensions in 1911 when the urban portion of the Parish of Tinsley, comprising about half the parish and including all the large works was acquired by Sheffield. Tinsley's population strenuously fought this change-over, and eventually the site of Steel Peech and Tozer's works was returned to Rotherham in 1917 in exchange for the site of the new electricity station at Blackburn Meadows.

The 1900 Act had added an area of 4,003 acres to Sheffield, and increased the population by 24,866. The 1911 extension added an estimated population of 5,334. A further small extension by the Corporation Act of 1914 added some 532 acres in the Rivelin Valley, extending up to the foot of the lower Rivelin Reservoir.

After the 1914–18 War a very ambitious scheme for extending the city boundaries was launched, which was strongly opposed at the local enquiry held in 1920. Resulting from this enquiry Sheffield acquired only Handsworth, the remainder of Tinsley Parish, the Sheffield sewage works, and the districts of Wadsley Bridge and Shiregreen.

Plans to clear the slum districts and the areas of crowded brick dwellings which had been erected for industrial workers were going ahead, and this meant the building of more modern housing estates towards the city outskirts and even well beyond its borders, to rehouse families. Roads and all services had to be extended, amounting in all to a vast undertaking. But the city still sought to extend its boundaries, meeting at times with a good deal of opposition. Between the years 1929 and 1934 two large villages on the city's south-west boundary were annexed, Dore and Totley. Citizens were still of necessity being rehoused in the newly established housing-estates beyond the city boundaries—and yet in 1947, 1950 and 1953 the council's efforts to extend the city boundaries to include these new estates, were unsuccessful. In 1967, however, the city succeeded in acquiring several important areas—Mosborough, Beighton, Gleadless, Frecheville and part of

Ecclesfield, an area totalling some 9 square miles; and the city's population rose to well over half a million.

But in the meantime there had been the dreadful Second World War, 1939–45.

As was the case in the previous war, Sheffield was the vital centre of an important part of the country's armament production. Perhaps the great steel firms were already preparing, for the outbreak of war in 1939 was not quite as unexpected as it had been in 1914. And again the needful cloak of secrecy enveloped the activities of the east end works. But it was known that the city was now open to attack by modern enemy aircraft—and thousands of children were evacuated to distant places in the country, where it was considered they would be safe. Throughout the first dark winter air-raid precautions were developed, and the work, of such life-and-death concern to our country, went on steadily, without pause night and day. Even today the story of those dark, dramatic years has not yet been written. The next summer brought news of the retreat from Dunkirk; and older people whispered to their workmates of their recollections of the First World War, and of the heroism and tragedy of Sheffield's City Battalion. And they knew that in Sheffield's east end, in the works of English Steel Corporation, was a vital piece of machinery—the only one in the country at that time—producing Rolls-Royce Merlin crankshafts for fighter aircraft. Messerschmitts had already made their fierce power evident; but in September 1940 they were faced by swerving, screaming Spitfires, and the world held its breath.

Hitler sent his bombers to Sheffield, and for nine hours throughout the night of 12th December bombs were rained on Sheffield. They came again for three hours on 15th December. They destroyed hundreds of houses and areas of commercial and business buildings, but the vital industrial areas were missed. Over 700 people were killed. There was no other direct air attack on Sheffield, but enemy planes often passed near the city as they went to bomb other places—and always there was a feeling of alarm, for there was no guarantee that they were not sent again to bomb Sheffield. Later, there came the 'doodle bugs', which spread damage over a wide area surrounding Sheffield. But Sheffield's people carried on steadily with the nationally important work which depended on them. And then in September 1945 the war ended.

Although the council departments had done their best, under very difficult conditions, to restore the disrupted essential services, it was not until the war had ended that it was possible to take stock of the ring of bomb-damage around and in the centre of the city.

XVII

ALL KINDS OF HOUSES

To appreciate our Portrait's record of domestic buildings throughout Sheffield's long history it is necessary to glance back to the coming of the founders of Escafeld—those sturdy capable Anglian settlers who reached this area via the Humber and Don Valleys early in the sixth century—for some of their buildings are still with us today.

They were timber users; they were skilled in the use of oak, and had no experience in stone-building. Their boats, their ox-ploughs, their ox-yokes, and their great cruck aulas were built of timber. The small dwellings of the families of the kindred were built much less sturdily and, like the humble dwellings of succeeding generations, they did not survive.

We have noted in an earlier chapter, that the great cruck building raised on the higher site at the confluence of the Don and Sheaf stood for many centuries, and that probably it was burnt with the rest of the township, during William the Conqueror's 'harrying of the North'. It is not known whether this devastated site in the virtually destroyed township was occupied by any person of importance until early in the twelfth century when William de Lovetot became lord of the manors of Escafeld and Attercliffe, and tenant lord of Hallam, and erected a castle—probably of the timber motte-and-bailey type. The obvious site was that on which the first building had been erected by the early settlers; and as de Lovetot stood on the highest part of his castle he would see the long, low cruck building on Wincobank hill, and the one on the hill to the south-east, which we know as Sheffield Manor. Only re-used crucks can be seen today at the Wincobank site, and only one remaining cruck in the long ruined building can be seen forlornly pointing to the sky at the manor. On each suitable hill-site surrounding his wide manor stood a

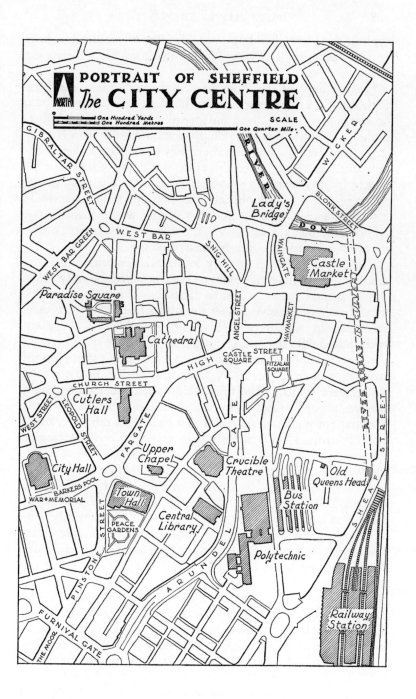

typical long, low, building with a group of smaller buildings nearby—and several of these historic structures are still standing today.

No buildings of the Norman period seem to have survived. Although the Normans were stone-builders, only their important buildings would be of stone, and for ordinary purposes the timber-building (but not cruck-building) method carried on for many years. And even if a few stone buildings were erected, they probably were destroyed, when the castle was destroyed, during the attacks by de Montfort's supporters in 1266-7. The then lord of the manor, de Furnival, obtained the King's permission to rebuild his castle, and in 1270 he erected a strong, well-defended stone edifice. But after the Civil War this was 'slighted' in 1648, thus destroying the town's only Norman building.

The late thirteenth and early fourteenth centuries ushered in another style of building, a compromise between the early use of timber and the later use of stone, a style we know as 'post-and-truss' building. Massive timber upright corner posts were used, erected for the support of the building's second floor. These posts, often placed with the root-end uppermost, had the space between them occupied by stone-walling, in which curved struts pegged from each upright post to the horizontal timbers of the second floor, were evident. The upper-floor walls had closer upright timbers, probably filled between with lathe-and-plaster. Only the dwellings of wealthier citizens would be built in this style, and if well constructed and well maintained they were certainly capable of lasting through the centuries. How many of this type of dwelling were built in Sheffield we shall never know, for only one still exists in the old part of the town. This is the 'Old Queen's Head', on Pond Hill, which has been known as the 'Hawle in the Pondes'. Much has happened to it at various periods, but its sturdy construction, despite alterations, is evident today. An interesting feature of this building is that there are still several remarkable carvings at the head of massive posts, where they support the overhanging storey. It is claimed that after the building of Sheffield Manor Lodge by the Earl of Shrewsbury early in the sixteenth century, the old building on Pond Hill (it was old then) down the hill to the north of the Manor Lodge and near the ponds by the River Sheaf, was used as the laundry for the Shrewsbury household. It is likely that it was used for this purpose when the

Another view of Sheffield from Wincobank Hill Fort

family still dwelt in the castle, as it was comparatively near the castle.

The early part of Broom Hall also is of post-and-truss construction. Being situated well beyond and to the north-west of the township, in delightful surroundings, it was, until comparatively recently, owned and lived in by wealthy families. The house has been added to several times, and today the post-and-truss section at the rear is the most neglected part. The famous Jessop family lived at Broom Hall over a period of several centuries. The vicar of the parish church, the Reverend James Wilkinson lived there until his death in 1805.

Carbrook Hall, in the former hamlet of Carbrook, east of Attercliffe, was originally of post-and-truss construction. Over the centuries it was enlarged and then parts were demolished. The present greatly reduced, stone-walled building has two rooms with fine oak panelling and plaster work.

The most spectacular of the three surviving post-and-truss buildings is now known as the Bishop's House, on Norton Lees Lane at the top of Meersbrook Park. This is a large house, which for many years has housed two families. Fortunately, few additions have appeared since its erection probably in the early fourteenth century. The surrounding area was developed as a residential area many years ago, and it will surprise no one who appreciates the type of site chosen by the first Anglian settlers to learn that this was an early settlement site, and a very desirable one. Almost a century ago the great cruck building, long used as a barn, which stood a few yards from the present house, was demolished.

There has been the usual interior modernization over the centuries; oak panelling has been added to several interior walls, staircases replace the original ladder-type access to the upper rooms, elaborately carved fireplace surrounds have been added, and fine plaster-work added to ceilings. It is known that the Blythe family of Norton at one period owned and occupied the house; sons of this family included Geoffrey Blythe, Bishop of Lichfield, and John Blythe who was consecrated Bishop of Salisbury in 1494—and the house was old even then. Several later modernizations are claimed to have been carried out by the Blythes, and their initials are in evidence. Fortunately, this very lovely house is being preserved by Sheffield Corporation.

The fine Tudor building period seems to have left no examples

14

Looking down the Haymarket to Waingate

in the township, but in the town's suburbs are several fine examples of stone-built Tudor-style residences. With the exception of several halls on the boundaries of the town and beyond, those in the town have been destroyed within the last century. Round the outskirts several small Tudor buildings survive, chiefly farmhouses; and there are Totley Hall, and Fulwood Hall (which shows evidence of several periods) as well as several Tudor buildings in the Stannington area. The buildings of this period were probably the loveliest and most attractively built of any period; their loss is a tragedy.

The Elizabethan period is represented today by only one still inhabited house, and that is the Turret House, at the manor. This small, three-storey building has an elaborately plastered ceiling in the upper room, and it was from here that Mary could mount to the roof of the Turret House to watch the hunting in the Park, and breathe the fresh air from the hills.

When the Howards succeeded the Earls of Shrewsbury as lords of the manor of Sheffield they did not live here. The castle had been 'slighted' after the Civil War, in 1648, but the Manor Lodge remained untouched; however, as the Howards had no interest in it, it was completely neglected and allowed to become ruinous, being largely dismantled in 1706. But the slightly later, small Elizabethan Turret House was left standing. Today it has been renovated and is again lived in.

A house of a very different type was built, about the year 1710, to the north of the town. This became known as Norwood Hall; it is a red-brick building with the tall windows of the Queen Anne period and with sandstone facings. James Wheat, a well-known lawyer in Sheffield lived here from 1775 to 1805, and his son and grandson also lived here. From 1917 to 1939 it was the home of the first Bishop of Sheffield, Leonard Hedley Burroughs, the name being changed to 'Bishopsholme'. Although this house is only about 260 years old, it has experienced several enlargements and alterations. An unknown artist made an interesting painting of Norwood Hall, viewed from the south, in the mid-eighteenth century. The painting, which is in the Graves Art Gallery, shows the house before it received additions, its isolated position and Queen Anne style emphasizing its unusual appearance—unusual, that is, for a Sheffield building.

An interesting example of Georgian-style building is found

quite near the cathedral, and is known as Paradise Square. Fortunately, this square is still largely unspoiled, for it is of historic as well as architectural importance. The buildings in the square were erected between about 1760 and 1772.

The observer should stand at the top of St. James's Row and look north. The line of the ancient trackway will be seen running steeply from Church Street (the former narrow Church Lane) down the east side of Paradise Square to cross the River Don by the ford at the foot of the present Corporation Street. When the town stocks, which formerly stood by the churchyard gate not far from the town hall (which was on a site now occupied by Coles' Corner) were moved, they were re-erected in the square. Before the square was built, Camper Lane ran below the north side of the old churchyard, and to the north below the lane, with the old track passing down its east side, was Hickstile Field. R. Gosling's map of 1736 shows the field, and so does Fairbank's map of 1759, but William Fairbank's map of 1771 shows Paradise Square on the site of Hickstile Field.

Paradise Row, at the lower, north side of the steeply sloping field seems to have been built first; and by 1771 the houses on the other three sides of the square were being built by Thomas Broadbent. The Paradise Row houses were a little superior, the dominant Masonic Lodge occupying the central position in the row. This fine building originally had a large meeting hall on the first floor entered via a door at the head of a flight of stone steps which extended about 18 feet out into the square; and on the ground floor under the meeting hall were "houses for various wares".

At a later date the elegant Paradise Square became known as Pot Square, and its sloping, cobbled surface was a favourite meeting place to hear important speakers. On 15th July 1779 John Wesley preached there to a large crowd, using the small landing at the top of the stone steps as his pulpit. Throughout the years many famous men spoke there, including, in 1874, Mr. Joseph Chamberlain. In the middle of the square part of an old cross stood on a low flight of steps, and some writers claim that this was the Irish cross, brought to this spot in about 1793 from the corner of Angel Street and Bank Street, others claiming that it was in fact the re-erected Townhead Cross. On the stump of the old cross a massive gas lamp was fixed at a later date, the forerunner of the present lamp. The top of these steps also was frequently used by speakers.

It seems certain that at one period pots *were* sold in the square, and it has been suggested that the "houses for various wares" may well have sold pots. It is known that there used to be a pot market by the churchyard gates. Moved to the square in 1790 the town stocks were actually in use until about 1832, a record stating that at one time several men were "put in" for "Tippling during Church time".

The house in the north-west corner of the square is remembered in connection with Sir Francis Chantrey, a plaque recording that in the years around 1802 Sir Francis Chantrey, R.A., worked there as a portrait painter. There is a plaque recording John Wesley's preaching, and another plaque records that Dr. David Daniel Davis, a well-known specialist who attended at the birth of Queen Victoria, lived there.

In the Masonic Lodge Meeting Hall a school was run by Mr. E. Hebblethwaite until about 1868. Some four years later the flight of stone steps was removed and a window inserted where the door had been. In 1886 Mr. A. Newell reopened the school, which was known locally as the Middle Class School, and this continued until well into the present century.

Lines written in 1827 by James Wills, a Sheffield poet, give a good description of Paradise Square:

> You may form to your fancy a stile which once stood
> Near the little Grape Tavern, and made up of wood,
> On the side of the field then belonging to Hicks,
> Where the children at that time have gathered sticks.
> It was called Hicks' Stile Field where corn oft has grown,
> But Paradise Row when the stile was took down.
> Many years it continued with only one row,
> But now 'tis a beautiful square as you know,
> With a Free-mason's Lodge and a flight of stone stairs
> And under it houses for various wares;
> But now 'tis a Johannes Chapel for prayers.
> This square on the hill is a market for pots
> That are sold some in odd ones, and others in lots.
> A column in centre, with lamp of pure gas,
> That lights all the square and the people who pass.

An admirable pre-Victorian building, 'The Mount', Broomhill, was designed in 1834 by a Sheffield architect, William Flockton. This building was designed as a block of eight private houses. Today it is used as office premises.

During the Victorian period building went on apace, and row upon row of brick houses appeared spreading out towards the suburbs, particularly after the introduction of tramcars. Many of these concentrations of brick rows have already been demolished, and whole areas are still being cleared as new accommodation is provided. The industrialists, whose works were expanding in size and importance were moving out to the western hills to build affluent new homes. The Ranmoor district, still having lovely, open countryside, was popular; from about 1860 large houses were built at Ranmoor, in extensive grounds, and to these Victorian palaces moved Sir John Brown; Mark Firth, who built Oakbrook, the Mappins, Stephensons, Jessops, and others. These huge homes still stand but are no longer used by the families of those who built them. They have been adapted for use as schools etc., and some of the surrounding grounds are being used for housing development. During the late Victorian and early Edwardian period many excellent houses were built in the suburbs, with lovely gardens. These homes were large, but not palatial. Most of them still exist.

By the time the Edwardian period arrived no more enormous residences were being built; wealthy people tended to move still further away from the east end and the works, and to live in smaller homes beyond the city's bounds.

In 1940, as we have seen, enemy action destroyed many houses and business premises, and it was obvious that plans must be made for the restoration, extension and modernization of the city. And the planning, in this city of steep hills and valleys, was by no means easy. It was a challenge.

One of the corporation's publications, "Ten Years of Housing in Sheffield", outlines the plans and achievements from 1953 to 1963. Three hills dominate the Sheaf–Don confluence, and it was on these hills that the three first new areas were planned. Many people deplore the fact that the use of timber and stone is a thing of the past, and that as the rows of ugly brick dwellings were demolished and cleared (although, regrettably, many quite well-built attractive houses were removed in the wholesale clearance plans) they were replaced by glass and concrete structures, a type of building dear to the hearts of many of today's planners, but a type which does not 'belong' to the area. It must be admitted that under the circumstances, with so many problems to consider, it would not be possible with other materials to build on such a vast scale.

The 1953 plans were for development on the city outskirts at Greenhill and Gleadless Valley together with extensive redevelopment projects near the city centre. Apart from Greenhill, on gentle, south-facing land, most of the proposed schemes posed considerable development difficulties, the sites being mainly on steep slopes, often north-facing, as is most of Gleadless Valley. The smaller sites were invariably those left over by previous developers as being exceptionally difficult and uneconomic on which to build. In the central area, slum clearance and the movement of old industrial buildings introduced problems which in the case of the Hyde Park site was further complicated by steep slopes and occasionally by old mine workings. The three hills mentioned above were crowned with the Park Hill, Netherthorpe and Woodside–Burngreave development sites. Of tremendous value was the fact that wide areas of the hillside were restored to their one-time green state by the siting of lawns, flowerbeds, and trees. The tall, tower-like housing blocks are certainly alien to Sheffield, but their cleanliness and pleasant surroundings have definite appeal. Across the steep valleys each site has excellent views of the others.

The Greenhill project, commenced in 1953, provided homes on a different plan, without the great tower-blocks; but the Hemsworth and Herdings sites had their hilltops crowned with sky-reaching tower-blocks overlooking the lower-type houses. Fortunately, much of the surrounding woodland has been spared providing delightful vistas.

The Park Hill site was selected for the city council's first redevelopment scheme after the war because it included the oldest outstanding slum clearance orders in the city, much of the land having been cleared before the outbreak of hostilities. The site, which rises steeply from the Midland Station (which is built over the River Sheaf) at 190 feet above sea level, to Hyde Park at 400 feet above sea level, forms the hillside to the east of the junction of the Sheaf–Don Valleys and commands extensive views to the west and south. This area was considered suitable for high-density multi-storey dwellings because it is near the city centre, it is close to but on the windward side of the heavy industrial area of the Don Valley, there are easily accessible permanent open spaces nearby, the topography of the site allowed scope for planning high flats with ample light, air and magnificent views, and the geological survey showed that the ground would take heavy loads.

The Park Hill–Hyde Park development proved to be quite fantastic—certainly it was a credit to the skill and vision of those who planned it—and today local authority planners from over half the world come to see it.

The Norfolk Park development, on rising parkland within sight of the city centre, is another striking illustration of the clever use of tower-block housing in charming park-like surroundings.

Considerable controversy was aroused when the city tried to acquire the attractive village of Mosborough in Derbyshire, to the south-east of the city. The council was looking for an area where overspill population could be housed, and where new industries could be introduced. Eventually the city council succeeded, and in April 1967 the village of Mosborough—a village of great antiquity—was taken into the city boundaries. Elaborate plans are afoot for the development of this area which stands high above the valley of the River Rother. All who love the area and appreciate its long, long story, are hoping that the old landmarks will be preserved.

Developments in the city centre have proceeded at a bewildering rate, and the work still goes on. It must be admitted the Sheffield's ancient centre *was* rather grimy and unimpressive; the new developments already have changed the long-familiar centre. Buildings have been removed almost overnight; roads have been discontinued and blocked off. New, wider roads have appeared; new, tall buildings reach upwards, and multi-storey car-parks have been built. The struggle between pedestrians and motor vehicles has been tackled by making under-passes and over-passes for pedestrians, in some cases with the convenience of escalators. But the corporation's pride is the recently opened 'hole in the road'. This amazing planners' dream occupies the middle of Castle Square. To quote the corporation's publication, "Sheffield —City on the Move": "Award winning Castle Square—known locally as 'the hole in the road'—serves a triple purpose as a roundabout, pedestrian underpass, and shopping precinct. This outstanding feat of engineering is a genuine continuation of the High Street, providing basement access to a wide variety of shops and kiosks. It even houses an aquarium!"

Castle Square attracts a good deal of attention, partly because it is of such unusual design, and partly because commercially the venture is a success, and the separation of pedestrians and traffic gives a feeling of greater safety to the former and permits of faster traffic-flow in the city centre.

With the 'hole in the road' in Castle Square—one of the oldest parts of the city—the development of housing sites and shopping facilities has been along similar outstandingly modern lines, and this, together with the building of new schools and entertainment centre has attracted the interest of architects and planners from all over the world.

An essential part of the modernization has been the construction of roads linking with the M-road system; this work has in some cases been responsible for the destruction of fine old sites and buildings. It is learned that in certain cases historic buildings must be destroyed because their continued existence would cause a difficult curve in the line of a proposed new motorway. This is the official reason advanced for the complete destruction of Jordan-thorpe Hall and its ancient Anglian cruck building. Although today's planners are quite brilliant at planning and designing multi-storey housing blocks, they could never erect a cruck building. This is the other side of the modernization picture. Sheffield's fine heritage of historic buildings should be saved.

One of the area's remarkable road-building achievements was the construction of the great two-level viaduct at Tinsley across the Don Valley, which at this point is 1 kilometre ($\frac{5}{8}$ mile) wide. The upper deck carries the M1 over the valley and the lower deck accommodates a dual-carriageway local road. This engineering feat is comparable with the fine viaducts built by the railway engineers. (See picture facing page 97).

In reviewing the almost incredible changes brought about by the re-planning of the city centre, the extension of the city boundaries and the new housing, shopping and industrial developments it must be remembered that, in addition to new roads, other services not so easily seen must keep pace with all the changes. And Sheffield's hills and valleys insist that services such as sewage and water supply will require much thought and skilful planning.

For many years Sheffield has enjoyed a very good water service; but supplies for future growth of population have to be thought about today.

In an earlier chapter we have seen that the corporation's purchase from the Waterworks Company in 1887 included the Ewden Valley sites of the Broomhead and Morehall Reservoirs. In 1913 the corporation started work on the construction of these reservoirs, and the work was completed in 1929. In the Little Don Valley work on the construction of the Langsett Reservoir began in 1898, and was completed in 1904; the building of Underbank Reservoir began in 1900 and was completed in 1907. The Barnsley Midhope Reservoir, the smallest of the three in the Little Don Valley, was completed early in 1903.

It was stated that by the completion of the Little Don Valley works the corporation had secured a water supply which would be adequate for the next forty years; yet in 1898 advances were being made towards securing future supplies from the Rivers Derwent and Ashop, in Derbyshire. This is yet one more example of the corporation's wisdom in looking far into the future, in the matter of essential services. Negotiations were put in hand, and eventually, after much discussion with Leicester, Derby, Nottingham, and Derbyshire County Council, the Derwent Valley Water Act was passed in 1899.

The original Act provided for the construction of six impounding reservoirs, of which Ronksley, Howden, Derwent and Bamford were in the Derwent Valley, and the Haggles and Ashopton in the Ashop Valley. Only one of these, the Howden Reservoir was constructed as planned, and this was opened in 1912. The Derwent Reservoir was brought into use in 1916 and actually is a modification of the one planned, and the other four were not constructed. However, it was decided to build the Ladybower Reservoir to replace the four which were not built, and this work was started in 1935. It was ready in 1945, and was opened by His Majesty King George VI. The building of this reservoir had involved the destruction of Ashopton and Derwent villages, and the building of a new Ashopton village. Derwent Hall also was demolished. In addition to many miles of pipes, $5\frac{1}{4}$ miles of new roads had to be made, and two large viaducts.

The question of compensation water has always to be remembered, and the fact that over half the supply available from the Loxley, Rivelin and Little Don reservoirs has to be released for compensation purposes posed problems, especially when, as in 1904–5, there was a long drought (lasting from April 1904 to November 1905). In 1921 there was again a prolonged period of drought.

Again the corporation seriously considered the water-supply problem in this rapidly expanding city, and it was agreed that an additional source of supply must be available by 1965 at the latest. The water supplies so far had been obtained only from moorland sources, but it was realized that other sources probably would have to be obtained. A good deal of surveying was carried out by officials of the water department, and at last it was agreed that a possible source would be the Yorkshire River Derwent. This seemed possible if water could be taken from the river in the region of Elvington, and it was realized that by the time that point is reached the river is already polluted. So for the first time in the history of Sheffield's water supply a polluted river source would need to be used, the water filtered, purified and softened, and a continuous pumping method used to forward the water to Sheffield, Barnsley, Leeds and Rotherham. As far as Sheffield was concerned, this would be a complete change from the construction of impounding reservoirs for water collection.

After all the preliminary difficulties had been resolved the Yorkshire River Derwent Scheme went ahead. It was the most modern method of water-abstraction and supply known at that time, and attracted the attention of water authorities all over the world. The water abstracted from the Yorkshire Derwent travels to Sheffield through an aqueduct 37 miles long. The work was designed to be carried out in three stages, and this has now been accomplished.

And already further sources of water supply are being sought. A plan to bring water from the headstreams of the Yorkshire Derwent has been successfully opposed, and perhaps other plans will be needed. The corporation still continues to look well ahead with plans to secure adequate supplies.

XVIII

CHURCH INTO CATHEDRAL

BEFORE the final touches are added to our Portrait it is necessary to review the story of an important building which, with its predecessors, has existed on the present site since shortly after the coming of our first Anglian settlers—our parish church, now the Cathedral Church of S. Peter and S. Paul.

Amazingly, there still exists an opinion that no church building existed in our town until after the Norman Conquest. This opinion may be based on the fact that Domesday Book (1086) makes no mention of a church in the township. The Domesday entries concerning many places in the north of the country make no mention of a church, although in some cases there is ample evidence that a church actually existed. The commissioners were not required to mention the existence of a church, though in many cases they did so; and in no case do they state that there was *not* a church at any particular place.

Where, exactly, our first settlers erected their church we do not know; but since the Escafeld folk obviously made a great success of their new settlement, a hamlet which soon became a township, it is likely that some time after their arrival, they erected their important place of worship on a significant, appropriate site. Standing today outside the east wall of our cathedral, disregarding the modern buildings and roads around, it can be seen that this site—sloping steeply to the north to the Don Valley, less steeply to the north-east to the little township with its great cruck building and down to the Don Valley, and to the south-east to the Sheaf Valley—would be on the highest land of the settlement and at the western edge. The heathen temple would be a timber building, probably quite small. Careful inspection of the whole area of the original settlement can suggest no better site than this.

Almost a century and a half later came the Christian missionaries, themselves Angles. They were welcomed by the ceorl, and perhaps after a stay of several days the ceorl agreed to call all the kindred together outside their place of worship. From the nearby woodland the missionaries would fell a tree, and with rope would secure together a vertical and a horizontal timber, to fashion a cross.

When the kindred of Escafeld accepted Christianity, their small heathen church would became the Christian church, for Pope Gregory had ordered Augustine not to destroy the heathen temple when the people were converted, but to consecrate it for Christian worship, and to use it. It is likely that Aidan's Lindisfarne monks adopted the same routine. From time to time missionaries would visit the township to officiate in the little church, and one day, perhaps in the eighth century, a stone-carver came with them—probably a Celtic monk, for the Celts were skilled stone-carvers. When the missionaries moved on they left a beautifully carved stone cross mounted in the churchyard on the south side of the church, replacing the timber cross. Today, that cross is in the British Museum.

Through the centuries Escafeld grew, and perhaps the small dwellings of the people reached almost as far as the church, although each would be surrounded by open land. Escafeld became a manor, and in 1066 it was held by Suuen. And then in 1067 William the Conqueror 'harried the north' following the rebellion in which Waltheof, lord of Hallam, took part. The township with its timber buildings was burnt, and probably the timber church also was destroyed or badly damaged. But the cross of stone was unharmed. Some of the inhabitants had managed to escape, and although their crops were destroyed a certain number managed to survive and eventually to grow crops again.

Little is known of our township until it was given to William de Lovetot early in the twelfth century. William evidently liked his manor's lovely setting for he built a castle, probably chiefly of timber, and came to live here. And soon he built a church, on the site of the old, probably ruined timber church, alongside the lovely cross. And he established the *Parish*. The little Norman church, which was built of stone, stood on its fine site until 1265, when Thomas de Furnival was lord of the manor. This was the period of the Baron's War, and the township of Sheffield was attacked and destroyed by one of the rebel barons, for de Furnival supported the King. It is not known whether the stone church escaped the destruction which the timber castle and houses suffered, but even if it survived it must have been seriously damaged. In about 1280 Wickwane, then Archbishop of York, "dedicated the Parish Church of Sheffield". This new, or restored, church was still on the same consecrated site, and would be built in the Early English style.

Little is known of the church's story until in the early fifteenth century it was again demolished and rebuilt, this time in the Perpendicular style which is in evidence today. The new church was cruciform in plan and had seven altars.

In the reign of Queen Elizabeth I the church began to suffer from lack of maintenance, and in this reign also it was ordered that stone altars in churches should be pulled down and destroyed. In 1864 the stone mensa of a Pre-reformation altar, with its five consecration crosses and three chamfered sides was discovered lying face down, having been cut in two pieces and used for paving. When he was vicar Dr. Gresford Jones had the stone restored and replaced below the east window in the Shrewsbury Chapel. Queen Elizabeth I also ordered that rood-screens and lofts be removed, so it was in 1570 that the parish church's rood-screen and loft, which originally spanned the eastern arch of the tower, were removed. Most of the central tower is of fifteenth-century work. At the same date the churchyard cross was removed and broken.

The neglected condition of the building was mentioned in Mr. Samuel Roberts's diary, towards the end of the eighteenth century. He wrote:

The town was then in a very rude state in every respect it being only partially flagged, with many stones loose: there were few lamps and these feeble and far apart—often not lighted or blown out. . . .

Nor was the scene within [the Parish Church] much more lively. The church itself was then one of the most gloomy, irregularly paved places of worship in the Kingdom. It seemed as if, after the work of pewing had begun, every person who chose had formed a pew for himself in his own way, to his own size, height and shape. There were several galleries but all formed, as it seemed, in the same way as the pews—some of them on pillars, some hung on chains. . . . All these things seen in the dimmest gloom with the feeble aid of a few candles. . . .

Church Street was known originally as Church Lane and was barely 20 feet wide; it was referred to as "that poor, narrow place with wood buildings projecting".

Thomas Asline Ward, who was about twenty years younger than Samuel Roberts, attended the grammar school. In a letter he wrote: "I well recollect the play that I, with other scholars educated at the Grammar School, enjoyed in the churchyard, and which consisted mainly in vaulting over the tombstones. The alabaster one, from its height and breadth, was very difficult. It required a knack, and I accomplished the feat by taking a running impetus to the tomb, and, planting my hands on it, threw myself over. This could not be done unless the hands were made to walk (as it were) a foot or two, while swinging over. The Charity Boys, too, enjoyed the churchyard, which seemed to belong to the school."

By the turn of the eighteenth century it was decided that the seriously neglected nave must be rebuilt. The old nave was demolished and a new one built, the work being finished in 1805. On 6th October 1805 Thomas Asline Ward recorded:

St. Peter's, or the Parish Church, was re-opened after having undergone a thorough repair and alteration; the old pews were taken down, new ones erected, the site of the pulpit and some of the galleries changed, the pillars diminished in bulk, and the whole greatly improved, which, beside the addition of an organ, has added much to the sanctity and sublimity of the place. The old outer walls have also, within the last century, been entirely taken down (small portions at a time) and rebuilt in a similar style to the former, discarding, however, some of its extravagancies. The re-opening of the church was deemed to be an excellent opportunity for collecting money in aid of the fund of the Sheffield General Infirmary. Several fine pieces of sacred music were introduced, and the first hymn sung by the congregation was "Lord of the Sabbath, hear us pray", etc. Rev. Edward Goodwin read prayers, and Rev. Thomas Sutton, our young Vicar, preached.

He further records, on 9th October: "In the morning my mother and I went to St. Peter's Church to hear the Oratorio of the 'Messiah'. Misses Parke and Munday are the principal female, Messrs. Bartleman, Harrison, Goss and Bradbury the principal male singers."

Although Thomas Asline Ward evidently approved of the

restoration, others were definitely critical. Part of the restoration entailed the building of a brick wall between the chancel arches, cutting off the nave from the chancel, and the new pulpit was of the three-decker type.

In 1880 Archdeacon Blakeney set in motion work to improve the nave in several ways.

In 1913 an important step was taken; a new diocese was formed, and Sheffield's old parish church was elevated to the dignity of a cathedral. During the 1914–18 War little could be done in the way of enlargements, but in 1919 plans were made for enlarging the parish church cathedral—plans which were not proceeded with. In 1935 Dr. A. C. E. Jarvis managed to re-awaken interest in the plan, and eventually it was decided that the nineteenth-century nave should be demolished and a new nave built at right angles with the main entrance being from Church Street. For thirty years various planned improvements were carried out and on 15th November 1966 a memorable service was held, attended by H.R.H. the Princess Margaret, Countess Snowdon. The enlarged cathedral was re-hallowed, and the sermon was preached by the Archbishop of York.

In his informative *The Cathedral Church of S. Peter & S. Paul; a Guide with some historical notes*, G. H. Rayner writes: "... at its centre, the Chancel and High Sanctuary ... the only whole and entire piece of mediaeval architecture left in the City. Disaster, triumph, disappointment, continuing faith and hope—all these symbolized by that one small window in the Chapter House."

The "small window" referred to is high in the east wall of the chapter house. Its lovely painted glass shows the Sheffield Cross.

Of the chapter house Mr. Raynor writes:

This will for ever be one of the treasures of the Cathedral and of the City of Sheffield. In its entirety it is the gift of Miss Fanny Louisa Tozer, her memorial to her father and mother. It is the first Chapter House built to conform with the Cathedrals Measure of 1931, which enacts that parish church cathedrals shall be governed by a Council as well as a Chapter, so that in addition to stalls for the Chapter, tables are provided for the Council.

The dominating conception of all the painted glass in the Chapter House is that it should speak of past history in Sheffield. . . .

As we have seen, the cross which had stood on the south side of the old church, in the churchyard, was removed and broken in the reign of Queen Elizabeth I, after having withstood the vicissitudes of some eight hundred years. There is still a wealth of these fine preaching crosses in Derbyshire and the neighbourhood of Sheffield, all having been removed and damaged, but 'found' again after the severe decrees no longer obtained, and re-erected. The parish accounts state that in 1570 the churchyard cross was pulled down and the stone sold for 12d. to George Tynker. The broken top of the cross has not been found, but the shaft, one side damaged, survived as an ornament in a private garden until 1924 when its origin was realized, and it was given by its owner, Mrs. G. M. Staniforth, to the British Museum. From this damaged shaft it is possible to envisage that originally it was well over 12 feet in height with an equal-armed cross-head, of typical Anglian craftsmanship.

The cathedral enfolds a wealth of interest. There are several sculptured memorials by Chantrey. In the Chapel of St. George is a stone in the floor by the entrance, stating that the chapel is dedicated to members of the York and Lancaster Regiment who have given their lives since the regiment was founded in 1758. Above are the colours, sovereign and regimental, of the York and Lancaster Regiment and the Coldstream Guards, which have been laid up in the cathedral. There is also the Union Jack and silk White Ensign of H.M.S. *Sheffield*. The ensign was made by the ladies of Sheffield and was flown from the peak when the ship was in action.

On the west wall of the chapel is a brass plate commemorating members of the Sheffield Police Force and Hallamshires who gave their lives in the South African Campaign, 1899–1902.

Above this is a brass plate to the memory of those of the 8th and 9th Battalions of the York and Lancaster Regiment who fell in the 1914–18 War, and above this is a memorial to the men of the 12th Battalion (the Sheffield City Battalion) "who at the call of duty and in the cause of freedom nobly made the supreme sacrifice".

In this chapel is the quarter-deck badge of H.M.S. *Sheffield* and a stainless steel plate giving details of her history from her commissioning in 1937 to her withdrawal from active service in 1961. Here also are the Books of Remembrance of the York and Lancaster Regiment.

In the south choir aisle is a marble tablet which reads: "To the Glory of God and in memory of the Rev. Samuel Earnshaw M.A.,

Senior Wrangler and Smiths Prizeman, 1831. This window is erected by his fellow-townsmen to commemorate his distinguished career at Cambridge; his earnest and successful efforts in the cause of education and his faithful labours as a minister of Christ. He was the last of a succession of assistant ministers or chaplains of this Church and officiated as such from 1847 to 1888. Born in Sheffield 1 February 1805, died 6 December 1888."

On a wall of the Lady Chapel is an interesting scratch dial, thought to be a thirteenth-century mass clock. The hole for the original gnomon is evident, surrounded by outward-slanting lines. The stone has a chamfered edge suggesting that it was at the end of a wall or on a buttress. It may have been brought in and built into this inside wall in the fifteenth-century rebuilding.

When the plaster was stripped from the sanctuary walls in the nineteenth century it was seen that many stones from the original stone church (the Norman building) are embedded in the walls.

Most of the roofs of the chancel and north and south choir aisles are the original fifteenth-century work.

An interesting item in St. Katherine's Chapel is a black oak portable sedilia, which is regarded as one of the great treasures of the cathedral. There are only two or three rare portable sedilia in the country.

Records mention an organ in the parish church before 1528, but, "In the year 1650 the organ was silenced by the Puritan spirit which prevailed in the Parish" (in the days of the Commonwealth). A record of 1770 states: "There was then no solemn, loud pealing organ: but before the West window, high above the gallery, was a kind of immense large box hung in chains, into which by the aid of a ladder musicians and singers, male and female, contrived to scramble, and with the aid of bum basses, hautboys, fiddles, and various other instruments, accompanying shrill and stentorian voices, they contrived to make as loud a noise as heart would wish."

The church registers commence in 1560, the early volumes being beautifully written. An interesting entry of 4th September 1574, in the burials section of that year records: "Petrus Roollett, Gallus." Roollett was the faithful secretary of Mary Queen of Scots, and he died during the time of her imprisonment in Sheffield Castle.

And finally, in our brief glance at the long history of this, our

15

city's oldest institution, is one which testifies to the age-long generosity of Sheffield people: "Paid, November 22nd., 1666 by me John Lee to John Wynch by order of the Lord Major of London the summe of Twentie Seaven pounds and ten shillings being collected in ye towne and p'ish of Sheffield towards the reliefe of those p'sons who have beene greate sufferers by the late sad fire within the City of London."

On leaving the cathedral by the door facing Church Street, just a few paces lead to the spot where for many centuries stood Sheffield's beautifully carved stone cross, recalling the period of its erection in the eighth century, when the small timber church stood here, well above the first little hamlet of Escafeld, and the surrounding hills and valleys were lovely, as they are today.

XIX

THE PORTRAIT IS FRAMED

BY THE year 1971 our Portrait is wide and well drawn, exhibiting lovely colours.

It shows the steel works and great industrial concerns, grown ever larger through the years due to amalgamation and the introduction of new techniques, occupying much of the Don's wider valley to the east. But the once so obvious smoke pall has been almost overcome by the introduction of smoke-control legislation. Rows of small red-brick houses have been demolished, leaving rather stark open spaces awaiting re-use, and the former occupants have been re-housed in modern homes.

The town centre has been drastically—almost bewilderingly— modernized, an undertaking not easy to carry out because of the changing gradients: but Sheffield owes its position and growth mainly to its hills and valleys, and loves them. The new developments reaching out to the suburbs and beyond have been controlled by the hills, and have accepted their challenge enthusiastically.

Sheffield has a population of 531,000, whilst nearly 1,000,000 live within a radius of 24 kilometres (15 miles) of the city centre. The population of the city is expected to increase to 570,000 by 1981.

Although it has the fifth largest population outside London, Sheffield has more open space than any other city. The rocky escarpments on the fringe of the western boundary are in places within the Peak District National Park and include some of the best rock-climbing faces in the country. No less than 6,741 acres of the City of Sheffield lie within the Peak District National Park.

In 1962 new wholesale fish, fruit and vegetable markets were opened, about 2 miles away from the city centre. This wholesale market with its restaurants, banks, car-parks, etc., with adequate railway sidings and access to the motorways, serves a population of over a million.

A few years ago an impressive new railway marshalling yard was opened at Tinsley and the Sheffield freight terminal was constructed at Grimesthorpe. These new developments are part of the British Railways' 'rationalization' plan.

Sheffield Corporation's most recent publication, *Sheffield— City on the Move* suggests a note of pride:

> Yorkshire's largest city and the finest shopping centre in the north; the city of quality, with an unrivalled reputation for skill and craftsmanship; the city dominated by trees and flowers, and surrounded by countryside of exquisite beauty: modern Sheffield combines the skills and traditions of the past with all the excitement of the '70s.
>
> Let no-one tell you that Sheffield is just another industrial conurbation. It is Britain's largest Garden City.
>
> Though Sheffield is traditionally associated with steel, cutlery and engineering, the range of activity within the City stretches far beyond these fields. Despite their varying jobs and skills, the people of Sheffield share three common characteristics—a pride in their work, a friendly disposition and a pride in their city. The good-natured humour of the Sheffielder percolates through the business and social life of the city.

It is well to climb Wincobank Hill again, to the hill fort of the Brigantes, to envisage the growth of our Portrait since the days when those first Anglian settlers early in the sixth century began to build our modern Sheffield.

On the hill rising beyond the first cruck building raised above the Don–Sheaf junction stands the cathedral—a building whose site speaks of ages past as well as the present, telling a story going back as far as the first small heathen place of worship, telling of the first Christian church, and on to the present parish church cathedral. The cathedral is not an elaborate, spectacular building; it is a friendly building standing sturdily on its ancient site; it is a building which *belongs* to Sheffield.

From our Brigantian vantage point we see the modernized city centre, and from there the eye travels to the hills—new housing developments climb the emparked nearer hills to the high borders of the city.

The hills, climbing from the Don–Sheaf confluence in Escafeld; always the magnificent hills, cradling a people who from early days have quietly used and developed their skills, their love of outdoor pursuits and of music and drama, and real art; who have pursued their quest for education to the highest standards; who have scored many 'firsts' in a variety of worthwhile fields; who have an inborn integrity and glance askance at those who exhibit 'side'. And who love the hills.

For this is Sheffield.

BIBLIOGRAPHY

Addy, S. O., *Historic Memorials of Beauchief Abbey, Sheffield*, Leader and Sons, 1878.

Anglo-Saxon Chronicle, J. M. Dent & Sons, Ltd., London, 1969.

Armstrong, A. Leslie; Jones, G. P.; Chapman, A. W.; *Sheffield and its Region. A Scientific and Historical Survey*, compiled for the Sheffield Meeting in 1956 of the British Association for the Advancement of Science, 1956.

Arnold, Dr., article in *Sheffield Courant* 1831.

"Abbeydale Industrial Hamlet" (pamphlet), 1970.

Baldwin, A. B., "The Yorkshire River Derwent Scheme. Stage 1."

Bingham, J. H., *The Period of the Sheffield School Board 1870–1903*. J. W. Northend, Ltd., Sheffield, 1949.

Brearley, Harry, *Steel Makers*, Longmans Green and Co., London, 1933.

Bunker, B., *Church Street, Dronfield. The Story of an Ancient Way*. W. Bishop and Sons, Ltd., Sheffield, 1963.

Cruck Buildings. An opinion as to their origin and dating, arising from a study of existing and recently demolished Cruck Buildings in North Derbyshire and South Yorkshire, G. C. Brittain & Sons, Ltd., Ripley, Derbyshire, 1970.

Articles in *The Sheffield Spectator*:

"A Brief Note on the History of Dronfield", July 1966.

"Water-highway to the Sea. The Sheffield and South Yorkshire Navigation", May and June 1966.

"A Brief Note on the History of Dore and Totley", January 1967.

"A Brief Note on the History of Ecclesall", May 1967.

"A Brief Note on the History of Sandygate", April 1967.

"A Brief Note on the History of Lodge Moor and Redmires", October 1967.

"The Wheels of the Porter Brook", July 1968.

"A Brief Note on the History of Paradise Square", July 1968.

"A Brief Note on the History of Wadsley", March and April 1968.

"Cargo for Sheffield", August 1968.

"A Brief Note on the History of Eyam", December 1968.

"A Brief Note on the History of Hathersage", January 1969.

"A Brief Note on the History of Castleton", March 1969.

Defoe, D., *A Tour Through the Whole Island of Great Britain*, J. M. Dent & Sons, Ltd., London, 1968.

Dunstan, J., *The Origins of the Sheffield and Chesterfield Railway*, Published by Dore Village Society, 1970.

Eastwood, the Rev. J., *The History of the Parish of Ecclesfield*, Bell and Daldy, London, 1862.

Gatty, A., *Sheffield Past and Present, being a Biography of the Town during 800 years*, T. Rodgers, Sheffield, 1875.

Hawson, H. Keeble, *Sheffield. The Growth of a City, 1893–1926*, J. W. Northend, Ltd., Sheffield, 1968.

Hunter, J., *Hallamshire*, Pawson and Brailsford, Ltd., Sheffield, 1869.

Leader, R. E., *The History of the Company of Cutlers in Hallamshire*, Pawson and Brailsford, Ltd., Sheffield, 1905.

Leland, J., *Itinerary in England and Wales*, 5 vols, Centaur Press Ltd., London, 1964.

Meredith, Miss R., "The Water-mills of Abbeydale", Sheffield City Libraries Local History Leaflet, 1966.

Miller, W. T., *The Water-Mills of Sheffield*. Pawson and Brailsford, Ltd., Sheffield, 1936.

Rayner, G. H., *The Cathedral Church of St. Peter & St. Paul, Sheffield*, The British Publishing Co. Ltd., Gloucester, 1967.

Roberts, Samuel, *Autobiography*. Longman, Brown, Green and Longmans, London, 1849.

Rolt, L. T. C., *Great Engineers*, G. Bell & Sons, Ltd., London, 1962.

Sheffield Independent, 3rd November, 1866.

Sheffield Morning Telegraph: Morgan, K., 5th September 1970. "Bell-pits" 25th November 1967. Williams, Max, 25th February 1971.

Sheffield Telegraph: Gardiner, D., 29th November 1961. Barry, J., 17th November 1962.

Sheffield Telegraph Year Book, 1919 and 1970–71.

Transactions of The Hunter Archaeological Society, Sheffield:
 Addy, S. O., "The Customs of Hallamshire", 1914. Seaman,
 A. W. L., "Reform Politics at Sheffield, 1791–97", 1957.
 Winder, T., "Sheffield Manor Lodge and Park", 1914.
Walton, Miss M., *Sheffield. Its Story and its Achievements*, Sheffield
 Telegraph and Star, Ltd., Sheffield, 1948.
Ward, Thomas Asline, *Peeps into the Past*, W. C. Leng and Co.,
 Sheffield, 1909.
Wilson, R. E., *Two Hundred Precious Metal Years*. Ernest Benn,
 Ltd., London, 1966.
Winning, A. L., (editor), *Recreation in Sheffield Parks*. The British
 Publishing Co. Ltd., Gloucester, 1968.